Imagining Bodies

IMAGINING BODIES

Merleau-Ponty's Philosophy of Imagination

JAMES B. STEEVES

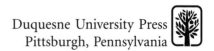

Duquesne University Press
Pittsburgh, Pennsylvania

Copyright © 2004 Duquesne University Press
All Rights Reserved

Published in the United States of America by:
DUQUESNE UNIVERSITY PRESS
600 Forbes Avenue
Pittsburgh, Pennsylvania 15282

No part of this book may be used or reproduced, in any manner or form
whatsoever, without the written permission from the publisher except in
the case of short quotations in critical articles or reviews.

Library of Congress Cataloging-in-Publication Data

Steeves, James B., 1971–
    Imagining bodies: Merleau-Ponty's philosophy of imagination/James B. Steeves
        p. cm.
Includes bibliographical references and indexes.
    ISBN 0-8207-0342-7 (alk. paper)—ISBN 0-8207-0343-5 (pbk.: alk. paper)
    1. Merleau-Ponty, Maurice, 1908–1961. 2. Imagination (Philosophy)
I. Title.
    B2430.M3764S74 2004
    128'.3—dc22   2003022705

∞ Printed on acid-free paper.

To Elizabeth,
whose love and imagination
know no bounds.

My art is an elusive art. It is making the abstract concrete and the concrete abstract. That is, making the invisible visible and the visible invisible . . . it is the art of illusion by itself.

— Marcel Marceau

Contents

Preface xi

List of Abbreviations xv

Introduction 1

ONE • Imagining Bodies 13

TWO • Perceptual Imagining 33

THREE • Aesthetic Imagining 51

FOUR • Fanciful Imagining 67

FIVE • Pathological Imagining 89

SIX • Self-Imagining 103

SEVEN • Elemental Imagining 121

EIGHT • Imagining Being 137

Notes 161

Bibliography 189

Index 201

Preface

*I*t is a most fortunate circumstance that when philosophers in France were beginning to focus on the body as a philosophical problem, the art of mime was undergoing a revolution in Paris. Under the direction of Jean-Louis Barrault, Pierre Verry and Marcel Marceau, students of mime became increasingly concerned with the purity of embodied expression. The renewed interest in mime also allowed it to emerge as an art form in its own right, distinct from theater and drama, and secured for itself a prominence that it had never known before. As these artists began experimenting in new ways with the body as an art form, French existentialists led by Maurice Merleau-Ponty, Jean-Paul Sartre and others were at the same time and in the same city also addressing the importance of the expressive body. Merleau-Ponty in particular explored the impact of the body on how we think about ourselves and reality.

Merleau-Ponty's philosophy has recently become more popular, especially among contemporary critics of deconstructionism and postmodern philosophy. Many philosophers are beginning to see in his work a prophetic voice that speaks to recent concerns in philosophy. These involve a shift in focus from the individual subject to the social and linguistic mediation of experience, and the recent interest in sexual difference and the question of alterity. The concepts of flesh and brute Being developed by Merleau-Ponty in *Eye and Mind* and *The Visible and the Invisible* suggest that it is possible to continue to pose traditional philosophical questions about the nature of Being, for example, without making the same assumptions about presence and subjectivity that have recently come under attack. While philosophers like Jacques Derrida have rejected the perceptual body of the individual as a sufficient theme for philosophical analysis, Merleau-Ponty's focus on both the imagination and the expressivity

xi

xii Preface

of the body as a ground for truth and knowledge allows for a philosophy of the flesh that escapes the confines of a philosophy of presence.

The renewed interest in Merleau-Ponty's philosophy generally overlooks the importance of his earlier works, especially *The Structure of Behavior* and *Phenomenology of Perception*, due to the belief that in these works Merleau-Ponty is still under the spell of modern philosophy and its emphasis on presence. The analysis of perception and the phenomenal body in these works sometimes seems to overlook the importance of absence and difference. If we look more closely at how Merleau-Ponty describes the body and the imagination, however, we begin to see traces of his later philosophy in which the imagination and perception are interrelated.

Perhaps one of the more remarkable characteristics of both Merleau-Ponty's early and later philosophy is the lack of attention he paid to disciplinary boundaries. He moved easily in his research and writing from perception to aesthetics, and aesthetics to politics, believing that the meaning of one topic relied on its relation to another. In the introduction to *Signs*, he describes his arrangement of the essays as "different," "incongruous" and "ad hoc" (S 3/SF 7), and the same could certainly be said about his philosophy in general. Merleau-Ponty believed that philosophy must describe the world as it appears in all of its immediate ambiguity and confusion, and called for an ad hoc approach that would consider as many perspectives as possible. No work of art is so lacking in political significance, and no perception so unconditioned by social influence, that art, perception or politics should ever be examined independently. The encompassing ambiguity of human existence necessitates a method in keeping with that of Merleau-Ponty and preserves a richness and concreteness in philosophy that often tends to be lacking.

Because I have taken this approach to Merleau-Ponty's philosophy, the work that follows is as much an original study as it is a commentary of his philosophy. References made by Merleau-Ponty to diverse topics including the body, perception, temporality, psychosis and neurosis will be incorporated into a general and explicit theory of the imagination. To a great extent, this work is based on the premise that a true reading of any philosophical text must allow it to remain open to new questions and directions in philosophy. A philosophical text is never complete and remains exposed to the questions of future generations. What Merleau-Ponty says of a work of art is thus also true of his own philosophy: "If creations are not a possession, it is not only that, like all things, they pass away; it

Preface   xiii

is also that they have almost all their life still before them" (PrP 190/ EMF 92–93).

*   *   *

This book is the result of the many contributions by family, friends and peers who have helped to shape my understanding of the body and the imagination. Without these contributions, this volume would not have been possible. The original research for this book was generously sponsored by the Ontario Graduate Scholarship Program and the Social Sciences and Humanities Research Council of Canada. The research was supervised by Jeff Mitscherling, who never failed to express his support and enthusiasm for the project. The careful analysis and helpful suggestions by Gary Madison were also crucial to the successful completion of the original draft and were matched by his generous hospitality on numerous occasions. Jay Lampert was also very helpful, at times even from a great distance. I wish to acknowledge the professionalism and patience of Susan Wadsworth-Booth, Kathy Meyer and the staff at Duquesne University Press for taking an interest in my work and for helping me to see this project through to publication. Informal discussions with many peers and friends, including Rodney Cooper, Darcy Otto, Daniel So and Shaun Gallagher helped to shape my thinking and to keep me motivated throughout the process. My parents and family have always shown an interest in what I am doing and have supported me in many ways; without this support I would never have been able to embrace such a project. To Elizabeth Loaring I am greatly indebted not only for her valuable editorial work, but also for her continual support for me as both a friend and spouse, her concern for making ideas matter in the world around us, and her limitless creativity in finding ways to make that happen.

Abbreviations

*T*he following abbreviations refer to Merleau-Ponty's texts. Wherever possible, I have used the same abbreviations for both the original French texts and the standard English translations. References to Merleau-Ponty's French texts always end with an "F." All italics and quotation marks found in quotations are from the original source unless otherwise indicated.

Works by Merleau-Ponty in English

AD   *Adventures of the Dialectic*. Trans. Joseph Bien. Evanston: Northwestern University Press, 1973.

CAL   *Consciousness and the Acquisition of Language*. Trans. Hugh Silverman. Evanston: Northwestern University Press, 1973.

HT   *Humanism and Terror*. Trans. John O'Neill. Boston: Beacon Press, 1969.

IM   "On Sartre's *Imagination*." In *Texts and Dialogues: Maurice Merleau-Ponty*, edited by Hugh Silverman and James Barry, translated by Michael B. Smith. Humanities Press: New Jersey, 1992.

IPP   *In Praise of Philosophy*. Trans. John Wild and James M. Edie. Evanston: Northwestern University Press, 1963.

PP   *Phenomenology of Perception*. Trans. Colin Smith. London: Routledge and Kegan Paul, 1962.

PrP   *The Primacy of Perception*. Trans. James M. Edie. Evanston: Northwestern University Press, 1964.

xvi Abbreviations

POW   *The Prose of the World*. Ed. Claude Lefort. Trans. John O'Neill. Evanston: Northwestern University Press, 1973.

SNS   *Sense and Non-Sense*. Trans. Hubert L. Dreyfus and Patricia Allen Dreyfus. Evanston: Northwestern University Press, 1964.

S   *Signs*. Trans. Richard McCleary. Evanston: Northwestern University Press, 1964.

SB   *The Structure of Behavior*. Trans. Alden L. Fisher. Boston: Beacon Press, 1963.

TFL   *Themes From the Lectures at the College de France 1952–1960*. Trans. John O'Neill. Evanston: Northwestern University Press, 1970.

VI   *The Visible and the Invisible*. Ed. Claude Lefort. Trans. Alphonso Lingis. Evanston: Northwestern University Press, 1968.

Works by Merleau-Ponty in French

ADF   *Les aventures de la dialectique*. Paris: Gallimard, 1955.

RCF   "Maurice Merleau-Ponty a la Sorbonne: Résumé de ses cours établi par les étudiants et approuvé par lui-même." *Bulletin de Psychologie*, no. 236, vol. 18 (November 1964); notes on courses delivered between 1949 and 1951.

HTF   *Humanisme et Terreure*. Paris: Gallimard, 1947.

IMF   "I'Imagination." *Journal de Psychologie Normale et Pathologique* 33, nos. 9–10 (1936): 756–61.

INF   "Un inédit de Merleau-Ponty." *Revue de Métaphysique et de Morale*, no. 4 (1962): 401–9.

IPPF   *Eloge de la philosophie et autres essais*. Collection Idées. Paris: Gallimard, 1960.

EMF   *l'Oeil et l'esprit*. Paris: Gallimard, 1964.

PPF   *Phénoménologie de la perception*. Paris: Gallimard, 1945.

PrPF   *Le Primat de perception et ses conséquences philosophiques*. Grenoble: Cynara, 1989.

POWF   *La Prose du monde*. Ed. Claude Lefort. Paris: Gallimard, 1969.

ROF   *Les relations avec autrui chez l'enfant*. Paris: Centre de Documentation Universitaire, 1967.

Abbreviations   xvii

TFLF   *Résumés de cours, Collège de France 1952–1960.* Paris: Gallimard, 1968.

SNSF   *Sens et non-sens.* Paris: Nagel, 1966.

SF   *Signes.* Paris: Gallimard, 1960.

SBF   *La structure du comportement.* 2nd ed. Paris: Presses Universitaires de France.

VIF   *Le visible et l'invisible: Suivi de notes de travail.* Ed. Claude Lefort. Paris: Gallimard, 1964.

Introduction

*E*very year on one of the hottest weekends of the summer, a small town is transformed into a festival of sound and light. The usually quiet main street of shops and cafés becomes a stage for buskers who sing and dance, swallow knives, and juggle balls and flaming torches. Farther down the street, a mime quietly performs her art. She is dressed in a black leotard, her face is painted white with exaggerated make-up on her lips and around her eyes, and her hair is tied back away from her face. With sweeping gestures she creates the illusion of a wall or a tiger, magically changing her immediate surroundings into a palace with kings and queens, or a dangerous jungle filled with lions and tigers.

How is it that the mime, so simple in dress and appearance, can communicate so clearly and "audibly" to her audience? The observer can tell instantly what the mime is experiencing. He feels her fear, senses the approaching tiger, shares her lust for power or her disdain for the criminal. The spectator is drawn into each of these illusions through the mime's skillful use of various techniques. By stretching her body as she pulls down on the imagined rope, the mime makes him feel the tension of climbing the rope. By moving her hands to the left while her abdomen moves to the right, she causes him to feel the tension between herself and the imagined wall, creating the illusion of action and space. The mime is aware of a number of gestures that bear an immediate significance for her

2   Introduction

audience, and by using these she is able to tell a story without making a sound.[1]

The secret of the mime's skill in storytelling is rooted in her capacity to make explicit what is implicit in the embodied experience of every individual. Each time a person speaks, his words are accompanied by gestures and facial expressions that add meaning to what he has said. The red face of a blush, the intense flush of anger or jealousy, and the drooping posture of timidity are all examples of how the body expresses feelings even in the absence of words.[2] From birth we find ourselves in a world of silent meanings. Young children in particular seem keenly aware of their bodies, making use of their natural gestures to communicate feelings and needs before they can do so with words. As we mature and are encouraged to find our voice and make ourselves heard, the language of the body often recedes into the background, with the ability it has to communicate increasingly taken for granted. From the quiet street corner, the mime encourages those who gather around her to recall the creative power of embodiment.

Like the mime, Merleau-Ponty challenges his readers to reconsider the expressive capacity of the body and the imagination. His commitment to this task is most clear and apparent in his philosophy of the body. From his earlier writing on perceptual experience to his later ontology of flesh and vision, Merleau-Ponty's philosophy is a celebration of the body. In his first two books, *The Structure of Behaviour* and *Phenomenology of Perception*, he is particularly concerned with how the body changes natural gestures into elaborate and personal modes of expression. Gesticulations and the simple skills of balance and posture are developed through practice into personal styles of living, and these shape the way that a person feels about herself and interacts with others. To understand the body as a whole structure of existence, Merleau-Ponty argues, it is important to recognize at the heart of embodiment an imaginative ability to modify the natural skills of the body into free and creative modes of existence.

Merleau-Ponty does not address the imagination of the body in a detailed or explicit manner. He focuses, instead, on embodiment in general and its role in perception, psychopathology and social relations. Within these contexts a theory of the imagination can be found, but most commentators on his earlier works fail to even discern Merleau-Ponty's thoughts on the creativity of the body. They tend to focus more often on the general themes of existence, freedom and the nature of perception.[3] It is also often assumed that it is only in Merleau-Ponty's later philosophy that a theory of the imagination begins to develop that is different from the theories of Edmund Husserl and Jean-Paul Sartre.[4] At best, his earlier works are thought to prepare the way for his later ontology. For instance, Gary Madison describes *Phenomenology of Perception* as an "anti-text" with "no positive theses" that is intended more than anything else to challenge traditional theories about perception and the body.[5] According to Madison, Merleau-Ponty's "positive" theses about perception, the body and the imagination can only be found in his later works. However, the ways in which Merleau-Ponty describes the body in his earlier writings suggest that a new theory of the imagination is already being developed. The perceptual basis of experience explained in these works is partially determined by the imagination. Indeed, every mode of existence for Merleau-Ponty consists of an imaginative dimension where new possibilities can be articulated and by which a particular situation can become a world of human possibility. To understand what Merleau-Ponty has to say about the imagination, it is essential to consider his thoughts on the imagination of the body as he presents them throughout his career.

A return to the imagining body as discussed in Merleau-Ponty's earlier works does more than simply provide a novel interpretation of his philosophy. It also presents a new way to think about the imagination in general. For centuries philosophers have attempted to arrive at a theory of the imagination that embraces all of its manifestations, from the role that it plays in perception and

4   Introduction

knowledge to the idle daydreams of fanciful thinking. The imagination has been associated with the artist or creativity in general and has also been viewed as the cause of psychopathology. As a potential vehicle for truth or error, creativity or destruction, the imagination is perhaps the most difficult phenomenon to understand or describe. Modern philosophers, including David Hume and Immanuel Kant, for instance, write mostly about the role of the imagination in perceptual and aesthetic experience. The writings of Romantic philosophers like Samuel Taylor Coleridge are primarily concerned with the imagination of creative genius and the role of the artist in aesthetic production. The theories of recent analytic philosophers, including Gilbert Ryle, Bernard Williams and Christopher Peacock, emphasize the imaginative mode of idle fancy and mental imaging at the expense of other modes of imagining. Some phenomenologists like Jean-Paul Sartre and Edward Casey focus mostly on fanciful thinking, while others, including Edmund Husserl, discuss the role of the imagination in perception and philosophical inquiry. Friedrich Nietzsche, Sigmund Freud and Jacques Lacan see the imagination as the source for delusion and neurosis, while postmodern philosophers such as Jean Baudrillard completely sever the image from its representational role and treat it as nothing more than a double in an endless series of simulacra. While each of these approaches has contributed in a specific way to a general discussion of the imagination, these theories have tended to overemphasize one aspect of the imagination at the expense of another.

In their attempts to develop a theory of the imagination, most philosophers have tended to do little more than list the different functions of the imagination. Peter Strawson, for instance, explains the imagination with reference to mental imaging, invention and false belief.[6] A simple enumeration of the functions of the imagination is likely to ignore contradictory relations between those functions, though. Mary Warnock suggests as much as she alludes to a tension that exists between the imagination as an aid to perception and as an aid to the creation of novel meaning. She writes: "We use imagination in our ordinary perception of the world. . . . So imagination is necessary . . . to enable us to recognize things in the world as familiar, to take for granted features of the world which we need to take for granted and rely on, if we are to go about our ordinary business; but it is also necessary if we are to see the world as significant of something unfamiliar, if we are ever to treat the objects of perception as symbolizing or suggesting things other than themselves."[7] Wondering how it is that the same imagination that facilitates mundane perception can also be the source for novel forms, Warnock exposes the problem of many functions being attributed to the imagination and the challenge of how to reconcile what seem to be incompatible meanings.

My response to this problem is to reject the search for a complete definition of the imagination. There is no single function of the imagination that can be used to make sense of its other meanings and functions, but this does not mean that the concept of the imagination is left with no meaning at all. This position is informed by Richard Kearney's suggestion that the different meanings ascribed to the imagination can be understood to bear what Wittgenstein describes as "family resemblances." While there may be no single meaning that connects the members of the group, there are many similarities that bind them together.[8] My brother might have my mother's chin, and I may have my father's, and we might both have eyes that resemble those of a grandfather. Taken as a whole, a stranger is quick to recognize the family resemblance I bear to my brother even though he may be at a loss to point out like characteristics. In the same way, it is possible to find resemblances between the different functions of the imagination. By searching for similarities and sifting through contradictions, a general theory of the imagination can gradually be developed.

What is common to each kind of imagining is a creative adaptation of habitual modes of embodiment to new situations or ways of seeing the world. The mime exposes the members of her audience

6   Introduction

to a creative dimension of their embodiment that grounds the meaning of their experience and which is capable of extension and development. The painter plays on habitual ways in which we perceive different situations with our bodies so that we are able to see the world in new ways. The psychotic and the neurotic exist in a restricted world because their compromised imaginations keep them from experiencing the world in terms of possibilities. Even the daydreamer continues to use her embodied sense of space and balance as she makes her way through the alternative world she has created. In every instance of the imagination, there is an imagining body that alters or escapes from the actual world, and which endows the world with meaning. The "family resemblance," or commonality, that unites each type of imagining is the ability of the imagining body to offer possibilities of existence.

The following will explore the role of the imagining body in the various kinds of imagination mentioned above: perception, aesthetics and fanciful thinking, to name only a few. Merleau-Ponty's philosophy of the imagination will be applied to many different types of imagining and will be shown to provide a solution to many of the problems posed by philosophers concerning the imagination, including its relation to perception, the nature of the mental image, and the role of the imagination in psychopathology. This will ensure that the general theory of imagination is not constructed in a vacuum, but is continuous with the history of the philosophy of imagination.

The first chapter introduces the concept of an imagination of the body. Merleau-Ponty's detailed analysis of the body explains the advantages of understanding the body in terms of a body schema, a concept that he borrows from psychological research to refer to the global awareness and motility of the body. This basic experience of the body can be developed into habits of perception and action, exposing a person to new ways of relating to his environment. Even within this very basic structure of existence, a virtual dimension of possibility is found in the form of a virtual body, a body that a person can imagine assuming and from which he can view the world from a different perspective. The chapter shows how this mode of virtual embodiment is a form of imagining. It also relates Merleau-Ponty's discussion to current research on the body schema, kinesics and kinesthesis. By exploring the creative aspect of the body as described by Merleau-Ponty, it is possible to arrive at a new understanding of the body and the embodied imagination.

The role of the imagination in perceptual experience will be considered in the second chapter. Merleau-Ponty's description of perception rejects traditional theories in favor of a new phenomenology of perception based on the methods of Husserl and the concepts of Gestalt psychology. The perceptual image is shown to occur within an interpretive context in which sense qualities make sense only in relation to each other and to the perceptual context in which they occur. In a way reminiscent of Hume and Kant, the imagination is central to perception in making possible the necessary structures for the appearance of a quality. But for Merleau-Ponty, the quality is also indicative of a mode of embodiment which the body experiences on the basis of the imagining body. A quality presents to the imagining body an entire perceptual structure that the body understands as a world of virtual and possible modes of embodiment. To focus on a particular quality is like choosing from a variety of possibilities that are imagined and assumed by perceptual consciousness. The role of the body in perception reveals a level of imagination that is essential for the experience of perceptual qualities.

In chapter 3, the imagination of the body and its role in perception is used to explain the significance of aesthetic experience. The artist, like the mime, is aware of the creative role that the body plays in perception and attempts to return the viewer's attention to the creative power of the body. Merleau-Ponty argues that an art form traces the path of the artist's body in relation to a particular way of "seeing" the world that the viewer is invited to explore and revisit by interpreting the art form in terms of her own embodied

8 *Introduction*

experience. A work of art arrests the attention of the individual to contemplate the way that the colors and surfaces of the work present a world to the body to interpret and inhabit. The inevitable abstraction in any work leaves gaps and fissures that the viewer is left to imagine. Since Merleau-Ponty's essays on aesthetics deal mostly with the art of painting, his aesthetic theory is further extended to the art forms of dance, cinema and music. Each of these aesthetic forms rely on the imagining body to communicate and express new ways of experiencing the sensible world.

Fancy and mental imagery is the main topic of chapter 4. Many of the most recent imagination theories from both the continental and analytic traditions of philosophy share the common theme of denying the existence of mental images. While Jean-Paul Sartre and Edward Casey treat the image as a mode of consciousness to be contrasted with perception, cognition and other modes of consciousness, Gilbert Ryle, Kendall Walton and Alan White see the imagination as an activity like pretending and make-believe. A careful analysis of Merleau-Ponty's references to Sartre and others suggests that at the same time that he accepts the view that mental images are not contents of the mind, he also believes that they involve a spatiality and embodiment that is unique and yet continuous with perceptual experience. The clear distinctions proposed by Sartre, Ryle and others between the imagination and perception are discarded for a complex range of experience from fancy to perception, which is determined by the different ways that the body is lived, be it as a means for engagement with reality or for an escape to the "private theater" of the individual. The spatiality of the image is supported by recent tests conducted by Jerome Singer, Stephen Kosslyn and other experimental psychologists, as well as by the writings of Jerry Fodor and Ned Block. Contrary to the popular view that fancy involves an escape from embodied experience, Merleau-Ponty's theory of the imagining body preserves the spatiality of the image and the virtual body of the dream without turning the mental image into an object in the mind.

Introduction 9

The next two chapters bring Merleau-Ponty's theory of imagination into contact with the theories presented by psychoanalysts. Sigmund Freud and Josef Breuer argue that the imagination is at fault for causing many forms of neurotic behavior. They claim that the imagination allows a person to conceal basic drives and instinctual desires by providing alternative ways of thinking about past or present experiences. These alternative interpretations accumulate to form confused and distorted messages so that it becomes difficult to understand what drives a person to do certain things or to feel a certain way. As a result, a person might react to particular drives or instincts without knowing why; the reaction, suggest Freud and Breuer, can be quite severe, resulting in neurotic behavior. Although Merleau-Ponty accepts the view that affective experience is mediated by images, he does not believe that original experiences become buried in an unconscious, or that the imagination's creation of garbled images and meanings must be overcome to unveil the true meaning of the patient's behavior. Rather, neurotic and psychotic experiences are the result of a person's losing the ability to switch easily from the real to the imaginary, resulting in a fixation on particular behaviors and an inability to consider alternatives. Between normal, neurotic, and psychotic behavior is a continuum of experience, with a healthy balance of reality and the imagination on the side of normal behavior and a weakening of the imagination through neurosis and culminating in psychosis. Research by Jerome Singer and James Morley confirms this claim. The psychotherapeutic method of the guided daydream, developed by Robert Desoille and J. H. van den Berg, illustrates how the imagination can serve as the cure, rather than the cause, of many of these conditions. By not overemphasizing the role of the imagination in psychopathology, Merleau-Ponty is able to address many of the concerns of psychoanalysis without relegating the imaginary to the whims of the unconscious.

Another issue to which Merleau-Ponty's philosophy of imagination can be applied is the genesis of the self and interpersonal

10 Introduction

relations. The experiments of Jacques Lacan on the mirror stage of a child's development suggest that a child first comes to understand herself through the recognition of herself in the mirror. On the basis of this externalization of consciousness, an image of the self is born. But the child is never identical with the image she has of herself, so that her self-consciousness is defined by a schism between the self as lived and the self as seen by others. Merleau-Ponty's innovative interpretation of Lacan's experiment shows that there is a reversibility between the roles of seeing and being seen that is held together rather than torn apart by the imagining body. As a person explores the imaginative abilities of his body, she experiences a reversibility between the body as seen and the body as a means for seeing the world. This reversibility provides the basis for a sense of self, as well as for a sense of others as sharing the capacity both to see and to be seen. The role of the imagining body in psychogenesis and social existence is illustrated in chapter 6 within the context of Lacan's analysis and some of the more recent concerns of contemporary feminist theory.

In chapter 7 the connection between the imagining body and psychological themes is extended to the question of the relation of the imagining body to the natural environment. It is shown how, for Merleau-Ponty, the traditional images of earth, air, water and fire play a crucial role in how we perceive ourselves and the world around us. The elements, he suggests, are not the fundamental material components of reality, as is suggested by pre-Socratic philosophy, but general modes of embodied comportment toward nature. These modes of embodiment are usually disclosed in dreams or poetry, and often consist of vague emotional values that effect how the world is perceived. These meanings have often been mistakenly thought to involve an unconscious determination of experience, whereas for Merleau-Ponty they are the products of a mutual creative activity of the body and the natural world. Through the four elements of earth, air, water and fire (and innumerable other elements), Merleau-Ponty finds a valuable example of the way that

Being appears to the phenomenal body and contributes to the meaning of the world in which we think and act and imagine.

The ontological implications of the imagining body are reserved for the final chapter. I will explain Merleau-Ponty's concept of flesh in detail and show in what way the virtuality of the body provides the site for the appearing of Being. The reversibility of seeing and being is found in both the body and the world that surrounds it, providing a complex interchange of roles that determine the various ways in which Being can appear. The Being of beings, as the force that makes them able to appear and assume a meaning for consciousness, is shown to be a form of imagining to which the imagining body responds by interpreting the traces of Being into various forms of embodiment, as well as being inspired by them to create words or images in which Being can present itself at the same time that it transcends its particular manifestations. With the concept of flesh, Merleau-Ponty provides a radical, new direction for the study of Being and the role of the body in ontology. The chapter concludes with an explanation of how the mediation of Being through flesh precedes the distinction of the real from the imaginary, introducing an imagination of Being that informs and enriches the imagination of the body.

ONE

Imagining Bodies

U nder the direction of Jacques Copeau, students at the Ecole du Vieux Colombier held their end-of-term theatrical performance in the summer of 1924. Etienne Decroux attended the performance and describes it as follows:

> Sitting quietly among the spectators, I beheld an astonishing show. It consisted of mime and sounds. The whole performance took place without a word, without any make-up, without costumes, without a single lighting effect, without properties, without furniture and without scenery.
>
> The development of the action was skillful enough for them to condense several hours into a few seconds, and to contain several places in only one. Simultaneously before our eyes we had the battlefield and civilian life, the sea and the city.
>
> The actors moved from one to the other with total credibility.
>
> The acting was moving and comprehensible, of both plastic and musical beauty.[1]

The performance marked the beginning of a new direction in mime and dance. Having grown tired of the flamboyance of the French stage he had observed as a theater critic, Copeau began his own school of mime, which he hoped would emphasize the purity of bodily expression. The success with which he and his students

14   Imagining Bodies

carried out this task after only one year was witnessed by Decroux on the night of that performance. Drawing from gymnastic techniques and the new science of motion displayed in photography and cinema, Copeau attempted to achieve in theater what Mondrian had achieved in the visual arts: the reduction of his medium to the purest and most powerful forms and images. The principles of the school, summarized by Paul Bellugue, consisted of "simplifying, purifying, and ordering gestures."[2] The school gained popularity with a new generation of artists who achieved Copeau's dream of a revolution in dance and mime. Jean-Louis Barrault and Etienne Decroux would both go on to feature the new techniques of Copeau's school in the legendary film *Les enfants du paradis*, while Marcel Marceau performed his own mime techniques around the world, giving to French mime an international reputation.[3]

In 1945, as the production of *Les enfants du paradis* was being concluded, Merleau-Ponty's most famous work, *Phenomenology of Perception*, was published. In the same way that Copeau wanted to bring attention to the general expressiveness of the body and to move away from a conventional focus on the mime's hand or face, for instance, Merleau-Ponty argues in this text that a philosophy of the body must consider the purity of expression and movement if it is to capture the essence of the phenomenal body, or the body as lived (*vécue*, PP xvii/PPF xii). His research on the psychology of perception gradually led him to reject traditional theories of the perceiving body and to pursue a more refined philosophy of the body. Borrowing from the methodology of Edmund Husserl, Merleau-Ponty argues that philosophy must involve a "reduction" of presuppositions about the body and a "pure description"[4] of the body as experienced and felt. But a total reduction and pure description becomes an impossible task, since there are always aspects of the body that remain essentially hidden to consciousness. Merleau-Ponty argues, in fact, that "the most important lesson which the reduction teaches us is the impossibility of a complete reduction" (PP xiv/PPF viii). A pure description of the body cannot be made because many of its essential modes are unavailable for direct observation. The philosophy of the body developed in Merleau-Ponty's *Phenomenology of Perception* is unique in that it allows for this ambiguity of embodied experience.

Merleau-Ponty refers to several bodily experiences in this text to show that these phenomena cannot be reduced to mere physiological or psychological explanations of how the body works. He argues that such theories on their own overlook the fundamental aspects of embodiment as a mode of existence. The phenomenon of "anchorage," for instance, represents for Merleau-Ponty the experience of being in the world in a way that cannot be measured or defined. When an individual looks at himself in a mirror, the most that he is able to see of his body is an image, or externalization, that fails to represent the experience of anchorage, or his particular experience and perspective from where he stands in the world. The image in the mirror seems to float in a virtual reality where it knows nothing of gravity and perspective (PP 91/PPF 107).[5] This experience of anchorage cannot be gauged or observed by others, either, since a person standing in the same room as the man in front of the mirror would only view his body as seen, and not as it would be experienced (PP 67, 100/PPF 81, 117).

Another experience discussed by Merleau-Ponty that escapes direct observation is that of double sensation, where a part of the body is sensed by another. Each part of the body passes easily from the role of sensing to being sensed, and Merleau-Ponty draws on the experience of a hand being touched by another hand in particular (PP 92/PPF 108). This experience, says Merleau-Ponty, involves "an ambiguous set-up in which both hands can alternate the roles of 'touching' and being 'touched'" (PP 93/PPF 109). The reversibility between these roles found in every part of the body is unable to be observed because observation can occur only for objects that are being sensed, and never for the activity of sensing itself. Merleau-Ponty explains that the awareness of the point of contact between sensing and being sensed, while offering something to be understood by consciousness, is not the same direct awareness that consciousness has of physical objects: "The body catches itself from the outside engaged in a cognitive process; it tries to touch itself while being touched, and initiates 'a kind of reflection' which is sufficient to distinguish it from objects" (PP 93/PPF 109). The point of contact between the two roles is understood immediately by the body. This "point" cannot be observed directly, however, and this makes a complete analysis of the body impossible.

Experiences like that of anchorage and double sensation are important for Merleau-Ponty because they point to some of the inadequacies of traditional explanations of the body. Two of the more prominent theories with which he takes issue are behaviorism and intellectualism. Merleau-Ponty rejects a behavioristic approach, which would allege that the experience of the phenomenal body is caused by physiological events. Behaviorism is based on the premise that all mental phenomena are caused by excitations of nerve endings and reflexive responses. A reflex involves "the action of a defined physical or chemical agent on a locally defined receptor which evokes a defined response by means of a defined pathway" (SB 9/SBF 7). An example often cited is the eye's movement as it follows an object in motion. The behaviorist would argue that the impression of the object on the retina causes the eye to dilate and focus, and then to move with the object as a response to the impression. I may claim to have tracked the bird voluntarily in accordance with an inner experience of free will, but the behaviorist would insist that I was motivated by causal factors. Merleau-Ponty attacks the behaviorist position by suggesting that it is not every experience of the phenomenal body that can be explained with reference to causal mechanisms. The body is not a passive receiver of sense impressions but is actively engaged, instead, in the interpretation of the context in which it responds to stimuli. For instance, I follow the bird with my eyes because I am already curious about the visual scene. Merleau-Ponty explains that "the excitation itself is already a response, not an effect imported from outside the organism; it is the first act of its proper functioning" (PP 31/PPF 31). The stimuli makes sense only as a response to a body that is always and already interrogating the world. If there is a causal relation to be found in the reflex, it assumes the form of a "circular causality" (SB 15/SBF 13) between the body and its environment. The body cannot be seen to be the effect of causal stimuli because it provides the reflex with its original significance.[6]

While behaviorism tends to focus on the physiological body and reflex action, intellectualism asserts that all experiences of the body are controlled by the mind. It suggests that every action follows a step-by-step procedure that is directed by explicit thoughts. According to the intellectualist, when I enter a narrow tunnel, I automatically calculate its size in relation to the size of my body and then adjust my posture in such a way that I pass through without injury. It is argued that such explicit judgments can become so habitual that we hardly notice ourselves using them in ordinary behavior. The instructions are translated into body movements and sensations, "as on a taximeter the distance is given already converted into shillings and pence."[7] There is no place for this translation of thought into action for Merleau-Ponty, though. The structure of behavior is actually based on an immediate awareness of how the world presents itself to the body in terms of possibilities. The body possesses what Merleau-Ponty calls an "inner communication with the world" (PP 96/PPF 113). I avert my head, in other words, because I am immediately aware of the relation of my body to the tunnel. I do not give recourse to explicit judgment because my body has an immediate and tacit awareness of the world.

Both intellectualism and behaviorism fail to explain the phenomenal body because they assume that the body must be understood either as an object or a subject. While the behaviorist attempts to explain the body in terms of laws that apply to physical objects, the intellectualist treats the body as an extension of the mind. Rejecting both of these traditional approaches, Merleau-Ponty attempts to explain the body as a global phenomenon that assumes both objective and subjective characteristics. The body can be seen or observed and in this sense it could be said to act like an object, but it also conceals itself from observation and becomes the vehicle for perception as the subject that sees. Rather than restricting the body to a particular realm of being, Merleau-Ponty stresses that the body possesses both subjective and objective characteristics and that this interchange between the subject and the object defines the phenomenal body.

Merleau-Ponty believes that a proper understanding of the body requires a discussion of the body as "lived," or as it is experienced as both subject and object. He manages to engage in such a discussion of the phenomenal body by referring to the concept of the "body schema,"[8] which is used in psychology to refer to a general awareness of the body as a whole and its capacity to move and be moved in the world. Merleau-Ponty draws from the research of Paul Schilder, who claimed as early as 1923 that embodied experience is best explained in terms of the "body schema." Through the body schema, Schilder explains, an individual knows at a tacit level where his limbs are and what they can do. When we are bitten by a fly, for example, we know instantly where the hand is and how to move it toward the flesh that has just been bitten (PP 105/PPF 122). What makes this kind of phenomenon possible, Merleau-Ponty says, is the body schema, which acts as "a compendium of our bodily experience, capable of giving a commentary and meaning to the internal impressions and the impression of possessing a body at any moment" (PP 99/PPF 115). The body schema is neither the result of reflex actions nor of explicit thoughts and judgments, and exists instead as a global awareness of the body that is maintained at every moment. The concept of the body schema allows for a more penetrating insight into the phenomenal body, in that it is able to account for both the subjective and objective characteristics of embodied experience.[9]

As fruitful as Schilder's work was in contributing to a discussion of the phenomenal body, he was not consistent in how he used the term "body schema," and created confusion about what the body schema actually involved. While Schilder sometimes referred to the body schema as an immediate awareness of the body and a medium for action, there were other instances in which he referred to it as an image in the mind.[10] In spite of Schilder's influence on his philosophy of the body, even Merleau-Ponty concedes that "[w]hen the term body schema was first used, it was thought that nothing more was being introduced than a convenient name for a great many associations of images" (PP 99/PPF 115). The same kind of ambiguity alluded to by Merleau-Ponty is apparent in more recent studies of the body schema as well, in which the terms "body schema," "body concept," and "body image" are often used interchangeably.[11] Although Schilder is helpful in laying the groundwork for an understanding of the body schema, Merleau-Ponty manages to resolve the confusion of Schilder and others by insisting on a clearer and more concise definition of the body schema.

Merleau-Ponty does this by developing "a second definition of the body schema" and uses this to describe the phenomenal body. For him, the body schema is "a total awareness of my posture in the intersensory world, a 'form' in the sense used by Gestalt psychology" (PP 99–100/PPF 115–16). He comes to this understanding of the body schema by rejecting the way in which some have thought of the body schema as a mental image. Instead, the body schema is, for Merleau-Ponty, an immediate and affective sense of the body. We experience the body schema when we spontaneously move our limbs and adjust our posture in a new situation in order to maintain our balance and a sense of control.[12] These experiences seem to occur on a deeper level of experience, beneath the level of conscious and voluntary action. Merleau-Ponty explains that the body operates on two levels: that of the "body at this moment" and that of the "customary body" (PP 82/PPF 97–98). The body at this moment works at the level of volitional action, while the customary body, which is more central to Merleau-Ponty's analysis of the body, exists at the level of the body schema. This customary level

20 Imagining Bodies

of existence is a general mode of being. It refers to a level of tacit abilities which constitute the majority of one's actions, including reaching, grasping, sitting, standing and walking. By means of the general level of existence provided by the body schema, or the customary body, one is aware of, or accustomed to, what the body can and cannot do. "My organism," he writes, "as a pre-personal clearing to the general form of the world, as an anonymous and general existence, plays, beneath my personal life, the part of an inborn complex" (PP 84/PPF 99). The body schema is not a conscious image of the body, but a tacit sense of its abilities and of its relation to the world.[13]

To provide a concrete example of the body schema, Merleau-Ponty refers to the phenomenon of the phantom limb. Some patients who have had a limb amputated experience a sensation of the limb after the operation. The cause of the sensation has been the subject of much debate. Some psychologists believe that the patient continues to receive messages from the brain, and that there is a direct relation between parts of the brain and sensation in parts of the body (PP 76/PPF 90).[14] There is evidence, for instance, that stimulation of some regions of the brain can make a limb feel larger or smaller.[15] It is therefore assumed by many researchers that there is a parallelism, or a direct link, between body sensations and neural stimulation. Merleau-Ponty rejects the possibility of such an explicit connection, however. He cites several experiments in which damage to the same part of the brain was shown to cause a variety of different bodily sensations, and refers as well to experiments in which the same bodily sensation was shown to be related to different parts of the brain (SB 62–63/SBF 66–67). He concludes that between the body schema and the central sector, "[o]nly a mixed conception of localization and a functional conception of parallelism can be accepted" (SB 72/SBF 79). Seymour Fisher and Sidney Cleveland have observed as much more recently in new amputees who slowly adjust their body schema to their body's new form. When patients were tested for two-point recognition in the upper arm or leg both before and after amputation, it was discovered that the sensitivity in the upper region increased after the lower part of the limb was removed.[16] Seymour Fisher and Sidney Cleveland draw the following conclusions from the study: "One may say then with some confidence that after amputation a radical change in the sensitivity gradient does occur, and the stump takes on an increased sensitivity usually found only in more distal areas. . . . At another level, these results suggest that following the amputation of a limb there are forces mobilized to maintain a pattern of body responses as closely similar to the preamputation pattern as possible."[17] The experience of the phantom limb is just one example of the body schema as a global awareness of the body, which cannot be based on a one-to-one causal relationship between parts of the body and innervations in the brain.

In addition to showing that the body schema involves more than just the inner workings of the brain, the example of the phantom limb also shows that the body schema, or the customary body, is never simply based on a memory. Such an argument has been put forth, but Merleau-Ponty refutes this premise by explaining that the limb assumes an "ambivalent presence" (PP 81/PPF 96) that makes it feel deformed and as though it were slowly shrinking (PP 76, 81/PPF 91, 96). This sensation recedes as the patient gradually adjusts to the new form of his body, a process that can be accelerated by massaging the stump. The phantom limb is not the result of a memory because the patient may continue to remember the previous form of his body when the sensation has finally disappeared. The experience of the amputee over a period of time suggests to Merleau-Ponty that the body schema is neither created by the brain nor based on memory alone. By referring to the embodied experiences of amputation and the phantom limb, Merleau-Ponty is able to provide a clear example of how the body schema is a general, or global, form of the body that adjusts when a radical change has taken place in the body's shape.

This flexibility of the body schema is apparent in the way it allows the body to acquire new habits apart from the "inborn complex" of possible movements of the body that an individual

22   Imagining Bodies

possesses from birth. The body schema makes it possible for a person to adjust and develop his initial abilities into more sophisticated behaviors. A child slowly learns to make use of his body to sit, stand and walk. In each instance, a basic skill becomes incorporated into the original body schema as simple behaviors are adjusted and modified. These simple behaviors are later combined in more difficult activities, like driving a car. Hubert Dreyfus explains that such an activity integrates many basic functions into a unified behavior that eventually becomes a general skill that is remembered by the body in the form of a habit. When I drive a car, I recall only the general behavior and find that my body automatically calls the more simple movements into action without explicit thought. Without this inner communication of the body schema, as Merleau-Ponty puts it, I would be unable to concentrate on the traffic or on my destination.[18] The acquisition of habits is what allows a person to have a sense of freedom and personal existence because it extends the stock of general behaviors that he shares with others into unique ways of living. The body schema, Merleau-Ponty asserts, is not an inert set of habits, but "has something of the momentum of existence" (PP 84/PPF 99).

Essential to the development of habits is an aspect of the body schema called the "virtual body" (*le corps virtuel*, PP 250/PPF 289). A proper understanding of the body requires in Merleau-Ponty's thought a thorough understanding of the imagining aspect of the body and its effects on the experience of the body in general. The virtual body is an imaginative ability to consider alternative uses of the body and to assume different perspectives from which to observe a situation. The original habits of the body can be extended and combined on the basis of an imaginative level of embodied existence. The virtual body allows for "a certain style of seeing, a new use of one's body; it is to enrich and recast the body schema" (PP 153/PPF 179). It allows a person to consider new possibilities for action and to establish a plan of action to acquire those skills.

Imagining Bodies 23

The plan does not need to be deliberate. A toddler may discover how to walk while attempting to accomplish something else or by imitating others; whether quickly or gradually, the toddler's virtual body moves her beyond her original stock of behavior. Merleau-Ponty observes how a cat learns to pull on a string to receive food by adjusting its action to perfect the movement. It begins by using its paw, and later changes to using its teeth. The cat is able to use its body in a general way so that its simpler movements serve as possible steps toward the new behavior. The toddler learns in the same way to use her feet and arms for various activities and becomes more and more efficient and effective in acquiring new habits as she observes and experiences the way in which her body offers a variety of possible or alternative movements. Merleau-Ponty explains that "to learn never consists in being made capable of repeating the same gesture, but of providing an adapted response to the situation by different means. Nor is the response acquired with regard to an individual situation. It is rather a question of a new aptitude for resolving a series of problems of the same form" (SB 96/SBF 106).[19] The body is a symbolic medium, with each of its members representing the possibility of countless activities and functions. Without the virtual aspect of the body schema, the body's original set of abilities could not be developed into more complex modes of behavior. This realm of possibility exists through the virtual body, which is an embodied mode of the imagination.

The virtual body also allows a person to assume alternative positions within a particular scene. It provides an individual with the "power of choosing and varying points of view" (SB 175/SBF 190). For instance, a man uses his mirror image to shave. He moves vicariously through the mirror image in order to accomplish the task at hand.[20] This capacity of the virtual body to obtain an alternative point of view is also drawn out for Merleau-Ponty in W. Kohler's famous experiments with primates. Kohler observed that chimpanzees are able to work with a limited ability to generalize their

24   Imagining Bodies

situation and to use a stick, for example, as a tool for obtaining food; they can learn to use their bodies in different ways. However, when a banana is placed behind an obstacle that is shaped like a U and which is turned away from the primate, a chimp is unable to push the banana with the stick from where it stands first away from the obstacle, or outside of the U, and then around the obstacle and back to itself (SB 98, 117/SBF 108, 127). Furthermore, while a chimp will make the connection between the food it desires and the tool in its presence when it is alone, the same chimp is unable to perceive the stick as a tool for fetching food if another chimp is using it for something else (as a seat, for instance) (SB 114/SBF 124). Humans, by contrast, invariably see the stick as a general object with various aspects and many different potential uses (SB 118, 175/SBF 128, 190). They also can imagine what it would be like to see the object from another perspective and can make use of this perspective to help them with the task at hand. They can imagine what it is like to be on the other side of the obstacle, for instance, and can see that if they push the banana away from them at first, they will be able to navigate it around the obstacle and back to them. This example reveals the way in which the virtual body provides us with "the capacity of going beyond created structures in order to create others" (SB 175/SBF 189), not only by developing abstract or complex movements, but also by creating or employing tools and machines to facilitate our goals.[21] The virtual body allows us to extend our habitual behavior beyond the actual situation to the limitless realm of the imaginary.

The imaginative dimension of the body schema is also manifest in the way that it allows the body to be "absent."[22] The virtual body is not just used to develop or extend the abilities of the body schema. It also allows the body schema to alternate between the roles of seeing and being seen, or of subject and object. For the most part, the body is experienced as a background for seeing instead of as an object to be seen. Merleau-Ponty describes this phenomenon: "If I stand in front of my desk and lean on it with both hands, only my

Imagining Bodies   25

hands are stressed and the whole of my body trails behind them like the tail of a comet. It is not that I am unaware of the whereabouts of my shoulders or back, but these are simply swallowed up on the position of my hands, and my whole posture can be read so to speak in the pressure they exert on the table" (PP 100/PPF 116). The body schema is usually experienced as a kind of absence in the form of a background for a person's activities. For example, while listening to a friend, I begin to lean on the desk in front of me. I feel the desk and have a tacit sense of my hand, but the rest of my body recedes into the background of the conversation. If I suddenly decide to shift my position due to fatigue, the presence of the first hand is replaced by the second, while the first hand joins the rest of my body in a form of absence. The body is not before me as an unquestionable presence, but often recedes into the background and becomes the _means_ for making _other_ things present.[23] The ability to change from seeing to being seen involves an awareness of an alternative that makes use of the imagination; only here the image involved is not of a particular skill or action, but the more general image of the body as a background for the world.

The importance and pervasiveness of the virtual body is especially made manifest in cases where this capacity has been impaired in some way, and in people for whom this background does not recede as smoothly or as readily as it does for the normal subject. Merleau-Ponty cites the example of a patient named Schneider, who exhibits several noteworthy behaviors as a result of a brain injury. He is able to perform normal tasks, such as continuing his work in a wallet factory, but when asked to perform abstract movements, such as pointing to his nose or saluting like a soldier, he can reproduce the movements only by thinking through them step by step (PP 103–5, 117/PPF 119–22, 136). For Schneider, "the world exists only as ready-made or congealed" (PP 112/PPF 130). When asked to assume an abstract or imaginary position, he must reconstruct the proposed movements in his mind and then apply the explicit image of those movements to his actual situation. His body

26   Imagining Bodies

is experienced as an "amorphous mass" (PP 110/PPF 128), an externalized machine that requires focused attention to fulfill a conscious intention. By contrast, the normal subject can readily imagine alternative positions. "He enjoys the use of his body not only in so far as it is involved in a concrete setting," says Merleau-Ponty, but also "he is open to those verbal and fictional situations which he can choose for himself or which may be suggested to him in the course of an experiment" (PP 108/PPF 126).[24] A professional actor does not recreate step by step the actual body movements of the imaginary character, but adapts his body to the character's style. In the same way, the normal subject is readily able to adapt the body to that of an imaginary character, such as the soldier or the virtual image in the mirror. "The normal man and the actor do not mistake imaginary situations for reality, but extricate their real bodies from the living situation to make them breathe, speak and, if need be, weep in the realm of the imagination. This is what our patient is no longer able to do" (PP 105/PPF 121-22).[25] What is lacking in the patient is an ability to "polarize the world" (PP 112/PPF 130) between actual and imaginary movements, and to move freely between these poles. The dialectic of the habitual, or customary, body and the virtual body has collapsed in the experience of the patient, so that a remedy to the patient's illness requires the development of the virtual body.[26]

The virtual body provides an imaginative basis for embodied experience and enables the body schema to move beyond instinctual behavior, acquiring for the individual a sense of freedom and personal existence. The body schema and the virtual body actually exist as two poles of a dialectic in which old habits are developed to meet new situations and general bodily structures are applied to consciously, or unconsciously, chosen projects. These levels of existence are caught up in an "imperceptible twist" (PP 88/PPF 104) in which they become more integrated in time, but "never quite coincide" (PP 87/PPF 103). They do remain grounded in the world and open to new possibilities, and the body schema and the virtual body as two poles of a dialectic constitute what might be called the imagining body. Two examples of the imaginative capacity of the body, or the imagining body, are the experiences of the body as an image in the mind and as a vehicle for expressive behavior, as we shall see. These phenomena are instances of this dialectic at work. An analysis of Merleau-Ponty's direct and indirect references to the body image and gesture allow for a more complete treatment of embodied experience because they present an implicit notion of the imagining body.[27]

In addition to having a global awareness of the body, or a body schema, a person also has a mental representation of her body.[28] Merleau-Ponty tends to refer to this representation, or the body image, by speaking of an individual's "specular image" (*l'image spéculaire*, PrP 125 n. 13/ROF 42) when he wants to talk about the image of the body in the mind. By specular image, Merleau-Ponty is not suggesting a visible image of the body, which might include a person's "mirror image" (*l'image du miroir*, ibid.).[29] He is referring instead to the way in which a person imagines her body to be. The difference between the visible image and the body image is apparent in the tendency of children in particular, and of adults who are less conditioned than others, to exaggerate parts of the body at the expense of others when they are asked to draw a picture of themselves. The head is usually out of proportion, for example, to the rest of the body. There seems to be a level of creativity in how an individual perceives her body, and this unique and personal perception can be used to manipulate the body and to develop new habits. Many patients seeking physiotherapy are asked to recreate their desired movements in their imagination and to use those images as a guide for recovering a lost ability until it becomes reincorporated into the body schema.[30] Shaun Gallagher refers to a similar scenario, in which a patient is reported to have lost all proprioceptive awareness below the neck. Although his body schema is fundamentally impaired, the patient claims that he can recreate some basic movements like walking by first creating a

28   Imagining Bodies

mental image of the movement.[31] The same kind of process could be said to be at work in the therapeutic treatment of people struggling with an inaccurate body image. Even though their use of the body schema continues to function appropriately, an inaccurate body image can cause people to believe that they are overweight, for instance. In extreme cases, a component of the required therapy is the development of a more accurate body image, with attention paid to the myriad of factors which inform how a person perceives his or her body in relationship to others. The body image is flexible and can be modified, allowing a person to alter the way in which he sees himself and his relation to the world.

This imaginative capacity of the body is also responsible for an individual's ability to express and communicate. Words are spoken and ideas are conveyed against the background of postural and facial expression. Such instances of body language at work can often betray thoughts or feelings that contradict the idea being voiced. The twitching of an eye can indicate dishonesty, a slouching posture may suggest a person's disinterest, a lack of eye contact might represent low self-confidence, and an excess of gesticulations may reflect a high degree of anxiety.[32] Because an individual is only sometimes aware of these physical manifestations, these instances of a body language might be more appropriately thought of in terms of disjointed words that only convey a partial or less articulate meaning than they might if they were joined together by the individual's intention to speak his thoughts or feelings. Many self-promotional books and marketing strategies alert people to body language and the power of more intentional nonverbal communication in setting first impressions and ensuring a favorable response from others. Julias Fast alludes to body language when he explains that there is a growing interest in the science of body language or kinesics. Fast argues that the body is so expressive on its own that people are amazed by how much they can communicate when they stop using words and rely on the body as a communicative medium in itself.[33]

The extent to which the body has its own articulate language is particularly apparent in the artistry of mime. Maravene Sheppard Loeschke explains that every mime sequence can be broken down into units of meaning much like the sentences, words and punctuation of language. For example, the mime sequence "The Big Date" includes a number of sections that include getting ready, leaving the house and starting the car. These sections are further divided into units such as looking at the clock and taking a shower, and these units are divided again into smaller units, or "beats," which include closing the shower curtain and turning on the shower.[34] Each of these units involves a particular movement of the body that is learned and developed by the body schema, and which is perfected by the constant practice and refinement of each movement. The language of the body, especially when used in an intentional way, points to the manner in which the body schema and the virtual body work together. They allow an individual to do more than simply move through the world with a particular set of skills and functions, and to incorporate them in a very real sense into an elaborate and creative mode of communication.[35]

Merleau-Ponty argues that the expressive medium of the body is more than just a special kind of language of its own, and that language is actually rooted in the development of gestures into a general symbolic structure of signs and symbols. The body is innately equipped with natural abilities to express its needs and fears and to communicate those feelings to others.[36] There is a sense in which language follows cultural rules that are not restricted to, or determined by, the stock of behavior with which an individual is born. "Speech is the surplus of our experience over natural being," admits Merleau-Ponty (PP 197/PPF 229). He does not believe, however, that a study of language can ignore the natural gestures and affective experiences out of which linguistic meanings are developed. This independence of language from the body is explained by Merleau-Ponty in terms of a distinction that he borrows from Ferdinand de Saussure between spoken language, or *parole parlée*,

30 Imagining Bodies

and the act of speaking, or *parole parlante* (PP 197/PPF 229). Spoken language involves a system of culturally determined meanings that can be considered apart from the natural abilities that make speaking possible. Merleau-Ponty explains:[37]

> If we consider only the conceptual and delimiting meaning of words, it is true that the verbal form — with the exception of endings — appears arbitrary. But it would no longer appear so if we took into account the emotional content of the word, which we have called above its "gestural" sense, which is all-important in poetry, for example. It would then be found that the words, vowels and phonemes are so many ways of "singing" the world, and that their function is to represent things not, as the naïve onomatopoeic theory had it, by reason of an objective resemblance, but because they extract, and literally express, their emotional essence. (PP 187/PPF 218)

Linguistic expressions are extensions of a language that is already present in the body in the form of natural expressions that are flexible and open to development. While there is a sense in which language does exist apart from the body, it is also fair to say, Merleau-Ponty suggests, that an integral connection exists between language and the body.[38] Language cannot be understood apart from the "emotional essence" and "gestural sense" to which Merleau-Ponty refers, so that words that are spoken and the bodies that speak them are at all times bound up in a bodily and imaginative dialogue.

The view of the body as a complex intertwining of subjective and objective characteristics, or of determinateness and creativity, represents a superior approach to the theories of behaviorism and intellectualism and an alternative to a reductionistic tendency in philosophical thought to focus on one aspect of the body at the expense of another. Merleau-Ponty's philosophy of what amounts to an imagining body reveals a dimension of bodily experience that allows a person to develop natural expressions and abilities into complex skills and a personal style of existence. The freedom to develop and change one's body schema through the imagination of the body is exemplified in the movements of the mime. Her gestures remind those who watch her of the power of expression that lies dormant in the embodied experience of every person. When she makes use of her body to create the illusion of a wall or a ladder, she creates on the stage a matrix of bodily forces that the audience is invited to assume and understand in terms of their own embodied experiences. Marcel Marceau's famous illusion of appearing to lean against a mantel, and the mime mentioned earlier who creates an imaginary wall by simple hand movements, builds on techniques that are universally understood even though (or perhaps because) the mime does not speak a word.[39] The expressive language of the body is also present in a variety of everyday experiences. It is at work when two children attempt to communicate underwater, when adults gesticulate at the stock market, when sign language is used in place of speech, when gestures are used to direct traffic or to conduct an orchestra, and in the liturgical worship of a congregational body. Each of these instances are rooted in the dialectic of the imagining body and demonstrates in an implicit way what the mime asks the members of her audience to recall: "If you look around," as mime Katherine Sorley Walker explains, "you'll be surprised how many gestures are quite instinctive with people. No one thinks of them as Mime. But of course, that's what they are."[40]

Two

Perceptual Imagining

The seashore is the site for a festival of the senses. The dark, purple waves betray hints of red, green and yellow, a palette that changes each moment as the waves roll into shore. Their translucent surfaces communicate to the eye their syrupy texture and the warmth of the sun that dances in their wake. From the crests of the waves, a dense spray of salt and foam is thrown into the air, creating a scent that is so strong that one can almost taste the salt. The sound of the waves crashing into the sandbar forms a rhythmic ostinato for the melodious cry of gulls overhead.

Merleau-Ponty was fascinated by perception. From *Phenomenology to Perception* to *The Visible and the Invisible*, his philosophy centers on perception.[1] The perceptual image contains a wealth of information about the physical environment and is a source of both pleasure and knowledge of the world around us. Each sense quality not only possesses a depth and hidden dimension of meaning, but is also supported by a context of related qualities. The body reacts to what it discovers in the sensible manifold by interpreting it in terms of what it can do, perhaps in the form of an affective response to the rhythmic sound of the waves, or a surge of energy one might receive from the rays of the sun. In either case, the imagining body is provided with new possibilities by the

34 Perceptual Imagining

perceptual scene that it can appropriate as actual modes of being in the world. Between the perceiver's body and the world of the sensible is a mutual dependence that constitutes the basis of human experience.

A major influence on Merleau-Ponty's philosophy of perception was the concept of the perceptual Gestalt that he borrowed from Wolfgang Koehler, K. Koffka and others. Gestalt psychology rejects traditional theories of perception that focused on individual sense qualities as independent bits of information. It was believed that consciousness combined these bits of sensory information into elaborate pictures in the mind that represented the sensible world as it appeared to consciousness. But experiments conducted by Koehler and others suggest that the "building block" approach to understanding sense experience failed to capture many essential aspects of perceptual phenomena. It has been shown, for instance, that a gray figure on a black background reinforces the color of the background, while the same gray on a gray background is made to look darker than the gray in the first example. In another experiment, a ring of gray on a yellow background is shown to appear blue (SB 80–81/SBF 89–90). In each of these cases, the color of the shape is altered by the context, suggesting that we cannot discern colors simply by combining bits of information. A common way to explain the nature of the Gestalt is to say that the whole is greater than the sum of its parts. Along with the Gestalt psychologists, Merleau-Ponty concludes that an essential structure of perception is that of a "figure on a background" (PP 4/PPF 10) that cannot be accounted for by traditional theories of perception. To understand the logic of perceptual experience, we must look beyond the mere sum of sense qualities and begin to consider the effect of the entire context on how we perceive colors, shapes and sounds.

A problem that arises concerning the study of the perceptual Gestalt is that the Gestalt is by nature ambiguous and resistant to analysis. When we turn to study the background of a particular sense quality, say the purple waves of the seashore, the color of its distant surroundings blurs into a pale blue that, at the margins of our visual field, "tends toward neutrality" (SB 82/SBF 91). If we try to focus on the color of the margin, the margin emerges into the foreground as a figure, such as when one looks into the sun and perceives its yellow center but loses hold of the original figure, the purple wave, which recedes to become part of a neutral background for the perception of the sun (PP 5–6/PPF 11–12). The perceptual world does not give to the perceiver a determinate set of sensory information. The significance of "blue" or "yellow" occurs only within a perceptual framework imposed on the visible scene. In another experiment, two lines of equal length appear to be unequal because of the use of arrows at the ends of each line. While the first one has the arrows pointing away from the line, the second has them pointing inward, making it look longer than the first (PP 6/PPF 12). If we were to measure the lines, we would notice that they are of equal length; but perception makes use of the entire context rather than measurement, picks up on the arrowheads as visual cues that inform the context of each line in a different way, and thus makes one look longer than the other. Merleau-Ponty explains: "The two straight lines in Müller-Lyer's optical illusion are neither of equal nor unequal length; it is only in the objective world that this question arises" (ibid.). On the basis of these experiments it can be seen that whether we are dealing with colors on a background or with parallel lines, "the perceived, by its nature, admits of the ambiguous" (PP 11/PPF 18).

In response to this problem, Merleau-Ponty turns to the method of phenomenological analysis. The preface to *Phenomenology of Perception* outlines Merleau-Ponty's version of phenomenology. The key task behind this method of analysis is to describe a particular phenomenon as it appears without imposing particular theories about how the world appears to consciousness (PP xvii/PPF xii). Because of the prominence of modern science, the observer's natural assumptions are that perception consists of individual sense qualities that are passively received by the observer. Another natural

36   Perceptual Imagining

assumption about perception is that it occurs in a world that is completely determinate and measurable. Alluding to the lines in Müller-Lyer's optical illusion and similar illusions, Merleau-Ponty explains: "Psychologists have for a long time taken great care to overlook these phenomena. In the world taken in itself everything is determined. There are many unclear sights, as for example a landscape on a misty day, but then we always say that no real landscape is in itself unclear. It is so only for us. The object, psychologists would assert, is never ambiguous, but becomes so only through our inattention" (PP 6/PPF 12). The phenomenologist, by contrast, argues that by ascribing precision and objectivity to the visual scene, the perceiver confuses the way in which the scene appears in itself to consciousness. Phenomenology involves precisely a return to the things themselves, in all of their ambiguity, before they are confined to conceptual categories like "straight" and "equal," "blue" and "yellow." "To return to things themselves," says Merleau-Ponty, "is to return to that world which precedes knowledge, of which knowledge always *speaks*, and in relation to which every scientific schematization is an abstract and derivative sign-language, as is geography in relation to the countryside in which we have learnt beforehand what a forest, a prairie or a river is" (PP ix/PPF iii). The geographical landscape makes sense only on the basis of an experience of the prairie or forest that is itself fraught with ambiguities that the scientist is at a loss to explain. Visual illusions, for the scientist, consist of aberrations of vision and say nothing about the way that the world is seen by the eye. The task of phenomenology "is to understand these strange relationships which are woven between the parts of the landscape, or between it and me as incarnate subject, and through which an object perceived can concentrate in itself a whole scene or become the *imago* of a whole segment of life" (PP 52/PPF 64). Phenomenology is the study of the perceptual scene or *imago* and the "immanent meaning" (PP 49/PPF 61) of the Gestalt that resists objective explanation.[2]

Perceptual Imagining 37

A phenomenological analysis of perception highlights two essential aspects of the experience: the logic of the sensible world as it appears to the observer and the role of the observer (and most importantly of her body) in the interpretation of that experience. Although neither aspect can be understood in isolation from the other, it is helpful to consider each in turn and then to take into account the effect of their convergence. When one considers the logic of the sensible world, one must start by accepting the ambiguity of the perceptual scene and engaging in a careful analysis of the way in which sense qualities appear within it. The goal is to discover the essential components of the sensible manifold that make it possible to be experienced as a whole.

The most important consideration in the study of the logic of perceptual experience is the law of synesthesis in which any given sense quality implies the qualities of other senses. The particular shade of blue that one sees in the ocean is not an isolated datum of information; rather, it relies on its location within a synesthetic structure for the particular significance that it assumes within the scene. The blue of the waves reveals an entire spectrum of color that is made visible when the rays of sunlight overhead become refracted in the water's prismlike texture. To even see the blue as a distinct color requires an awareness of its place within a spectrum of color and in terms of its different modulation of the entire visible field in comparison with the other colors. This can be explained by considering the way that colors are identified. Children learn colors not by recognizing individual shades but by making distinctions within the field of color as a whole. They begin by distinguishing general shades of light and dark, the general color distinctions of cool and warm, and after a long process they become able to distinguish many different colors from each other and to recognize them within a complex spectrum of blues, reds, yellows and greens (PP 29–30, 175–76/PPF 38, 204–5). In the reverse case when color awareness is lost, the patient experiences a

38   Perceptual Imagining

gradual blurring of colors until there is only a single nondescript hue.[3] Color spectrums allow us to make distinctions in the field of color and to apply these distinctions to a variety of scenes. We do not perceive the scene in terms of individual colors that are combined within an optical illusion, such as one finds in the paintings of Georges Seurat; rather, the distinctions of colors are more like forces or currents within the medium of color that combine to offer the scene its particular synesthetic structure.

This relativistic theory of color may appear to deny the universality of color, the fact that I can recognize red in a variety of contexts, implying to some psychologists that there must be a universal shade for each color. Many studies of color experience have been based on the belief that there is a standard shade for all colors when represented as "color areas" within white light. Merleau-Ponty, however, suggests that this is only one way of experiencing color, and that there is no reason to grant it the status of being a standard for color. These "color areas," he says, are "only one of the possible structures of colour, and already the colour of a piece of paper or a surface of colour no longer obeys the same laws."[4] Color areas, for example, do not capture the phenomenon of gloss, glow and brightness found in the color of stained glass or traffic lights (PP 306/PPF 353). Color areas involve abstractions of how color usually appears when observed, for example, on the surface of objects. Merleau-Ponty explains:

> Colored areas are indeed located at a distance, though vaguely; they have a spongy appearance, whereas surface colors are dense and hold the gaze upon their surface. Colored areas, moreover, are always parallel to the frontal plane, whereas surface colors may show any orientation. Finally colored areas are always more or less flat, and cannot, without losing their distinctive quality as such, assume a particular form and appear curved or spread out over a surface. (Ibid.)

If we were to choose a standard for any color, we would do better to choose the surface color and not the color area, since it captures more of the mystery of vision. But other studies show that we need to reject the concept of a standard shade of color altogether. Experiments show, for example, that a white object in the shade will be experienced as white even though the shade of color that reaches the retina is gray. When an impressionist painter uses gray to depict the white object (such as when Monet paints a picture of white linen), the object is perceived as white. Another example of color recognition is when a blue piece of paper is seen to be blue in gaslight even though the color registers as brown on a photometer (PP 307/PPF 353). When we say that we see an object as white regardless of the lighting or the context, what is being shared between contexts cannot, then, be an absolute shade. To understand the significance of color, it is not sufficient to choose a particular appearance of a color as a standard to compare with other experiences. It is better to say, with Merleau-Ponty, that a color is based on its position within an entire spectrum that will change its shade depending on the context and the lighting of the scene. There are no absolute shades of color, but rather differentiations within a global phenomenon of color that is modified from situation to situation. Exactly what these differentiations consist of will make more sense when we consider synesthesis in general, and then relate this structure of experience to the imagining body.

In addition to containing a complex logic of the interrelation of qualities within a particular dimension of sense (such as color), perception also involves an intertwining of the various sense qualities within a common synesthetic experience. An understanding of perception, says Merleau-Ponty, requires an analysis of synesthesis as a basic structure that is irreducible to the sum of individual sense qualities. An example of synesthesis is when the foam of white-caps reveals to the perceiver the other sense qualities involved in the experience: the salty taste and smell of the waves, their frothy texture and the sound of the water as it tosses and turns with the tide. The sounds and smells do not simply accompany the color of the whitecaps, but are part of the color and intrinsic to it. The color

40   Perceptual Imagining

of the whitecaps contains the roar of the water and the salty taste of the foam. Merleau-Ponty observes that "the subject does not say only that he has the sensation both of a sound and a color: it is the sound itself that he sees where colors are formed" (PP 229/PPF 265, 264). Another example is the relation between texture and sound when one can detect the sharpness of the sound of breaking glass and the hollowness of a sounding bell (PP 230/PPF 266). Cézanne claimed to be able to paint smells (SNS 15/SNSF 26). All of these examples suggest that every particular quality indicates an entire system of sensible information that contributes to the significance of the perceptual scene.

Without synesthesis we would be unable to recognize perceptual objects at all. The global synesthetic structure of a scene provides "a way into the thing" (PP 305/PPF 352) as an "intersensory entity" (PP 317/PPF 366). The whitecaps appear as white, frothy, roaring and salty. We understand the essence of the wave as a unity of these meanings that corresponds with the unity of the synesthetic experience. The thing is "an organism of colours, smells, sounds and tactile appearances which symbolize, modify and accord with each other according to the laws of a real logic" (PP 38/PPF 48). The internal law of the thing is not a form or idea, but is immanent in the landscape as a "distinctive perceptual style" (PP 39/PPF 49). The whiteness and the frothiness determine each other to become the white and froth "of this particular wave," so that the wave appears as a single perceptual object. What is primary is not the wave's essence but the synesthesis of particular qualities and the immanent law of the perceptual scene in which the object appears.[5] Phenomenology as the study of the things themselves must resort to the phenomenon of synesthesis if it is to discover the essence of the perceptual object.

In *Phenomenology of Perception*, Merleau-Ponty does not elaborate on the structure of synesthesis; the work does not, explicitly at least, provide a comprehensive treatise on perception. Only in the working notes to *The Visible and the Invisible* are we given a more detailed description of synesthesis.[6] There Merleau-Ponty suggests that sense qualities can assume both the role of the figure of a given phenomenon and the role of the background when other qualities become the figure of the phenomenon. If we focus on the color of the whitecaps, our experience is informed by the background information of the smell, the taste and the sound. When we decide to switch our focus to one of these other qualities, the color becomes part of the tacit background of the experience. Sam Mallin provides an elaborate explanation of how this occurs by means of cues within a particular dimension of sense. He argues, for instance, that the differentiation of colors will vary depending on the texture or the sound or the taste involved. This sound and taste, for example, would assume a particular color differentiation in the visual field.[7] Although it is believable that we can tell depending on the intensity of a color whether it is made of glass or wood, thus lending support to Mallin's theory, it becomes difficult with this kind of analysis to determine within a given color the implied tastes and smells of a particular phenomenon. A better illustration of the relation between different sense qualities is provided by Merleau-Ponty's image of the inside and the outside of a glove where each side implies the other and is the reverse of the other (VI 263/VIF 317). If the glove is inverted through a small hole on the surface of the glove, its shape will be completely different; but this alternative shape or dimension remains implied by the appearance of the glove in its normal form. Likewise, the texture of an object is implied by its color without assuming a particular color value itself. Synesthesis is the juncture of the sensible fields that takes the form of "the pivot of a system of equivalencies" (VI 205/VIF 258), the pivot, in other words, of a variety of sense dimensions which imply each other without being reducible to any one of them (like vision in Mallin's example). Synesthesis involves the ability of qualities to *not* appear, to remain invisible as the background and as a hidden dimension of another quality. It requires a separation of the senses in order to facilitate their unity within the phenomenon, so that they can encroach on one another without losing their richness by becoming reduced to only one of them. "It is *that separation*

42   Perceptual Imagining

(*écart*) first of all," concludes Merleau-Ponty, "that is the perceptual *meaning*" (VI 197/VIF 250).

A helpful commentary on Merleau-Ponty's description of synesthesis is provided by Jacques Garelli in "Voir ceci et voir selon."[8] He argues that fields of sense should be understood as a *means* for seeing qualities and not as objects of vision. He cites one of the working notes from *The Visible and the Invisible*: "Perception is not first a perception of things, but a perception of elements (water, air . . .) of rays of the world, of things which are dimensions, which are worlds, I slip on these 'elements' and here I am in the world, I slip from the 'subjective' Being."[9] I step out of my "subjectivity" and into the world by perceiving a given sense quality upon the background of other qualities. While I focus on the color, the other qualities are there, but in the form of an absence and the possibility of becoming a future figure of the phenomenon. If I shift my focus to another quality, it becomes the figure while the color joins the background. To see color thus implies seeing a relation of the color to the other qualities; in order to be a color, the quality must refer to the possibility of exploring the other qualities that are related to the color (such as texture and smell). The perception of color also implies that the color itself is experienced as possibly becoming the dimension for another quality. Perception involves "an interlacing of significations such that, when certain among them are perceived and pass into actuality, the others are only virtually intended" (SB 217/SBF 234). There is an elaborate structure of presence and absence, of actuality and possibility, that constitutes the phenomenon of synesthesis. The visible quality involves a complex relation to the other senses and to its own possibility as a dimension for the others. Renaud Barbaras concludes that perception involves the ability to recognize dimensions of sense and not the passive reception of information on the retina. The perceptual image is not "in front of me, as an object that I can exhaustively reveal, but around me; I do not perceive *it*, I perceive *by means of* it."[10] It is on the basis of an interchange

Perceptual Imagining 43

between the different qualities and their respective fields that the perceptual image is able to appear.

With the logic of the perceptual world comes a particular way for my body to engage with the scene. One essential difference between Merleau-Ponty and Gestalt psychologists is that for him the context of synesthetic experience is not a static phenomenon that appears in isolation of consciousness; rather, the context is a living mode of existence in line with what Edmund Husserl called the "lifeworld" (*Lebenswelt*) of experience.[11] The lifeworld consists of "the intuitive surrounding world of life, pre-given as existing for all in common."[12] The perceptual scene is a context for living that makes sense in terms of the actions and behavior of the perceiver. In particular, the visual scene presents itself as a "muddled problem for my body to solve" (PP 214/PPF 248). To illustrate his point, Merleau-Ponty refers to experiences of perceptual foreshadowing, such as when an object is discerned only slowly as one continues to enter and explore a particular context, identifying a ship's mast upon the background of trees, or the shape of a rabbit that is hiding in the grass, for example. Each object is at first unnoticed to the observer, but the scene offers itself as being confused or indeterminate and in need of further exploration.[13] Foreshadowing is often overcome by habits of perception, when we come to see patterns of qualities coalescing into a common style or essence by which we identify particular objects. When we see a face upside-down, for instance, we instantly recognize it in its proper setting because of a pattern of experience that we have come to make use of (PP 19–20/PPF 27–28). Our experience consists of an immediate interpretation of the sensible manifold in terms of modes of behavior; the perceptual phenomenon makes sense in terms of what my body can do.

The context of the perceptual scene, or the lifeworld as Merleau-Ponty likes to describe it, is interpreted by the perceiver as offering virtual modes of embodiment. There is a correspondence between the perceptual world and the body's motility: "The visible world

44   Perceptual Imagining

and the world of my motor projects are each total parts of the same Being."[14] The problem posed by the perceptual world is solved "by the body" by walking toward the object and grasping it by the hand, or by calling upon more sense organs to make sense of the phenomenon. Between the body and the phenomenon is a "kind of knowledge that is very close to praxis."[15] Merleau-Ponty argues that qualities are even experienced as ways of living the body and of occupying space. For example, the red carpet implies a series of possible bodily experiences such as the sensation on the hand of its fibrous texture and the experience of hearing the particular sound the carpet makes when I walk across it. It is also well known that colors have different effects on the body: reds and yellows excite the body while blues and greens have a calming effect (PP 213–14/ PPF 247–48; see also PP 311/PPF 359). Qualities are first experienced as "different modalities of our co-existence with the world" (PrP 5/INF 403). The original meaning of the perceptual world is interpreted in terms of the body's motility.

Merleau-Ponty is not suggesting, however, that perception and motility are identical. In one passage he seems to make this mistake when he says that "we are not to be understood as having in mind two distinct facts, a sensation of redness and motor reactions — we must be understood as meaning that red, by its texture as followed and adhered to be our gaze, is already the amplification of our motor being" (PP 211/PPF 245). In another passage he appears to identify perception with kinesthesis, the body's internal awareness of its own movement. He writes that they are both "synonymous" (VI 255/VIF 308), suggesting that one cannot be understood in isolation of the other. "Perception," agrees Barbaras, "is not to be understood apart from motility, the truth of perception resides in self-movement."[16] What Merleau-Ponty is suggesting, however, is not that perception is reducible to kinesthesis, as some critics have claimed.[17] Their synonymous relation is rather only a virtual relation, a "failure" (VI 255/IVF 308) to achieve an actual conflation. Kinesthesis, for example, reveals nothing about the objects of perception and provides us with information only concerning our disposition and posture. The mystery of perception, although related to kinesthesis, cannot be explained solely in terms of the experience of motility. Renaud Barbaras explains: "The subject's movement is equally distance and proximity to [the perceptual object], placed in a nascent state, always already begun and never deployed, dynamism without extension."[18] Because of the divergence opened between movement and perception, the object is made visible as both related to the body and separate from it, as both close and yet distant from the body's self-movement. Another way to understand the relation of perception to kinesthesis is to see them as involving the same relation that was found in synesthetic qualities. Just as qualities imply each other without being reducible to each other, so perception and kinesthesis, as different modes of embodiment, participate in a relation of "proximity at a distance," in which each serves as the potential background for the other within a common diacritical field that is embodiment in general. Within the divergence created by perception and movement, the perceptual object is able to appear as both a mode of existence and as an independent object in the sensible world.

Merleau-Ponty expands on the relation between the logic of the perceptual scene and the experience of the body by suggesting that the unity or logic of perception assumes a similar form to that of the unity of the body or the body schema. The perceived object and its particular synesthetic structure presents to the body different ways of relating to the world. These qualities are gathered into a "synergetic system" that is "the same in kind" (PP 234, 185/PPF 270, 216) as the body schema. The implied synesthetic system of the red carpet is experienced not by combining individual actions related to each sense quality but by a single movement of the entire body, a "general action of being in the world" (PP 234/PPF 270). Without the unity of the body, the perceptual scene would never be able to assume an order for the body.[19] "It is my gaze which subtends color," exclaims Merleau-Ponty, "and the movement of my

46 Perceptual Imagining

hand which subtends the object's form" (PP 214/PPF 248). It is only later, when the body assumes the habit of passive observation, that the perceptual object is seen to possess measurable and distinct properties, and even these make sense only with respect to the action of measuring, an action requiring the motility and unity of the body schema. The unity of the perceptual world would not be possible without the unity of the body schema. Merleau-Ponty stresses this point by concluding that "the theory of the body schema is, implicitly, a theory of perception" (PP 206/PPF 239).

It can now be made clear in what way the body involved in perception is the imagining body discussed in the previous chapter. The traditional theory of perception treats the body as a passive agent that receives sense data, which as a model for perception could not account for the virtual dimensions of meaning that are found in every phenomenon of color, sound and texture. The body of perception implied by Merleau-Ponty's theory of synesthesis is "a system of systems devoted to the inspection of a world and capable of leaping over distances, piercing the perceptual future, and outlining hollows and reliefs, distances and deviations — a meaning — in the inconceivable flatness of being" (S 67/SF 83). The experience of the red of the carpet is made possible by the fact that it conceals the related qualities of texture and sound; but the very meaning of this red contains the possibility of surpassing itself as a mere surface and as serving as a dimension for other qualities. To see the relation between the figure and the background, we must recognize them as reversible; the red of the carpet is reversible with its dimensions of sense as a potential dimension for the other qualities that it implies. If we were to ignore this reversibility, we would cease to see the red within its synesthetic structure and thus would no longer be studying the things themselves but rather an abstraction of color, such as the "color areas" discussed earlier. To see the red within its particular context, we must see it as the figure of a perceptual structure that by its very nature can be modified to reveal the other qualities; we must, in short, see the virtual dimensions of the experience along with its actual manifestation in the form of the quality of color. Perceiving a color on a background thus requires an entrance into the virtual, a recognition within perception of "an interlacing of significations such that, when certain among them are perceived and pass into actuality, the others are only virtually intended" (SB 217/SBF 234). A passive body could not encounter qualities as virtual modes of existence, suggesting that the imagining body is essential for perception.

The bodily attitudes presented by qualities are recognizable as potential modes of creative embodiment. Merleau-Ponty comments that "there is an immediate equivalence between the orientation of the visual field and the awareness of one's own body as the potentiality of that field" (PP 206/PPF 238). Between the imagining body and the perceptual phenomenon is a relation of "communion" (PP 212/PPF 245–46) such that the phenomenon becomes "a kind of inner diaphragm which determines . . . what our reflexes and perceptions will be able to aim at in the world, the area of our possible operations, the scope of our life" (PP 81/PPF 95). Qualities offer virtual modes of embodiment that we slip on by virtually extending our body in imaginative ways.

Consider the example of color. Individual colors are first recognized as modes of embodiment. The red carpet, we have seen, causes the body to engage with the world in a particular way, and to be exposed to its unique structure of touch, sound and smell. The relation of the qualities in a perceptual object can thus be seen as the relation of various modes of embodiment. In order for the object to be seen as an object, it must appear within the structure of foreground and background, with one quality standing out as the focus and the others receding into a kind of absence. This means that the appearance of the perceptual object requires a unique structure of presence and absence: the presence of the red of the carpet implies the absence of softness and of the smell of fibers; the absence of the texture and smell is based on their virtual presence as the focus of perception, which would also imply the virtual absence of the

48   Perceptual Imagining

color. There is a reversibility implied between the different sense qualities that is essential to seeing the perceptual object as a whole with different qualities, and that betrays an essential virtuality in perception without which synesthesis would no longer be possible. The virtuality of perception, however, resembles the virtuality of the body because the virtual qualities implied by the actually perceived quality are also modes of virtual embodiment. "The synthesis of the object," Merleau-Ponty explains, "is here effected, then, through the synthesis of one's own body, it is the reply or correlative to it" (PP 205/PPF 237). The synthesis of the object is the correlate of the synthesis of the body and, like the body, partakes of the virtual as well as the actual. Just as the actor engages in a virtual body to explore the world of the fictional character, so the perceiver must engage with the virtual modes of embodiment implied by the receding qualities to perceive the focused quality as an instance of a particular structure (as the red of the carpet, for instance, PP 104 5/PPF 121 22). Thus to perceive is to engage with virtual qualities that are essentially virtual modes of embodiment.

There is a tension in Merleau-Ponty's description of perception between the creativity of the perceiver and the natural origin of the perceptual scene. As an instance of virtual embodiment, perception is like a creative activity with the various qualities serving as the colors on a palette that we make use of in creating the masterpiece of our experience. Perception involves, to some extent, what Gary Madison calls a "metaphorical innovation"[20] in its use of patterns of seeing and hearing that are altered and applied to new experiences. "It must be poetry," Merleau-Ponty tells us; "that is, it must completely awaken and recall our sheer power of expressing beyond things already said or seen" (S 52/SF 65). Colors, for example, are like words or symbols that allow us to see the perceptual scene as involving various possibilities of embodiment; and, like words and symbols, their significance is constantly changing and being revised to better suit our experience of the sensible manifold (SB 85/SBF 94). But in perception, the creativity of the body is always in response to the logic of the scene itself which does not always conform with the wishes of the observer. The perceptual scene offers a "modality of a general existence, one already destined for a physical world and which runs through me without my being the cause of it" (PP 216/PPF 250). Before I perceive the waves of the ocean, they already open for me a particular way of being in the world and provide me with a "perceptual tradition" (PP 238/PPF 275) that I do not determine. Merleau-Ponty explains: "My act of perception, in its unsophisticated form, does not itself bring about this synthesis; it takes advantage of work already done, of a general synthesis constituted once and for all, and this is what I mean when I say that I perceive with my body or my senses, since my body and my senses are precisely that familiarity with the world born of habit, that implicit or sedimentary body of knowledge" (PP 238/PPF 275). When the body explores the virtual modes of embodiment implied by the qualities that it encounters, it develops and expresses the sensible world itself, and not the emotions or ideas of the observer alone. "All perception," says Merleau-Ponty, "is already primordial expression" (S 67/SF 84). The task of phenomenology, grounded in the primacy of perception, is to "reveal the mystery of the world" (PP xxi/PPF xvi), to express the sky and the waves so that they may appear in themselves, in terms of modes of virtual embodiment that can be appropriated and further developed, and yet remain rooted in an originary meaning that the perceiver does not constitute. To imagine with the body is to resonate with the imagining of the sensible world, to participate in its original script and to bring its meaning to fruition.

Perception provides the body with a basic mode of existing in which the world is offered in the form of possibilities of virtual embodiment. The art of mime and the imagining body in general expand on the basic perceptual experiences of space, sound and color to create complex structures of meaning that can be repeated and shared with others. At a more basic level, the creative development of habits of perception in response to the sights and sounds

50 Perceptual Imagining

of the perceptual scene enables us to develop a general set of behavioral patterns so that ordinary objects can appear immediately to us without the need to rediscover their significance as they are first presented to the senses. One of the lessons that we learn from the mime is that our stock of behavior is not locked into ordinary habits of perception but is susceptible to change and development. Later in this book I will explore the various results that are possible when we go beyond our habitual modes of seeing and listening to either the creative acts of genius or to the flights of fancy of the insane. Far from being merely the passive reception of information, perception provides the most basic expression of the imagining body that is taken up in different ways in all other modes of human existence.

THREE

Aesthetic Imagining

Filled with wonder before the waves of the seashore, I decide to take out my pad and charcoal to draw. I trace with my hand the sweeping curves and the movements of the waves to express their impact on my body and my imagination. When I am done, I place the sketchbook before me, and I trace the curves on the page with my eyes instead of my hand. The finished sketch becomes the object of my attention, providing a communion at a distance between the waves and myself.

In addition to being a unique visible object, a work of art can have a powerful effect on perception itself. The perspective drawings of the Renaissance, for instance, allowed for the birth of a new experience of space; the vanishing line, a single dot at the center of the landscape, exposed the canvas to the third dimension and changed forever the way that space is experienced. More recently, the Impressionists used their technique to present the world as a two-dimensional spectacle of color and light, and Andy Warhol's use of computer graphics have made the visible world plastic and dispensable. The artistic battle is more than a struggle to represent objects, it is a fight to reinvent the very way that we perceive the world.

52 Aesthetic Imagining

Merleau-Ponty's later philosophy gives special attention to the phenomenon of the work of art. Much of his research after the publication of *Phenomenology of Perception* concerns the aesthetic experience and the activity of artistic production. The arts that interested him the most included painting and literature, especially the artworks of Paul Cézanne and Paul Klee, and the literature of Honoré de Balzac and Marcel Proust. He admired the sculptures of Marcel Duchamp and Auguste Rodin, and he even wrote an essay on the new art form of cinema. Merleau-Ponty was also aware of many of the most popular art critics of his time: André Malraux, Erwin Panofsky and Sigmund Freud to name a few. But he does not simply express the ideas of others. What is unique about his essays on art and literature is the appreciation that he shows for the expressive body and the role that it plays in every form of art. Be it a painting or a sculpture, a novel or a film, what is common in every artwork is the way that it uses the imagining body to extend the experience of perception to a heightened sense of beauty and creativity.

The art world during the 1940s and 1950s, when Merleau-Ponty was writing many of his essays on aesthetics, was in a state of transition. The popularity of classical realism started to wane as the Impressionists began to experiment with painting. Photography and cinema were beginning to assert themselves as legitimate art forms that surpassed their original mimetic function. The art of mime was undergoing a radical transformation that gave to the body a new expressive power. Each of these developments created a tension between those who believed that art was meant to hold up a mirror to nature, and those who claimed for art the role of emotional expression.

Until about the middle of the nineteenth century, the arts in France had been mostly representational in nature. Artworks had traditionally remained a part of the general landscape, a fresco decorating the wall of a place of worship, or a statue commemorating the victory of a great general as part of a public square. For this reason,

Aesthetic Imagining   53

art has traditionally been treated as mimetic.[1] Even today sketches and photographs are often used primarily as an aid to memory, painted landscapes are frequently used to adorn the walls of commercial buildings, and the digitized reproductions of classic masterpieces now litter the expansive regions of virtual reality.

Pictorial art gained support from several technical innovations during the early ages of modern science. Merleau-Ponty mentions the story of how Brunelleschi, the great master of the duomo in Florence, built a device to show how a scene of the Battistero was subject to the laws of perspective (S 41/SF 52). Shortly after his invention, his contemporaries, including the sculptor Ghiberti, began using perspective in their artworks, replacing the mystical space of medieval art for the new spatial order of perspective. In one of the panels of Ghiberti's doors to the Battistero is an Old Testament scene of Jacob sending his sons to buy corn from Egypt. Behind the figures stands a round temple, portrayed in perfect perspective, displaying exceptional skill and design.[2] Since the creation of his famous doors, artists from around the world have attempted to achieve the detail of Ghiberti and to universalize Brunelleschi's conception of perspectival space.

During the sixteenth century the universalization of perspective was further extended to the heavens when some artists switched their medium from oils to optics. René Descartes reports the invention of the first telescope by Hollander Jacques Métius, which opened the skies to human measurement. With the discovery of the telescope the entire world could be subjected to what Husserl later called the "mathematization of nature," the projection by artists and scientists of a particular way of seeing reality.[3] As a result, the traditional mimetic function of art became the function of representing the world as a mathematical *Idea*. The concern for the artist became one of design and precision as he or she represented the world according to the idealized space of perspective.

Painters during the seventeenth and eighteenth centuries perfected the representational arts with new techniques and a refined

54 Aesthetic Imagining

use of perspective. Artistic revolutions during this period included the use of light, skillfully developed by Flemish artists, and the depiction of velvet found in the portraits of Jean-Honoré Fragonard and in the peaches of Jean-Baptiste-Siméon Chardin. Merleau-Ponty describes the attitude of the French Academy as follows: "A painting makes us see in the same way in which we actually see the thing itself, even though the thing is absent. Especially it makes us see a space where there is none" (PrP 172/EMF 44). Added to this attitude was the conviction that, thanks to the spatial innovations of perspective, the only task remaining for painting was to overcome the limitations of its medium to achieve the perfect representation of reality.

What is most important to Merleau-Ponty about each of these innovations is the way that they make use of space as a medium of expression in its own right. Perspective frees the artist from the hierarchical and symbolic spaces of medieval frescoes for another space that centers around the human body. Each technique involves only one of many possible ways of depicting space. The discovery of perspective, then, although rekindling an interest in how we experience space, does not offer a definitive statement on the matter. Merleau-Ponty explains that we do not always see according to perspective; distant objects, for example, do not vanish along the horizon, but look larger and assume a shape that defies perspective (S 49/SF 61). If you attempt to find a vanishing point in nature, you will not find one because each visual fragment of the world teases the eye to see further, to see objects on the horizon where there should be a flat line, to explore the virtual meaning of the horizon as a dimension of space. "These techniques were false," Merleau-Ponty argues, "only in so far as they pretended to bring an end to painting's quest and history, to found once and for all an exact and infallible art of painting" (PrP 134/EMF 49). While Renaissance perspective ushered in a new era of spatial representation in painting, it could not put an end to the mysteries of vision.

The idea of art as representation soon came to be replaced by a concern for aesthetic expression. In 1863 a group of Parisian artists opened an exhibit of paintings in protest against the French Royal Academy of Painting and Sculpture. Called the Salon des Refusés, the exhibit consisted of paintings that had been rejected by the Academy because they failed to make use of established techniques in French portraiture. Included in the exhibit were paintings by Cézanne, Pissarro, Whistler and Manet, including Manet's famous canvas, *Le déjeuner sur l'herbe*. These novel artworks, the early examples of French Impressionism, freed painting from the confines of a mimetic discipline for a world of pure painting, a world of the work as *work*. In these paintings, the artists invite the viewer not to see a world where there is none, but to see the world according to the artist's cues and style of perception.[4] Consider, for example, the multiple paintings by Monet of Rouen Cathedral, or by Cézanne of the Montagne Sainte-Victoire. The artist is not, in each case, attempting to correct his depiction of the landscape but to produce a picture in its own right "to challenge existing pictures."[5] With the Impressionists the artist's task became the attempt to create a universe of color, and not to use a universe of color to depict ordinary objects; the work of art no longer represented an absent reality, but invited the viewer into the private universe of the artist.

The change from the work as a representation to the work as *work* led artists and critics to consider the significance of art in general. A popular response, led by Leo Tolstoy, was that art involved the expression and excitation of emotions. He writes: "To evoke in oneself a feeling one has once experienced and having evoked it in oneself then by means of movements, lines, colors, sounds, or forms expressed in words, so to transmit that feeling that others experience the same feeling — this is the activity of art."[6] For more recent artists, the suggestion has been made that what is different about art is the particular emotion that is expressed,

56   Aesthetic Imagining

and not simply the expression of any emotion, placing it on a par with natural expression. After placing a white square on a white background, Kasimir Malevich claimed to have achieved the purest expression of unidentified emotion, emotion qua emotion, on a canvas transformed into "a desert in which nothing can be perceived but feeling. . . . The square = feeling, the white field = the void beyond this feeling."[7] Even Jean-Paul Sartre describes the emotional power of a work to be objectified in the colors and lines of the work itself. The emotion, he writes, "is a grief which does not *exist* any more, which *is*," and which is found in the "yellow rent in the sky over Golgotha." Malraux seems to be saying something similar to Sartre: "All art is the expression, slowly come by, of the artist's deepest emotions *vis-à-vis* the universe of which he is a part."[8] Merleau-Ponty does not believe, however, that the aesthetic value of a work is the memory and objectification of a prior emotion. "For not all the painting is in those little anguishes or local joys with which it is sown: they are only the components of a total meaning which is less moving, more *legible*, and more enduring" (S 55/SF 69). The meaning of the work can be found in the scene itself and in the law that guides the painter to choose this color over that one, to choose marble instead of bronze, and that tells the artist when the work is complete. There is an objectivity to the work that cannot be reduced to the emotions of the artists. For Merleau-Ponty, the meaning of art "is not the subject — it is the allusive logic of the perceived world" (S 57/SF 71).

Merleau-Ponty's aesthetics elaborates on the "allusive logic" of the painting, revealed in both the way the artist represents reality and the expressive nature of the work itself. His hope is to show that a consideration for both expression and representation is essential for understanding the work of art. Beginning with the artist, Merleau-Ponty argues that the artist's style cannot be overlooked when considering the aesthetic value of a portrait or a novel; what is of concern to the critic or viewer "is that life itself, to the extent that the life emerges from its inherence, ceases to be in possession of itself and becomes a universal means of understanding and of making something understood, of seeing and of presenting something to see — and is thus not shut up in the depths of the mute individual but diffused throughout all he sees" (S 53/SF 66). The life of the artist Merleau-Ponty is referring to is not made up of the idiosyncratic character traits of the artist, or the artist's psychobiography, as Freud and others have argued.[9] The life of the artist, rather, is found in how the artist reveals the way the sensible world is made manifest to him; in the words of Malraux, it is "his lifestory as an artist, the growth of his faculty of transformation."[10] To give an example, the work of Cézanne, with its brutal reworking of traditional forms and its unique use of color to depict the contours of objects, suggests a particular way of expressing the visual world that became the signature of Cézanne's art. The technique arose from a particular problem of painting that "called for this life" (SNS 20/SNSF 35) and that allowed the artist to see the world in new ways. The goal of the art critic is to understand how the artist's style allows him to communicate his "private universe" to the world, and to transform his life into a recognizable style of painting.[11]

The artist does not, however, work solely from the heart; his art is inspired by the sensible world around him and the way that it already offers ambiguous meanings that guide the artist's choice of color and medium. Few artists claim to work completely from emotion or memory, and most spend countless hours observing the perceptual world. What they see is a world in the making that requires interpretation and completion. In particular, the artist notices visual cues that allow the perceiver to see the world as synesthetic and as flooded with light. Monet, for example, discovered the ambiguity of color that allows flecks of white to appear not as positive elements of the painting (like the dark blues or reds that he used to depict clothing) but as the light that energizes the painting and presents the scene as it was originally experienced, full of light and life, movement and laughter. Painting highlights the fact that the visible world contains visual cues that open the

58 Aesthetic Imagining

scene to alternative dimensions of sense, white suggesting the medium of light that filters through the trees overhead, or a particular brushstroke revealing through color the velvety texture of the peach. Perception always contains the opening of the visible onto the invisible dimensions of the other senses. "The proper essence of the visible is to have a layer of invisibility in the strict sense, which it makes present as a certain absence" (PrP 187/EMF 85). Perception, Merleau-Ponty says, "must have its *imaginaire*" (PrP 178/EMF 59). Usually the perceiver passes over this inner life of perception, overlooking the "inner traces of vision" (PrP 165/EMF 124) and focusing on objects as things with defined properties. But even ordinary perception involves the creative interpretation of the allusive logic of the world, and the unity of the object reflects "a certain structural co-ordination of experience, a certain modulation of existence" (PP 193/PPF 225) rather than a determinate world that was passively perceived. It is the artist who breaks apart habitual modes of seeing, who creates "a coherent deformation" (S 54/SF 68) of ordinary vision and presents the invisible traces of the visible that the ordinary perceiver tends to ignore. The work of art is a "visible of the second power" (PrP 164/EMF 22) that presents "a general way of expressing being" (S 56/SF 70) rather than a particular object or emotion. Merleau-Ponty explains: "I would be at great pains to say *where* is the painting I am looking at. For I do not look at it as I do a thing; I do not fix it in its place. My gaze wanders in it as in the halos of Being. It is more accurate to say that I see according to it, or with it, than that I *see* it" (PrP 164/EMF 23). The work of art offers not another visible object but a visible presentation of "the genesis of things" (PrP 183/EMF 74) and of the visual cues that make the appearance of visible objects possible. Art provides an inward glance at the way we perceive by arresting the assumptions of ordinary perception and revealing, in ways unique to each artist, the secret ciphers of vision.

Merleau-Ponty refers to the art of Cézanne to illustrate the way the artist's line serves as a mode of seeing rather than as something

Aesthetic Imagining   59

to be seen. In the still lifes of fruit or ordinary objects, Cézanne used a series of overlapping colors to depict the curving sides of objects, their depth and volume, giving to their contours a physical meaning as weighty and textured (SNS 14–15/SNSF 25; PrP 179–80/EMF 65–67). This "flexuous line" (PrP 183/EMF 73) is the visible cue of depth that remains, itself, invisible; we do not see lines around actual objects, but assume that they are there because of habits of vision. The contours of the cup are the result of particular modes of existence, the rim that separates my mouth from the drink, the sides that are made present in the same way every time I grasp the cup with my hand. The artist brings these assumed contours into question by emphasizing the line as the power to distinguish objects in the visual field. "The line not only looks like something," writes Alan Munchow, "it also looks at us. It engages the boundaries of our body. It depicts, but also hides, demanding that the work of the painter be undone so that a more intimate relation to the world is attained. The line installs itself diacritically between viewer and world and testifies to an invisibility."[12] What is particularly important about the aesthetic line is the alchemy by which it makes visible the invisible traces of experience. The artist allows us to explore the line with our eyes, to contemplate its depth, and to offer to our eyes a new way to see the world around us.

Merleau-Ponty elaborates on the aesthetic value of the work by showing in what way it relies on the human body. The significance of the work, consisting of the logic of perception and its coherent deformation according to aesthetic style, is understood and communicated primarily through the imagining body. Grounding aesthetic value on the body is most obvious in the art forms of dance and mime, where the entire body becomes the medium for the artist's expression. The mime communicates by means of the body the idea of the piece that is recognized immediately by her audience. A large elephant is shown on the stage by the manner in which she pulls on its imaginary rope, her signs of fatigue and her exaggerated smallness in comparison to the large imagined animal at

60 Aesthetic Imagining

the end of the rope. Maravene Sheppard Loeschke explains that the mime makes use of bodily forces and stock movements to re-create the massive body of the elephant and its force against the body of the mime. By recreating the contortions on her body that a real experience of the elephant would cause, the mime is able to make the elephant appear. What the mime calls to view are the visual signs of the body as it makes the objects of the world appear in various ways. The mime also adds to these movements a certain style and grace that is usually lacking in ordinary experience and that makes her sequence one of beauty and skill.[13]

The analysis of dance provided by Maxine Sheets-Johnstone helps to reveal the role of the imagination in mime and dance. She explains that the dancer's body is "a center of force which presents changing linear designs." By moving about on the stage, the dancer creates a "spatialization of force" that the audience can see by fol-lowing the intricate patterns of the dancer's movements on the stage.[14] Dance is a "form in the making," the activity of creating a form with the body. But the form is not experienced (by either the dancer or the audience) as a visual spectacle. The dancer does not attempt to picture her movements from a bird's eye perspective, and the members of the audience do not watch the dancer as they might watch a fireworks display. The dancer becomes absorbed in the entire experience of the movements, from head to foot, from inner motivation to external gesticulation. Sheets-Johnstone ex-plains: "The dancer has a fund of lived experience of her body in movement, and consequently, a highly developed pre-reflective awareness of the moving spatial presence of her body" (117). The dancer draws from her body schema the movements that are pos-sible to express the idea of the piece, which the audience member recognizes by virtually extending his own body schema onto the bodily movements of the dancer.[15] The viewer follows the dancer not only with his eyes but virtually with his entire body and its experiences of forces and kinesthetic impressions that are repre-sented on the stage by the dancer. A similar experience occurs in ordinary perception, when a person watches an athletic event and virtually experiences the force of the ball on the player's hand when he receives a pass from a teammate, and the vibrations felt in the feet of the player when the ball is bounced against the gymnasium floor. The difference in the case of dance is that the movements themselves become the focus of one's attention. "What differentiates dance from movement is that lived form-in-the-making is created as a sheer form in and of itself, and unlike other movement activities, such as basketball, gymnastics, and the like, it has no meaning beyond itself" (Sheets-Johnstone, 148). The dance focuses our attention away from everyday objects and toward the images of the body created by the dance.

There is an important distinction, however, between Sheets-Johnstone's analysis of dance and that of Merleau-Ponty. Sheets-Johnstone suggests that the body is only a means to the end of having the audience imagine a particular idea. She admits that the image exists only within the movements of the dancer's body, so that the "linear and areal qualities [of the dance] exist within the total illusion of force and have no existence apart from that global phenomenon" (115). But she maintains that there is a radical difference between imagining the image represented by the dance and experiencing the dance kinesthetically. She claims that a "spontaneous shift occurs from the imaginative mode to the perceptual mode" when the dancer switches her focus from the image to the body. The audience meanwhile experiences only the image through the analogue of the dancer's movements.[16] The separation of the image from the experience of the bodily movements of the dance, however, does not conform with how we experience the dance. The members of the audience understand the dance on the basis of their own bodily experiences, which means that they must be aware of both the forces on the dancer's body *and* the image that is created by means of it. There is no shifting back and forth from perception to imagination; the audience imagines by means of shared kinesthetic and bodily experiences.[17] By means of the figurative movements

62   Aesthetic Imagining

of the dancer or the mime, the audience members are invited to explore the aesthetic image not within the realm of the fanciful but in the virtual dimension of their own embodiment. Dance and mime both make use of the imagining body to communicate to the audience and to disclose the creative power of embodiment.

Although Merleau-Ponty does not comment on mime or dance, he provides an elaborate description of the role of the body in the visual arts. It may seem that painting only concerns itself with vision, and that the rest of the body is unimportant to the art form. But Merleau-Ponty suggests that implied in any aesthetic experience is the rest of the body as the background for that experience. The artist expresses his own embodied relation to the world, and his own manner of completing its vague meaning in the visible form of the painting or sculpture. This general mode of embodiment is revealed by the style of the artist,[18] which is neither reducible to the "feeble movement of the brush or pen" (S 45/SF 57) nor to "a certain number of procedures or tics" (S 53/SF 67). Like the dancer, the artist "did not have in his mind's eye all the gestures possible, and in making his choice he did not have to eliminate all but one" (S 45/SF 57). The embodiment involved is a more general mode of being, the action of the eye on the world, and of the body as it forms the background for the artistic vision. For some artists, this style is savage and emotional, as in the work of Cézanne and Jackson Pollack; for others, it is polished and refined, like the paintings of Fragonard and Chardin. These styles, unique to each artist, are essentially ways of being embodied in the world that are universalized in the visible work of art, available for all to see and to virtually explore with their own imagining bodies. The artwork is an expression of the artist's style of embodiment. The contours of Matisse's women, for instance, are not mimetic but "veins, as the axes of a corporeal system of activity and passivity."[19] The work of art, writes Merleau-Ponty, provides us with "new organs" (S 52/ SF 66) with which to see the world. Without this implied embodiment, the painting could not bear the meaning that it does, composed

Aesthetic Imagining 63

out of "certain gaps or fissures, figures and grounds, a top and a bottom, a normal and a deviation" (S 54/SF 68). The viewer does not simply look at the artwork, but must employ her virtual body to understand the artist's "private universe" depicted by the painting and to "take up the gesture which created it" (S 51/SF 64).

The essentially carnal nature of painting is shown especially in paintings that represent motion. Merleau-Ponty compares Gericault's *Epsom Derby* to a photograph of a running horse in order to show how art captures the embodied experience of movement. The horse in the photograph appears to be floating, with all four legs outstretched. By contrast, the painting represents the movement itself by having the horse's hooves in different places so that some of the legs are touching the ground while others are not. The painting provides a structural story of how the horse moves through time, with each hoof signifying a different moment in time. The Gestalt created by the four hooves represents a temporal passage and an embodied experience that is lacking in the photograph. Merleau-Ponty explains that while the photograph attempts to depict the body as it actually is at a given moment, the painting endeavors to capture the embodied, temporal experience, complete with its virtual future and remembered past. "[T]he art of painting is never altogether outside time, because it is always within the carnal" (PrP 186/EMF 81). As carnal, the aesthetic image is not merely a sign of movement, like the blurring that occurs in photographs of speeding objects, but the very embodiment of movement, the transposition of movement from kinesthetic impressions to the colors and lines of the artwork. "Painting does not copy movement point by point or by offering us signs of it," says Merleau-Ponty; "it invents emblems which give it a substantial presence, presenting it to us as the 'metamorphosis' (Rodin) of one attitude into another, the implication of a future within the present" (TFL 10/ TFLF 19). The painting presents a virtual body in an aesthetic space that the actual body could never occupy or mimic point by point; it is by means of the deformation of ordinary experience that the painting is able to expose the imagining body to a deeper sense of its experience of time and motion.

Merleau-Ponty argues that the imagining body is essential for film as well as painting and dance. He explains the progression of film from a mimetic device to the expressive medium that it had become by the 1940s (TFL 10–11/TFLF 19–20). Film directors quickly discovered the effectiveness of the close-up and montage to allow a scene to be observed from a variety of perspectives. Juxtapositioning the perspectives allowed the director to present particular moods or scenarios in ways different from other art forms. An example is when a director has a distant shot follow a close-up to create emotional tension, or when a distant shot is combined with the sound of intimate conversation of characters that could not be heard from that distance in reality. Montage establishes a rhythm and a coherence to the film whose meaning is known immediately to the viewer, "just as the meaning of a gesture may immediately be read" (SNS 57/SNSF 103). The mode of embodiment that the film presents is an extended body that can assume all of the presented perspectives, an imaginary body that can see through walls to observe a couple in bed and that can see around walls or from above.[20] The virtual body can look at two people from afar and yet at the same time listen to an intimate conversation. The viewer understands the sequence and combines the various shots by exploring the virtual modes of embodiment they express. The imagining body assumes a unique role in film where it is able to combine a variety of perspectives into a single experience, the experience of the film.

The imagining body also plays a significant role in the experience of music. The performance of a piece is based on more than simply the plucking of strings; the guitarist enters a different world and allows his entire body to sway to the music. Sound opens a new dimension onto the sensible that one inhabits by means of the entire body, through the eardrums initially as they are made to vibrate by the sound, and eventually through the rest of the body as it responds to the sound. The musician knows how to use synesthesis to create a world of sound, using the harsh tone of brass to elicit the attention of the audience, or the soft tones of the harp to relax the listeners. To experience the music requires a virtual body that positions itself in various dimensions of the sensible, exploring the timbre of certain sounds and the silences between them. One of the best examples of this can be found in Glenn Gould's recordings of J. S. Bach's Brandenburg Concertos, in which the music is slowed and structured around carefully constructed silences. Between the notes lies a wilderness of sound and, in effect, an affective abyss that lies at the heart of the most ordinary sounds: the crescendo in the voices of customers at a diner or the sound of trees swaying in the autumn wind, which, in the nimble fingers of the pianist, become the silences that open a new world of sound to the appreciative listener.[21]

One last example of the imagining body's prominent role in art is found in Merleau-Ponty's description of literature. Reading a book seems to involve little bodily activity. The reader follows the text with her eyes, word for word rather than quality for quality, once removed from the world of sense and engaged in the world of linguistic meaning. This is often seen to be in contrast with the immediacy of music or painting. But reading involves becoming absorbed in the world of fiction, virtually exploring the experiences of the characters, inhabiting their virtual bodies and participating in their virtual encounters. Over time a mode of existence emerges from the pages: the poverty of Oliver Twist, or the artificial love of Françoise for Pierre in Simone de Beauvoir's *l'Invitée*. According to Merleau-Ponty, literature and philosophy "can no longer be separated" because they are both involved in "formulating an experience of the world, a contact with the world which precedes thought about the world" (SNS 28/SNSF 48). This contact takes the form of a certain mode of existence, presented not in the meaning of the sentences but "between them, in the hollows of space, time, and signification they mark out, as movement at the

66   Aesthetic Imagining

cinema is between the immobile images which follow one another" (S 76/SF 95). The significance of the novel is the existence of the characters and the world in which they appear, and it is experienced by the reader's imaginative positioning of the virtual body in the modes of embodiment suggested by the fictional characters.

These examples should suffice to illustrate how the imagining body plays an essential role in appreciating artworks. The mime serves not only as an example of aesthetic imagining, but as a prototype of the embodiment found in many examples of aesthetic experience. The close relationship among the sensible, art and embodiment makes the creative and virtual body central to the creation and appreciation of great works of art. It also finds within the ordinary experience of the body a hidden art that is available to all. Merleau-Ponty remarks that the artist appeals to others only because "there is a little of him in every man" (S 64/SF 81). The common bond between the artist and the observer is the creative potential of the imagining body.

Four

Fanciful Imagining

*I*n a conference brochure for the American Association for the Study of Mental Imagery, Jerome Singer provides a convincing definition of mental imagery: "Mental imagery, in general, is a sensation-like or perception-like experience that occurs in the absence of the stimuli that would ordinarily be present to elicit it. It is a constructive process, but in contrast to true sensory or perceptual images, it is far more flexible and creative."[1] Singer's description of mental imagery reflects the common view of the imagination as a fanciful activity, appearing in some respects to be like sensory experience while escaping the confines of the laws of perception. Lying on the beach, I close my eyes and imagine a ship appearing on the horizon; I then shift the scene so that I am the captain at the helm, safely navigating the vessel toward the shore. In the first scene, I seem to "see" the vague outlines of a ship with my "mind's eye," a brown-colored vessel surmounted by an expanse of white canvas for a sail and surrounded by the blue of the sky and the sea. In the second scene, I seem to feel the grain of the wooden helm in my hands, to feel the salty spray splashing against my face, and to hear the cry of gulls overhead. On the whole, I seem to have total control over the experience, switching effortlessly between the roles of spectator and participant, as well as between entire sequences

68   Fanciful Imagining

when I become bored of one scene and begin to imagine another. We are left, however, with a series of unanswered questions: in what way is fanciful thinking like perception? How is it different? What exactly am I seeing when I imagine the ship at sea? And how is fanciful thinking related to embodied experience?

Because of the elusive character of mental images and fanciful thinking, philosophers continue to disagree about how to define them. While many theorists tend to ignore the differences between imagination and perception, others overlook the similarities and argue that they are mutually exclusive experiences. Merleau-Ponty's philosophy of imagination falls between these positions. He admits, with Jean-Paul Sartre and others, that the image is not a mental content or a copy of perceptions. The mental image is a particular mode of consciousness. But he also argues that the image involves a spatiality that is continuous with the space of perception. According to Merleau-Ponty, fanciful thinking and perception occur within a continuous spectrum of experience that is mediated and determined by the imagining body.

The traditional view of the imagination is based on the philosophies of David Hume and Immanuel Kant. Hume argues that the mental image is a picture in the mind. Images, he writes, involve copies of sense impressions that are either recalled from memory or spontaneously created to allow consciousness to see absent objects as if they were present. The only difference between images and sense impressions is that the former strikes the mind with less force and vividness.[2] The lack of an essential difference between images and impressions means for Hume that there is no apodeictic knowledge concerning reality. All knowledge, he claims, is based on associations made between impressions and ideas that are imagined rather than observed. For example, when a person claims that a particular object persists through time, she does not actually see the association between past and current impressions of the object but only imagines their union within a mental image. Hume concludes that the imagination is not only continuous with perception, but also provides the illusion of a unified world of experience. Although Kant also believes that the imagination is central to knowledge, he does not think that all mental images are pictures in the mind; he suggests another kind of mental image in the form of a general schema that enables consciousness to relate abstract concepts to sense experience. The image, he writes, is not simply an object in the mind, but rather serves as "a rule for the determination of our intuition."[3] The imagination is also, for Kant, the power to contemplate objects without restrictive concepts in aesthetic experience in which the mind is able to engage in a free play of ideas and images, which he describes as a "purposiveness without purpose," a meaningful activity that surpasses the confines of conceptual thinking.[4] On the basis of the theories of Hume and Kant, mental images have come to be seen as either objects in the mind or mental schemata that play an essential role in perception and in the acquisition of knowledge.

Many philosophers today reject the modern view of the mental image as an object in the mind; they also tend to treat the imaginary as an escape from reality rather than as an essential aspect of perceptual experience. Mental imaging is generally associated with fancy and caprice. Jerome Singer provides many examples of people who engage in fanciful thinking in order to escape the boredom that they experience in their daily activities. When I take a moment to engage in fanciful thinking, I am allowing the imagination to enrich my ordinary life or at the very least to make that life more bearable for the moment. Singer describes daydreaming as "a neutral skill available for adaptive enrichment of the life of otherwise ordinary persons as well as being a manifestation in many persons of escape, evasion of responsibility, or self-dissatisfaction."[5] Edward Casey's study of the imagination also suggests an escape from perceptual activity toward a realm of possibility that we are free to explore. Imagination involves a disengagement from reality and the freedom to think about whatever comes to mind. "Imagination," Casey writes, "multiplies mentation and is its freest form of

70 Fanciful Imagining

movement. It is mind in its polymorphic profusion." But this free play of imagination provides more than simply an entertainment; Casey adds that imagining also allows us to discover the mind's potential to create images without prompting, and thus provides a sense of "self-completion" and "self-enchantment" that is often lacking in ordinary experience.[6] For Jean-Paul Sartre, the imagination becomes the fullest expression of the freedom of consciousness to endow its own meanings on the objects that it encounters. Since the imagination surpasses the confines of perceptual experience, it allows consciousness to freely explore new meanings in a free play of imagining that negates reality and makes it subject to our will. The imagination, in this sense, is identical to the negating activity of consciousness that Sartre later discusses in *Being and Nothingness*. The imagination, he writes elsewhere, "is the appearance of the imaginary before consciousness which permits the grasping of the process of turning the world into nothingness as its essential condition and as its primary structure." Thus the imagination is not a mere entertainment: "We may therefore conclude that the imagination is not an empirical and superadded power of consciousness, it is the whole of consciousness as it realizes its freedom."[7]

As an escape from reality, fancy also seems to be quite different from perception. Analytic philosophy has tended to downplay the relationship between imagination and perception, suggesting that the traditional view of the image as a copy of sense impressions is no longer acceptable. Gilbert Ryle, for instance, criticizes the view that the imaginer sees mental pictures "in a gallery which only he can visit," and rather asserts that "there are no such objects as mental pictures." When a child imagines a smile on her doll's face, for example, she is not observing a smile in her mind: "There is not a smile at all, and there is not an effigy of a smile either. There is only a child fancying that she sees her doll smiling."[8] Sartre, Casey and other continental philosophers have also argued for a separation of imagination from perception. The main objection is that we cannot explore and verify our imaginings in the same way that we can explore and verify our perceptions. To see the cup, I can adjust my position and explore its hidden sides and assume that it has an unseen inner side as well. The image, by contrast, is given all at once in its totality, with nothing left behind or within it to teach us something new about the world.[9] Many philosophers deny an essential relation between the imagination and perceptual experience.

If mental images are not mental pictures, then what are they? It could be argued that imagining is simply an illusory experience caused by physiological movements. J. S. Antrobus and Jerome Singer found that oculomotor activity increased when a subject claimed to be imagining a moving object, just as they would in ordinary perception.[10] More recent tests by G. E. Schwartz and S. L. Brown found a similarity between the facial movements involved in expressing various emotions and the facial movements of subjects who were asked to imagine a picture of a face expressing those emotions. "In brief, there is a substantial body of evidence that attests to the fact that physiological measures of imagery are sensitive to different kinds of images, and this evidence is particularly extensive with respect to images of different affective states."[11] Thus it could be possible to identify certain affective images with correlating physiological events.

Another possibility is that images are really a different way of acting toward an object. Ryle argues that imagining can include a number of different actions, all of which are different from perceiving, including especially the action of pretense. "There is no special faculty of imagination, occupying itself single-mindedly in fancied viewings and hearings. On the contrary, 'seeing' things is one exercise of imagination, growling somewhat like a bear is another; smelling things in the mind's nose is an uncommon act of fancy, malingering is a very common one, and so forth."[12] Kendall Walton's *Mimesis as Make-Believe* involves a detailed account of an imagination theory based on pretense. To imagine a stump to be a bear, and to imagine the formal relationships of an abstract painting, are

72 Fanciful Imagining

both instances of participating in a game of make-believe.[13] For Sartre, the image becomes a mode of consciousness, different from that involved in perception. The object of both imagination and perception, my friend Pierre (to use Sartre's example), remains the same in each mode of consciousness rather than being two different things, the object and the image, as was suggested by modern philosophers. In perception I see Pierre sitting at a table in a café, or I witness Pierre's absence from a smoky room; in imagining, I negate Pierre's absence from the café and intend his presence even though he is not there.[14] In each of these explanations of the existence of the image, there is an assumption that it can no longer be seen as an object in the mind.

According to recent studies on mental imagery, the view of the imagination as a flight from perceptual experience is questionable. Tests concerning the mental rotation of objects and the spatiality of the mental image have shown that the common sense identification of images with "weak" or "quasi" percepts bears within it some truth. Stephen Kosslyn and his colleagues compared the behavior of subjects approaching both perceived and imagined objects and found that the reactions of patients in both situations were the same. It is known, for instance, that we can recognize a set of vertical lines from further away compared to a set of oblique ones. When subjects were asked to imagine the sets of lines in an imaginary space and to (actually) walk toward them in real space, they were able to recognize the vertical lines from further away, just as they were able to when perceiving the lines for real.[15] Another test consisted of identifying the point at which an image can no longer be seen in its totality, such as when we approach a building and eventually can no longer see the whole structure at once. This point, Kosslyn found, was similar in both the experience of a perceptual object and of an imagined object.[16] It has also been found that a subject who analyzes the points on an imaginary map take the same amount of time to complete the exercise as subjects who analyze a similar map in reality.[17] These tests suggest that imagining possesses its own spatiality and that mental images are in some sense spatial like their perceptual counterparts.

It does not even seem, according to some psychologists, that we need to discard Hume's belief that images are like pictures in the mind. It has been argued that if mental images were like perceptual pictures, then they would require the amount of detail that we find in a photograph. And as Daniel Dennett observes, a mental image of a tiger need not involve a determinate number of stripes; the image of a tiger is often vague and sketchy, rather than a literal picture that can be analyzed with a magnifier.[18] Thus he concludes that mental images are not like pictures at all, but are rather based on descriptions of the absent object that we entertain in our minds. Dennett's analysis, however, commits what Ned Block calls the "photographic fallacy,"[19] the assumption that all forms of picturing are similar to a photograph or detailed picture. It may be true that a photograph of a person, for instance, will usually provide all of the details of the person's appearance, such as whether or not he is wearing a hat or has a small nose. And it may be true, as Dennett argues, that a literary description of the person can leave many parts of the person's appearance undetermined. But it is wrong to think that all forms of picturing are reducible to a photograph. To borrow an example from Jerry Fodor, a stick figure would fall between a photograph and a description, and yet would be more like a "picture" than a description. Likewise, mental images can be like pictures in some ways while maintaining an indeterminacy such as the image of "many stripes" or of "many columns" that could assume no determinate number.[20]

From what we have seen so far, it is difficult to determine what mental images involve, and what exactly their relation is to perceptual images. In some ways they are like pictures because they contain a "quasi" spatiality that is nevertheless different from the pictures and spaces of perceptual experience. An experiment by

74 Fanciful Imagining

C. W. Perky, conducted with the intention to show that images and percepts are similar in many ways, only intensified the debate that was going on at the time Merleau-Ponty began his philosophical career. Perky had subjects look at what appeared to be a blank screen and invited them to imagine a yellow banana. He then projected a faint image of a banana onto the screen without telling the subjects. All of the subjects claimed to be "imagining" the banana while they were in fact perceiving a faint image of a banana on the screen. The subjects, claims Perky, were confusing a perception for an image. And for such confusion to be possible, the two experiences must be similar in kind.[21]

On the other side of the debate, many philosophers, including Sartre, claim that there is no confusion on the part of the subjects in Perky's experiment, and that imagination and perception continue to be radically separate. Since Sartre denies the existence of an image, he turns to consciousness itself in order to distinguish between imagination and perception. He argues that we know immediately whether we are imagining or perceiving, and that confusion exists only with respect to identifying the object of the particular experience. The subjects in Perky's experiment, for example, did not confuse a percept for an image, but engaged with the object, in this case a banana, in an imaginative rather than a perceptual manner. The case is the opposite, he suggests, of a perceptual illusion in which a person mistakes a distant tree for a man. The error involved is not "to form an image of a man, but merely to perceive a tree poorly. One remains on the terrain of perception, and up to a point one perceives rightly: there is indeed an object in the shadows, ten feet away. It is indeed a thin body, slender, about six feet tall, etc. But the deception lay in the manner of grasping the import or meaning of the object."[22] Casey adds that in Perky's case, the subject could be imagining the object *in spite of the image*, so that regardless of what is actually perceptible and appearing on the screen, he is clearly in the act of imagining and not perceiving.[23] It is not clear that Perky's experiment proves without a doubt that mental and perceptual images are similar in kind.

When we turn to Merleau-Ponty's philosophy, a response to this debate and to the question of the mental image begins to emerge. At first Merleau-Ponty appears to be on the side of Sartre. One of his first published articles, a review of Sartre's *l'Imagination*, praises the book for "the rigour and vigour of its critical thought and its uniformally felicitous expression" (IM 114/IMF 761). In *The Structure of Behavior* and *Phenomenology of Perception*, Merleau-Ponty echoes Sartre's attack against the idea that images are objects in the mind, suggesting that the image is a mode of consciousness that is different from perception. It is not the case that the image is a mental copy of the perceptual object. Merleau-Ponty explains that "the experience of a real thing cannot be explained by the action of that thing on my mind: the only way for a thing to act on a mind is to offer it a meaning, to manifest itself to it, to *constitute* itself vis-à-vis the mind in its intelligible articulations" (SB 199/ SBF 215). Perception does not involve the experience of an independent perceptual object that is then copied by the imagination; rather, both the percept and the image are different ways of intending the meaning of the *same* object, be it the object as it is explored in perceptual experience or the object in a state of imaginary nonexistence. It seems in these early texts by Merleau-Ponty that he agrees with Sartre's belief that the image is a mode of consciousness.

Merleau-Ponty also seems to adopt Sartre's belief that the imagination and perception are radically different and incommensurable modes of consciousness. While perception offers to consciousness a plenum of meaning that can be explored and verified (such as when I observe the other side of an object), the imagination offers only a transient world based completely on the whims of consciousness. "In the realm of the imagination," he writes, "I have no sooner formed the intention of seeing than I already believe that I have seen. The imaginary has no depth, and does not respond to our efforts to vary our points of view; it does not lend itself to our observation" (PP 323–24/PPF 374).[24] This claim seems to support Sartre's view of the imagination as a distinct mode of consciousness. The difference between an image of the Pantheon and a percept of

76 Fanciful Imagining

the same is not one of degree or intensity, as Hume suggests, but a difference of kind, such that while the latter has a determinate number of columns that can be verified by closer observation, the former is vague and coexistent with the act of consciousness itself.[25] The image can instantaneously change into another image and is thus unable to be subject to extensive inspection. "The alleged richness of the image," concludes Sartre, "is, therefore, but a *fancy*."[26] Poignant images are powerful only due to their affective quality, their ability to sharpen our emotional attitude toward a particular situation. The image, according to both philosophers, is an instance of fancy, of separation from perceptual reality, diverting consciousness from the limitations of perception and freeing it for a moment of free association. This is made possible, alleges Françoise Dastur, Glen Mazis and others, because Merleau-Ponty sees the imagination and perception to be radically different modes of consciousness.[27] At one point perception is even described by Merleau-Ponty as "the antithesis of imagination" (PP 35/PPF 44). This seems to be in stark contrast to his statement in *The Visible and the Invisible* that criticizes Sartre's view of imagination as "the negation of a negation" which "reduces the imaginary. This assumes then a bipartite analysis: perception as observation, a close-woven fabric, without any gaps, locus of the simple or immediate nihilation" (VI 266/ VIF 320). Thus it seems that Merleau-Ponty's earlier works merely echo Sartre's theory, and that only his later works provide an alternative to Sartre's theory.

In other places, however, Merleau-Ponty discusses a form of imagining that is more in line with Kant than Sartre. This mode of imagining, what has come to be called "imaginative variation," is explained by Merleau-Ponty as a central concept of Husserl's phenomenology. One of the first steps in Husserl's method of determining the essence of an object is to "bracket" all unfounded theories concerning the ontological status of the object and to focus on the way in which the object's meaning is intended by consciousness.[28]

Imagination provides an effective way of "neutralizing" our presuppositions about the object so that we can observe it in the very way that it appears to consciousness. The imagination also allows us to contemplate the various "perspective variations" of the object so that we can synthesize them into an "intentional unity."[29] Merleau-Ponty refers to Husserl's phenomenology as an extension of Kant's aesthetic imagination, which creatively determines the meaning of a given experience: "It is no longer merely the aesthetic judgment, but knowledge too which rests upon this art, an art which forms the basis of the unity of consciousness and of consciousnesses" (PP xvii/PPF xii; see also PP 386/PPF 443). Like Kant, Husserl was claiming that the imagination plays a central role in knowledge. Merleau-Ponty explains that "when we try to comprehend, in direct reflection and without the help of the varied associations of inductive thought, what a perceived movement, or a circle are, we can elucidate this singular fact only by varying it somewhat through the agency of imagination, and then fastening our thought upon the invariable element of this mental experience" (PP 63/PPF 76). By providing a neutralization of traditional theories about the object, the imagination allows consciousness to determine the object's essence, making it a valuable tool for phenomenological research. Imaginative variation is a second mode of imagination in addition to fanciful thinking which, like the imagination in Kant and Hume's philosophies, contributes to the acquisition of knowledge.

Unfortunately, Merleau-Ponty is not always clear in *Phenomenology of Perception* about which mode of imagining he is discussing. For example, while at times he seems to treat the imagination and perception as polar opposites (such as at PP 35/PPF 44, cited earlier), at other times he claims that they are simply different modes of presenting objects to consciousness (and thus not necessarily mutually exclusive of each other, as Sartre would say; SB 196/SBF 211–12). It is also unclear how his allegiance to

78   Fanciful Imagining

Sartre's theory of imagination is supposed to complement his discussion of imaginative variation. Perhaps the reason for this ambiguity was that his primary concern in this volume was to develop a new version of phenomenology that would be based on perception and embodiment; it is easy to imagine that Merleau-Ponty may not have been as concerned in this early study to provide a comprehensive and consistent philosophy of imagination. But despite the lack of an explicit theory of the imagination in this work, it is perfectly consistent with Merleau-Ponty's writings in general to say that he intended to treat the imagination in a broader manner than is found in Sartre's philosophy. Even the statement above that the imagination and perception are opposed to each other could be taken to mean only that a *kind* of imagination is so opposed to perception, namely fanciful thinking, in that it approximates a Sartrean negation of reality. Other kinds of imagination, such as artistic creation and the observation of perceptual images, could then be seen as coextensive with perception rather than as opposed to perception.

Another ambiguity that emerges from the text is the extent to which Merleau-Ponty gives priority to perception over imagination. He writes, it is true, that "our power to imagine . . . borrows from vision" (PrP 187/EMF 83–84; see also PP 296, 424/PPF 342–43, 485). But the fact that the imagination often makes use of perceptual images is still consistent with the claim that perception requires the imagination in order to have the structure that it does. Merleau-Ponty writes, with equal conviction, that "our waking relations with objects and others especially have an oneiric character as a matter of principle: others are present to us in the way that dreams are, the way myths are, and this is enough to question the cleavage between the real and the imaginary" (TFL 48/TFLF 69). Far from stressing the radical separation of imagination from perception, Merleau-Ponty articulates their mutual dependence and implication. Without perception the imagination would have no possibilities to explore and develop; without the imagination perception would be flat, with no depth and structure.[30] Thus, while holding that fanciful thinking is similar in many ways to how Sartre describes the imagination, Merleau-Ponty does not intend to see the imagination in general as conforming to that description.

Another issue that is addressed by Merleau-Ponty's theory of imagination is the spatiality of the mental image. We have already seen how Kosslyn and others have conducted experiments to show the similarities between perceptual and imaginary space. Even Sartre and Casey admit that there is some degree of spatiality in mental images. Casey concedes that images are not completely depthless, but have a "quasi-depth" and a pseudohorizon or background, but he claims that this depth "resists exploration, since it does not *remain* to be explored." This is because "everything in the presentation . . . is in some sense apprehended since the presentation itself is nothing *beyond* what it is apprehended as being." This margin or background is *"unthematizable."* He adds that "we imagine it through a kind of lateral or tandem consciousness."[31] A careful analysis of Casey's argument, however, shows that he is begging the question. It is one thing to say that a fanciful image contains "less" depth than a perceptual image and to say that it is on the verge of becoming depthless, but it is quite another thing to say that the fanciful image is completely without depth and is unexplorable. When I imagine the number of columns in the Parthenon, my fanciful image fails to provide me with the opportunity for exploration and verification that a perceptual experience would provide. But perceptual experience is often like this as well; I may notice an approaching automobile out of the corner of my eye as part of the margin of my experience and be able to react to the warning without analyzing the experience. Likewise, the image can often offer details when I decide to switch from laterally experiencing it to focusing on its symbolic value. It is true that we are usually content with the indeterminate image, but this is also frequently the case in perceptual experience. Lateral seeing suggests depth-seeing, the possibility of exploration, even if such exploration

80   Fanciful Imagining

will not produce an exhaustive report. Contra Casey's claim, I can attempt to explore the margins of an image that provides it with a quasi space that is, nonetheless, a "space" in many ways similar to that of perception. This infusion of space into the mental image cannot be explained as something that is immediately given to consciousness, nor can it be adequately explained by referring to it as a "quasi" space. It is better to say that perception and imagination are both spatial and that their respective spaces are similar in many ways.[32]

It is interesting to note that while Sartre believes the image to be nonspatial, he admits that there is a necessary spatiality in the experience of the image in the form of what he calls a material analogue. He writes: "I have recourse to a certain material which acts as an *analogue*, as an equivalent, of the perception." A photograph, for example, provides the material for seeing my absent friend. When I imagine my friend, the material of the photograph operates as a background for the experience. I see by means of the photograph, but I negate it for the imagined object. "I really do see something, but what I see *is nothing*." Although his theory works well with instances of imagining that make use of visual aids, it becomes less convincing when it deals with the experience of pure fancy. The analogue in such cases is said to be nothing perceptual and so is seen to be "solely from the intention that animates it." Sartre concludes by saying that an analysis of the analogue of fanciful thinking inevitably becomes "reduced to conjectures."[33] By his own admission, Sartre's discussion of the spatiality of the mental image becomes reduced to a study of the probable (the second part of *The Psychology of Imagination* is entitled "The Probable.")

Most critics of Sartre's theory of imagination, including Mary Warnock, argue that he would have been more consistent had he stuck to his position of the imagination as a pure negation of reality and rejected the concept of a material analogue for the image. Warnock is correct when she claims that Sartre ends up replacing the intentionality of consciousness with the intentionality of the

Fanciful Imagining 81

analogue, beginning an infinite regress rather than explaining the phenomenon of the image.[34] With the photograph serving as an analogue of the absent friend, it now becomes the focus of the experience. In place of imagining an object (rather than perceiving it), the person is imagining an object through another object. There are only three possible conclusions that can be drawn from Sartre's argument. One is that the object is imagined in spite of the presence of the object, implying that the analogue is irrelevant to imagining altogether. A second possibility is that the analogue is perceived, but since Sartre does not believe that we can experience images and percepts at the same time, this position would suggest that the person is no longer imagining the object at all. The third possibility is that the person is imagining the analogue in place of the object, which raises again the question of relevance. In all of these cases, Sartre seems to have led himself into a contradiction by introducing the concept of a material analogue.

I suggest, however, that Sartre's inclusion of the material analogue for the image betrays a reliance of his theory on perceptual experience. In order to explain the nihilating power of the imagination, Sartre is basing his theory on the experience of that which is to be nihilated. As Thomas Flynn suggests, "Absence presupposes presence; de-realization realization."[35] We can only see Pierre's absence from the café through an awareness of what it is like for him to be present. Although it is correct for Sartre to treat the image as something that is not strictly *present* to the mind, it is impossible to engage in Pierre's *absence* without an understanding of presence. Sartre admits as much by claiming that we are able to see the absent object through the content of the analogue. Sartre's imaginer is making use of the secret ciphers of the visible analogue that make it possible for the imaginer to make the absent present. Although Sartre recognized the essential materiality of the analogue for the image, he was unable to explain it because of his theory that the image and percept can never be experienced simultaneously. While we can learn from his discussion of the analogue

82 Fanciful Imagining

of the image, we are required to reject his assumptions about the relationship between perception and imagination.[36]

Merleau-Ponty avoids Sartre's problems concerning the spatiality of the image. He describes space as a "setting for co-existence" (PP 221/PPF 255) that already gives to our environment a particular meaning. We find ourselves in a world of significance that surpasses the geometrical meaning of Euclidean space. To use Heidegger's famous example, when we enter a room, we do not at first understand the objects in the room in terms of their shapes and sizes, but rather as items of equipment made available for our use; the objects are related to each other within a practical configuration before they are experienced as mere objects coexisting in Euclidean space.[37] Merleau-Ponty suggests that it is better to think of space as something created rather than as something that we discover ready-made. We create space on the basis of the significance that we place on our environment, a significance that rests on our abilities and immediate interests (PP 221/PPF 256). Making space involves endowing the world with a particular meaning and directionality, both of which are captured by the French word *sens*, which Colin Smith translates as "sense, significance, direction" (PP 253 n./see PPF 292–93). Space as described by Merleau-Ponty is thus a general mode of existence that is found in every experience, including perception and imagining. "There is a determining of up and down, and in general of place, which precedes 'perception'" (PP 285/PPF 330). This suggests that the mental image is neither a mental content, as Kosslyn and others have come to believe, nor a nonspatial mode of consciousness, as Sartre and Casey suggest. Although the image involves a spatiality, that spatiality assumes the form of a general mode of existence. To explain what he means by space, Merleau-Ponty compares the directionality of the dream with that of perceptual experience. He writes: "The movement upwards as a direction in physical space, and that of desire towards its objective are mutually symbolical, because they both express the same essential structure of our being, being situated in relation to an environment, of which we have already stated that this structure alone gives significance to the directions up and down in the physical world" (PP 284/PPF 329). Although the two spaces, that of the dream and that of the percept, are not reducible to each other, they possess an "emblematic value" (PP 284/PPF 329) such that similar general relations to the world can be transposed from one version of space to another. The significance of physical height is metaphorically developed to include the pursuit of desire in the dream, not because of a primacy that is given to the physical direction but because between the two spaces is a shared structure of being in the world. Likewise the spatiality of the mental image shares with its perceptual counterpart a general structure of existence that is shared by both experiences.

Merleau-Ponty's discussion of the virtual body helps to clarify what the spatiality of the mental image and of the dream would be like. Space, he says, is based on the body's "spatial level" (PP 248/ PPF 287), which is a basic directionality that allows us to orient our bodies and to maintain our posture and balance. The nature of the spatial level of the body is shown in an experiment by Stratton in which a person is given lenses that correct the inversion of images on the retina. The person first experiences the world as being upside-down, causing much confusion and a sense of imbalance; but eventually the person comes to adjust himself to the illusion so that he can regain his balance and walk about the room without difficulty. When the lenses are removed, the person experiences the same confusion and gradual adjustment. Merleau-Ponty argues that the person does not attempt to correct his posture by means of a correspondence between the altered visual orientation and the tactile information that he continues to experience as before. Rather, he corrects his situation by giving recourse to the virtual body and its ability to adjust its coordinates so as to make sense of its immediate surroundings (PP 244–46/PPF 282–84).[38] Merleau-Ponty explains: "What counts for the orientation of the spectacle is not my body as it is in fact, as a thing in objective space, but as a system of

84 Fanciful Imagining

possible actions, a virtual body with its phenomenal 'place' defined by its task and situation" (PP 249–50/PPF 288–89).[39] The new spatial level is the virtual bodily disposition called for by the new situation in the form of "a certain gearing of my body to the world" (PP 250/PPF 289).[40] This bodily disposition is mediated by the body schema that we already have and that we can alter and develop in the new scene; the body schema involves an "already acquired spatiality" (PP 253/PPF 293) that brings the body into contact with the world. By means of the body schema and its establishment of a spatial level, we have a balance or reference point in terms of which the body as virtual activity can be related to a new situation. Thus, the body provides a "primary spatiality" that determines our existence as a mode of being in the world (PP 283/PPF 328; see also PP 294/PPF 340).

With space defined as a mode of embodied orientation, it will no longer suffice to describe the fanciful image as being a quasi percept or picture, or to describe the imagination as a quasi perception. Both fancy and perception involve different ways of the body's making space, along a continuum of possibilities of embodiment. The difference between the spaces of imagination and perception concern the focus of the subject, and not a difference between the objects of each experience. While not being bound to actual experience, fanciful thinking is still bound to the virtual body and its relation to reality, providing the imaginer with the basic orientation and groundedness that are necessary for experiencing an alternative world. But the connection to the real world remains "part of the background of conscious experience," as Albert Gilgen explains: "Regardless of the center of attention (the focus), there is at least a vague awareness of 'being-in-the-world.' . . . The focal changes, on the other hand, generate the sense of 'being engaged in something.'"[41] While fancy focuses on an alternative world, directing itself away from the habitual body and everyday activities — indeed, according to Jerome Singer, fleeing these mundane activities in the search for enrichment — perception remains focused on the world at hand with virtual possibilities persisting on the margins of the experience. The spatiality of the image is thus continuous with the spatiality of perception because both are grounded in the directionality of the imagining body.

The spatiality of fancy is illustrated in an experiment conducted by James Morley on five subjects who were asked to engage in daydreaming. He noticed that daydreaming involves a shift in focus away from ordinary experience and toward the world of the daydream. But essential to this shift was the sense of assuming at least three different perspectives or "subjects" at any given moment in the daydream: the engaged subject, the habitual subject and what Morley calls the "director-spectator." The engaged subject "was the one that carried the emotional accent of reality" and that played the central role of the experience. On the margins of the experience of the daydream, the habitual subject continued to perform basic bodily movements such as walking to an office or driving a car. Between these two perspectives was the director-spectator. Morley explains: "It was the director-spectator that seemed to orchestrate and 'direct' these intra-subjective or egological relations incorporated within the entire project of daydreaming." The focus in each daydream was on the person's emotions, which usually remained on the margins of everyday experience. The daydream provided for each subject "an entire alternative 'world'" consisting of an affective content which, within the dream, became an "idealized presentation." Within the dream-space, "objects are idealized; colours tend to be brighter, sounds clearer, all sense experience is intensified. Objects are meaningful as general impressions, which assume their meaning solely through their fulfilling relation to the subject." The affective space of the daydream remained continuous with the space of habitual action because of the dreamer's ability to slip easily from one to the other through the perspective of the director-spectator.[42]

Morley's experiment also lends support to the idea that the imagining body is central to fanciful thinking. The participant and the

86 Fanciful Imagining

habitual subject in Morley's description of the daydream are held together by the imagining body. The habitual subject remembers and tacitly employs the stock of behavior of the body schema, such as walking and driving. The participant plays the lead role in the drama, absorbed in the new world of emotional meanings and affective symbols of depth and intimacy. The director-spectator is the virtual body, passing easily from the real to the imaginary, anchoring the daydream in the perceptual world while exposing the latter to its virtual dimension. Morley writes: "Subjects lived out the dramatic scenes of the daydreams as spatially positioned participants within these scenarios. Their bodies, albeit imaginary, were emotionally anchored or rooted within that narrative while the perceptual world was emotionally neutralized."[43] In the daydream there are not two worlds — the real and the imaginary — or two bodies and two spaces. There is rather the one space, the primordial space of the body, that has marginalized everyday concerns to allow for the exploration of and enact the significance of desire. While the fictional world presents an alternative spacing of one's experience, centered around the significance of desire, the perceptual world remains on the margins of the imaginer's experience as an alternative setting. The point of transition between each is the virtual body, equally ready to assume the fictional body of the dream or the perceptual body that is absorbed in everyday concerns. The person who becomes most comfortable with adventures into the imaginary is one who is able to return to the real world, refreshed and enriched. A healthy imagination is one that remains connected to reality by means of the virtual body in the form of the director-spectator.

Understanding the mental image as a form of imagining one's body better equips us for understanding the significance of the Perky experiment. Merleau-Ponty's broader view of the imagination allows him to say that, in the Perky experiment, there is no confusion between perception and imagination (in agreement with Casey and Sartre) and yet, at the same time, that the space of the image and that of the percept are continuous and similar to each other in many ways. He admits, with Sartre, that perceptual illusions do not involve a confusion of fancy with perception but rather a confusion within the perceptual scene that leads the subject to investigate further.[44] But this need not lead to a radical separation of imagination from perception. Edward Casey agrees to the extent that he criticizes Sartre's all-or-nothing approach to philosophy when he writes: "Combination or compromise is ruled out: you must choose either the real or the imaginary, never both. Yet no such strictly exclusive choice operates in ongoing human experience, which is often composed of a subtle mixture of real and imaginal elements."[45] In a broader sense of imagination, the sense that treats the virtual dimension of perception as a mode of virtual embodiment, the imagination does, in fact, become an essential component of the perceptual illusion.[46] It is not necessary, then, to reduce imagining to fancy, as Sartre does, because the imagination and perception are found within a single range of possible experiences. While accepting the view that the imagination is a general mode of human existence, Merleau-Ponty retains within it a sense of spatiality that is lacking in other theories.

Merleau-Ponty's approach to the question of mental images also explains the phenomenon of multiple-aspect seeing. An example of multiple-aspect seeing is Wittgenstein's duck-rabbit, an ambiguous form that lends itself to both the interpretation that it represents a duck and that it represents a rabbit.[47] Sartre would be required to say either that the imagination is at work and that there is no "seeing," or that the interpretation is intrinsic to the perception.[48] Due to the multiple meanings of a more polyvalent form, such as an inkblot, it becomes difficult to believe that the imagination is not involved; but we seem to detect the image immediately as one thing or another and we struggle to see the other aspect, implying that the experience cannot be guided by imagination alone. While Wittgenstein believed the case to be a unique blend of perception and cognition, Warnock and Casey both see it as an obvious instance of the imagination at work in perception.[49] In one place

88 Fanciful Imagining

Merleau-Ponty seems to agree with Sartre, stressing that a two-dimensional picture of a cube can be seen as sitting on the ground or as suspended from the ceiling immediately without recourse to thought (PP 263/PPF 304; see also PP 17/PPF 24–25). But he never denies that the imagination is aiding the perception, nor does his theory of imagination force him to deny such a role for the imagination. Again, Merleau-Ponty's theory of imagination is less problematic and extreme than that of Sartre, allowing the imagination a role in the interpretation of perceptual experience.

Even flights of fancy — idle daydreams on the beach or momentary musings while waiting at a taxi stand — are instances of the imagining body. The daydream especially reveals how the real and imaginary worlds are continuous and virtually interchangeable with each other. Mental images push the real into the background and allow us to engage in fanciful ways of relating to objects and emotions. The pivot between these two spaces is the imagining body, straddling the difference between the real and the imaginary in the form of the director-spectator. As long as the imagining body maintains this precarious balance, the subject passes easily between the roles of perceiver and imaginer. But it is precisely when the knot of the real and the imaginary becomes unraveled that the imagining body stumbles into pathological experience.

FIVE

Pathological Imagining

*H*armless as they are in ordinary experience, flights of fancy can lead to neurosis. While walking along a beach I become moved by the expanse of the ocean and the darkness of the water and sense a cosmic calling to become absorbed by the massive ocean. I translate the resounding sound of waves into the song of Sirens, or I mistake the waves caressing my feet to be the tentacles of an octopus pulling me back to its abysmal domain. I know, at some level, that there are no Sirens and no tentacles, that my imagination has gotten the better of me. But is pathological experience only a step away from ordinary experience? Are cases of neurosis the result of an imagination gone too far?

I will show how, for Merleau-Ponty, pathological behavior can be explained in terms of the imagining body. Through the virtual body we are able to move easily between reality and the imaginary, between wakefulness and the dream, along a continuum of experience. This continuum can be extended into pathological experience, so that healthy and neurotic experiences are not radically opposed to each other. Even the more severe cases of psychosis, as in hallucinatory experience, can be understood to result from an eclipse of the virtual body and a fixation of a particular set of

90 Pathological Imagining

behavior. But even in the case of psychosis, the virtual body is present, making it possible at all times to return to normal behavior. There is thus a continuum between the healthy and the pathological imagination, proceeding through dreams and minor instances of neurosis to the more severe cases of psychosis.

It has often been said that dreaming involves an escape from reality and assumes some of the characteristics of neurosis: a focus on particular images, a detachment from reality, and an emphasis on emotions, to name a few. Like the daydream described in the previous chapter, the dream transforms the spatiality of the body from physical into affective space, providing the dreamer with an oneiric world that abides by the dreamer's wishes with no concern for reality. When Merleau-Ponty considers the significance of dream images, he refuses to relate them to the same categories that govern ordinary experience. The images of falling or ascending, for example, possess general affective meanings that are made determinate only upon reflection when the dreamer is awake. Within the dream, these images do not obtain a specific sexual meaning, for instance, but remain "blurred outlines, distinctive relationships which are in no way 'unconscious' and which, we are well aware, are ambiguous, having reference to sexuality without specifically calling it to mind" (PP 168/PPF 196; see also PP 160/PPF 191). As experienced in the dream, the images have only a vague significance for the dreamer that lends itself to a specific sexual meaning only when the patient reflects on the dream. Within the dream, the emotion is identical to the scaling of a mountain, or the flight of a bird, and the patient inhabits the emotion and explores its possibilities for her imagined body as "the pulse of [her] existence" (PP 285/PPF 330). There remains, however, a strong connection between the dream and reality. Like perception, the dream maintains a spatiality for the virtual body and "conditions a space peopled with phantasms, just as, in waking life, our dealings with the world which is offered to us conditions a space peopled with realities" (ibid.). The dream and reality are also never completely separated;

reality is held at the margins of the dream so that the dreamer can be roused by a loud noise or by hunger. Without this contact with the real, dreams would be "no more than instantaneous modulations, and so would not even exist for us" (PP 293/PPF 339) because we would never be able to reflect on their significance. Between the dream and ordinary experience there is an unbreakable link that is mediated and guarded by the virtual body as director-spectator which adjusts the focus between the real and the imaginary depending on the needs and wishes of the subject.

The connection between the real and the imaginary begins to unravel when one approaches neurotic behavior. Examples of such behavior include various obsessions (over people, objects, or one's own appearance), an inability to perform basic functions (such as to speak or to eat), and other forms of abnormal behavior. Merleau-Ponty's example is a girl who developed anorexia and aphonia after her parents forbade her to see her lover (PP 160–64/PPF 187–92). Merleau-Ponty argues that the girl did not experience a loss of memory or a physiological impairment, because she was later cured not by memory recovery or physiotherapy, but by gradually being reintroduced to social interaction (PP 163/PPF 190). The traditional psychoanalytical interpretation of her neurosis would be that she was forced to suppress the affection that she had for her lover to satisfy her parents, but that she was unable to overcome her feelings and became healthy only when she could express them to others. Since Merleau-Ponty agrees with and borrows much from psycho-analysis, it would help to consider the theory in greater depth.

The father of psychoanalysis, Sigmund Freud, found that at the base of our experience are instinctual drives and wishes that are exemplified in sexual impulses, a quest for wealth and power, and a fascination for death. Because these impulses are often opposed to peaceable, social living, we come to suppress them so that we are able to participate in society. The psychogenetic history of a child thus involves a series of repressions leading to adulthood. The process of suppressing these desires requires a reinterpretation (through the use of the imagination) of them so that they will be rejected as taboo. According to Freud, the reimagining of these desires occurs below the level of consciousness and provides a deep reprogramming of how the child sees himself and his world.[1] But since the imagination cannot get rid of these drives and instincts altogether, the attempt to suppress them can sometimes lead to neurosis. The inability to express emotion, for instance, or the sudden loss of a close relative, can intensify the conflict between these instincts and conscious attempts to control them to the point of crisis, such as when a set of behavior shuts down or when instinctual responses, especially in the form of obsessions, begin to dominate conscious experience. The result is often a form of neurotic behavior.

The task of the psychoanalyst is to attempt to decipher which drives or instincts are at the root of the neurotic behavior. Freud claimed that instinctual behavior is below the level of consciousness in what he called an unconscious level of experience. The difficulty for the analyst is deciphering the significance of a patient's behavior that has become convoluted over years of reimagining the meaning of the particular drives and instincts, resulting in a nucleus of confused and disjointed messages that Freud refers to as "overdetermination."[2] The point of psychoanalysis is to penetrate beyond the level of consciousness and the distorted defensive images generated by the pathological imagination to discover at the level of impulses and repressed emotions the cause for the patient's behavior. On the basis of the knowledge obtained through the process of analysis, the analyst will have a better understanding of the patient's behavior and, ultimately, of how he can help the patient come to deal with his instincts in a healthier way.[3]

While accepting many of the claims of Freud and traditional psychoanalytic theory, Merleau-Ponty is skeptical about the existence of an unconscious. Although the meaning of our experience is essentially ambiguous to him, he does not see it as removed from the level of consciousness. Freud was wrong, he says, to have treated "under the name of the unconscious a second thinking subject whose creations are simply received by the first" (TFL 48–49/TFLF 69). He suggests that Freud's theory of the unconscious explains consciousness in terms of another subject, the unconscious, without explaining why this second consciousness is not itself controlled by a third consciousness, and so on. The claim that this second consciousness is an unconscious level of the human psyche only avoids the question of why it is allegedly inaccessible to consciousness. To Merleau-Ponty there is no inner self controlling our behavior, but only embodied consciousness as it is immersed in a world of ambiguous meaning.

In what way, then, can the ambiguity of experience account for neurotic behavior? Merleau-Ponty answers this question by considering Freud's description of overdetermination. According to Freud, the analyst must unravel the various structures of meaning that the patient has come to place on his instinctual drives. But this suggests, says Merleau-Ponty, that the analyst's focus should be not on a level of meaning beneath the patient's consciousness but on the images that give it meaning for consciousness. "Instinct may well exist as a source (*Quelle*) of a psychological life," admits Edward Casey in support of Merleau-Ponty, "but its biological format is insufficient to explain the vagaries and vicissitudes of that life: a life that is resolutely representational and that takes the form of fantasies, wishes, memories, etc."[4] Thus Merleau-Ponty argues that Freud's "most interesting thought" is not the existence of an unconscious but "the idea of a symbolism which is primordial, originary, the idea of a 'non-conventional thought' . . . which is the source of dreams and more generally of the elaboration of our life" (TFL 49/TFLF 69–70). Merleau-Ponty agrees that the source for these images remains a mystery buried in the psychology of desire, but the work of the analyst should focus on the expressions that occur in the realm of consciousness. It is neither the business nor the jurisdiction of the analyst to make claims about what the source for these expressions is, and whether or not it is "conscious"; the

94   Pathological Imagining

analyst, rather, must unravel the meanings of the images and determine their relation to the patient's behavior. "Even if there is perception of what is desired through desire, loved through love, hated through hate, it always forms round a sensible nucleus, however small, and it is in the sensible that its verification and its fullness are found" (PP 293/PPF 339). Every human experience, including instincts and desires, lends itself to symbolic and linguistic expression: "Because we are in the world, *we are condemned to meaning*, and we cannot say or do anything without its acquiring a name in history" (PP xix/PPF xiv–xv). The analyst must help the patient reinterpret the convoluted expressions of his experience.[5]

It would be instructive at this point to consider the elusiveness of the perceptual horizon. The moment one tries to grasp the horizon as figure, it ceases to be a horizon and another background takes its place. "Perception is unconscious and unperceived," writes Martin Dillon, "in the manner that backgrounds are overlooked. Nonetheless, backgrounds are given, present; they are explorable, thematizable — although that thematization necessarily involves an alteration and distortion of their horizonal character."[6] Merleau-Ponty claims that all references to the "unconscious" are merely references to the ambiguity of perception that we find, "not at the bottom of ourselves, behind the back of our 'consciousness,' but in front of us, as articulations of our field" (VI 180/VIF 234). While admitting that existence bears a meaning that one does not always understand, Merleau-Ponty denies that there can be meanings that are essentially inaccessible to conscious observation. When the analyst interprets the meaning of a neurotic image, the meaning is sharpened and made more determinate just as the meaning of a background is made more determinate when it becomes the figure or foreground of a perceptual scene. The unconscious is not an inner self, driven by impulses and repressed desires, but is the silent side of what becomes expressed by the way that we live and in the words that we say. The unconscious is merely the ambiguity of personal expression; what the analyst attempts to understand is not

Pathological Imagining 95

a deeper level of meaning but the ambiguity of behavior and its symbolic expression.

Merleau-Ponty further explores the ambiguity of experience by considering its effects on the interpretation of historical events. In political history, acts that are considered to be terroristic at one moment can later be seen as revolutionary and heroic. Conversely, attempts at diplomacy can at one time be seen as visionary and at another as being too conservative. In *Humanism and Terror*, Merleau-Ponty illustrates how the Moscow Trials are paradigmatic examples of the ambiguity of history. He shows how those condemned to death for treason under the Stalinist regime had committed actions they deemed to be necessary for the cause of the Russian Revolution. But the court decided that the actions were undermining the extreme policies of Stalin, and that they could eventually lead to the fragmentation and dissolution of the communist cause internationally. Thus, the well-intentioned actions of the defendants who opposed Stalin's politics of terror could only be seen within their political context to be a threat to the revolution itself. This example suggests that to anticipate the future meaning of action, one cannot rely on the "good faith" of intentions alone.[7] "Consciousness is not a good judge of what we are *doing* since we are involved in the struggle of history and in this we achieve more, less, or something else than we thought we were doing" (HT 104/ HTF 112). This does not lead, however, to historical determinism. To understand the meaning of history, one requires an active imagination that can consider a variety of interpretations and a keen vision that can determine vague, general patterns of meaning developing over the course of time. History offers us a field of possibilities that is limited on all sides by economic and material conditions and by the difficult task of creating meaning in the company of others. The historian must approach her subject with suspicion, as the analyst approaches the utterances of the patient, interpreting the direction of its themes and failures while remaining open to what the future has in store. The analyst correspondingly

96 Pathological Imagining

must consider the relation of the behavior of the patient to the patient's own emotional and personal history, and interpret the significance of the patient's behavior accordingly.[8]

Now that we have considered Merleau-Ponty's criticism of Freud's early theory of psychoanalysis and have examined his description of the ambiguity of embodied experience, we are in a better position to understand how Merleau-Ponty explains neurotic behavior. The aphonic and anorexic patient discussed by Merleau-Ponty did not experience a loss of memory or a physiological injury. Rather the patient's future had become "arrested in a bodily symptom" as "the place where [her] life hides away" (PP 164/PPF 192).[9] The illness was overcome not by attempting to restore her speech word for word, but by restoring for her the intersubjective world by holding her hand (PP 163/PPF 190). This suggests that "existence is not a set of facts (like 'psychic facts') capable of being reduced to others or to which they can reduce themselves, but the ambiguous setting of their intercommunication, the point at which their boundaries run into each other, or again their woven fabric" (PP 166/PPF 195). What the patient had begun to lose control over was the ambiguous chiasm between the imaginary and the real, the hinge between becoming lost completely in the imaginary and being completely absorbed in everyday affairs. While experiencing her neurosis, the patient became too focused on her actual situation to be free enough to consider alternative possibilities, to the point where it began to affect her behavior. Neurosis, then, is the result of a gradual closure of the imaginary for the present.

Merleau-Ponty's analysis of neurotic behavior suggests that its cure, more often than not, is found in restoring the imagination. Often it is by means of reviving the imagination that therapists are able to help neurotic patients. By asking their patients to imagine particular situations and by monitoring their responses, therapists can determine their patients' attitudes and detect situations with which their patients are uncomfortable. They can then ask their patients to reimagine those situations in ways that facilitate a reorientation toward the problem, and to resymbolize those situations so that the patients can visualize them as involving possible alternatives. Jerome Singer explains that a cure can be found by preparing the patient "to reverse his stream of thought over the previous few minutes so that he can detect the particular image, memory, or scene which, perhaps by slightly delayed reaction, triggered a long-standing conflict or fear. In effect, such activity greatly broadens the scope of the person's capacity to deal with his own ongoing behavior and frees him from the apparently automatic behavior that so often characterizes neurosis."[10] It is through the imagination, then, and not in spite of it, that some instances of neurotic behavior can be eventually replaced by normal behavior.

Another therapeutic application of the imagination is found in the guided daydream (*rêve éveillé dirigé*) designed by Robert Desoille in the 1930s. In this form of psychotherapy, the patient is asked to engage in a daydream and to describe the imagined figures and actions. The patient inevitably encounters barriers to forbidden places and experiences vertical movements, although the content of and reaction to the dream vary from patient to patient. On the basis of these variations and the way that the patient reacts to suggestions by the therapist, it can be determined what fears or concerns are at the root of the patient's behavior. An example of the guided daydream provided by J. H. van den Berg involves a woman who had a history of breaking off her engagement to marry. The woman's husband had been killed during the war. At one point in the guided daydream, she was in a state of danger and claimed to be alone. When asked by the therapist if she could call for help, the answer was no. After further visits, however, the woman came to see her need to allow others to become intimate with her, and within two months she was able to marry without hesitation. Van den Berg reflects on the experience, reporting that "it is difficult to doubt that the *rêve éveillé* proved to her that it was unnecessary to be alone and that it was very well possible for her to go farther with her fiancé, and that this imaginary experience opened the gate

98 Pathological Imagining

to a reality in which a marriage without doubts was possible."[11] Rather than providing the cause for the neurosis, the imagination has been shown to be a cure.

The experience of becoming focused on the actual at the expense of the imaginary is most poignant in psychosis. Citing cases recorded by Minkowski, F. Fischer, Schröder and others, Merleau-Ponty eliminates the possibility of explaining psychosis in terms of a malfunction in the patient's perceptual or cognitive abilities by highlighting the fact that patients can tell the difference between their psychotic behavior and ordinary behavior. A patient who has tactile hallucinations, for example, jumps when pricked by an actual needle, but remains seated when experiencing the hallucinatory sensations. Another patient who reports visions of a man standing under his window is astonished when a real man assumes the same position (PP 334/PPF 385). The patients also correct themselves when reflecting on their experiences, so that at "the level of judgment they distinguish hallucination from perception" (PP335/ PPF 386).

For Merleau-Ponty, what occurs when a patient is experiencing hallucinations is a breakdown in the continuum between the real and the imaginary. The normal subject passes easily from daydream to reality, and is able to both imagine and put into action behaviors that are different from what is being done at the present moment. But the patient becomes fixated on a particular behavior and unable to free himself from it. The patient exists as if in a private world, unable to embrace the dimension of the possible and condemned to a particular course of action. "Hallucination," suggests Merleau-Ponty, "causes the real to disintegrate before our eyes, and puts a quasi-reality in its place" (PP 334/PPF 385). The quasi-world feels artificial to the patient, as shown by the fact that many hallucinatory images are said to be of technological instruments, such as the sound of a telephone or a radio (ibid.). In the private world of psychosis, the patient also feels objectified and reports being seen by others or talked about behind his back. The patient paradoxically feels locked in a private world over which he has no control. "The schizophrenic no longer inhabits the common property world," says Merleau-Ponty, "but a private world, and no longer gets as far as geographic space: he swells in 'the landscape space,' and the landscape itself, once cut off from the common property world, is considerably impoverished" (PP 287/PPF 332). Merleau-Ponty illustrates this point by comparing psychosis not to the dream, as many other theorists do, but to walking in the dark.[12] He explains: "Night is not an object before me; it enwraps me and infiltrates through all my senses, stifling my recollections and almost destroying my personal identity. . . . Night has no outlines . . . it is pure depth without foreground or background, without surfaces and without any distance separating it from me" (PP 283/PPF 328). The dark dissolves the clear distinction of exteriority and interiority that we experience by daylight, exposing my subjectivity to its opacity while providing an opportunity for my phantasms to appear real. Likewise hallucinations shrink the world of the patient to the world of the actual, dissolving the difference between interiority and exteriority so that imagined sounds and scenes appear to be part of the external world. "Sometimes," explains Merleau-Ponty, "the lived distance is both too small and too great: the majority of the events cease to count for me, while the nearest ones obsess me. They enshroud me like night and rob me of my individuality and freedom. I can literally no longer breathe; I am possessed" (PP 286/PPF 331).

The description of psychosis provided by Merleau-Ponty is in stark contrast to the traditional view that it is based on the imagination. Merleau-Ponty finds that the patient usually does not find comfort in an imaginary world, but rather experiences a discomfort with the world in general. To understand the root of this discomfort, Merleau-Ponty reminds us of the "perceptual faith" (VI 3/VIF 17) that we have in ordinary experience that involves a "confidence in the world" (PP 297/PPF 344) such that our experience can be analyzed and verified upon further inspection and can be shared and discussed with others. On the basis of this faith, we engage with the world and maintain a tie and a balance between our own subjectivities and the objectivity of the world around us. For the patient, this trust is not replaced by a trust in the imaginary, but is lost altogether. "My perception brings into co-existence an indefinite number of perceptual chains which, if followed up, would confirm it in all respects and accord with it," explains Merleau-Ponty. "The victim of hallucination enjoys no such belief; the hallucinatory phenomenon is no part of the world, that is to say, it is not *accessible*, there is no definite path leading from it to all the remaining experiences of the deluded subject, or to the experiences of the sane" (PP 339/PPF 390). The patient suffers not from too lively an imagination, then, but from the loss of a "world" to live in. James Morley observes that the patient is no longer able to share her experiences with others, is no longer able to distinguish subjective experiences from the objective world, and as a result experiences the world as actual and rigid.[13] The problem arises because of an obsessive fixation on a particular feeling or project to the extent that the rest of the world comes to lose its meaning as background, reducing the world of the patient to the immediate feeling or intention. Merleau-Ponty explains: "The victim of hallucination does not see and hear in the normal sense, but makes use of his sensory fields and his natural insertion into a world in order to build up out of the fragments of this world, an artificial world answering to the total insertion of his being" (PP 341/PPF 393). The symbols of the hallucination become the emotions themselves that the patient is fixated on: the poison is not an objective threat but the personification of fear; a word becomes a threatening experience, an incantation that is not subject to rational explanation. Unlike the dream, the hallucination becomes rigid, depersonalized and inaccessible to others. For the patient there is a loss and not an overabundance of the imagination, and it is only by restoring the imagination that the patient is able to alter his behavior.[14]

Although psychosis involves the most extreme case of a loss of the imagination, the virtual body can still be found on the margins of psychotic experience. Merleau-Ponty stresses that the patient's world and the world of perception "are not, in so far as they are different, hermetically sealed within themselves; they are not small islands of experience cut off from each other, and from which there is no escape" (PP 292/PPF 338). Even the patient acknowledges that her experience is not real and can distinguish between the real and the illusory upon reflection, precisely because the initial tie to the objective world is never completely lost and only momentarily eclipsed. This link between the imaginary and the real assumes the form of a dialectic (as discussed in chapter 1) between imagined possibilities, entertained by the virtual body, and actual limitations and environmental conditions. In some situations, we give priority to the actual, such as when we attempt to overcome obstacles or engage in ordinary activities; at other times we focus on what is possible, either while deliberating or daydreaming. Our existence consists of a rhythm of openness and closure, of focusing more or less on either the actual or the possible — what Merleau-Ponty calls "the systole and diastole" of existence (PP 164, 285/PPF 192, 330). In psychosis this dialectic collapses into the present, and the patient is no longer able to switch readily from the possible to the actual. The virtual body, in other words, becomes absorbed by the actual body. The analyst must invite the patient to regain a faith in the intersubjective world and to slowly reintegrate her experience with the experiences of other people. The analyst, one might say, is more of a priest than a scientist, with the task of "converting" the patient to regain her perceptual faith. It is only when the patient retrieves the power of the imagination to reinterpret her situation that she is able to free herself from her psychotic behavior and restore a healthy balance between the actual and the virtual body.

It is has been shown that between the daydream and psychotic behavior lies a continuum of existence. This continuum at each and every point consists of a dialectic of the imaginary and the

102 Pathological Imagining

real, and is defined in terms of the priority that the subject places on one or the other pole. The research considered by Merleau-Ponty implies that the traditional view of neurosis and psychosis as involving an excess of imagination is false, and that they more often involve a reduction of the imagination and a fixation on reality. In such cases what is needed to return to ordinary behavior is not greater control over the imagination but the freeing of the imagination from the rigidity of neurotic and psychotic experience. The imagination, it should be added, is more specifically that of the virtual body which enables the subject to maintain a balance between real and imagined space, an essential balance for the consideration and application of alternative modes of embodiment. The imagination, then, is not primarily the cause of neurotic and psychotic behavior, but a neutral and essential mode of existence. The imaginer, no doubt, runs the risk of becoming too detached from reality, or of becoming overly anxious about the possibilities that he might have to consider. But as Jerome Singer explains, "what his increased inner capacity offers him is a fuller sense of being intensely alive from moment to moment, and this may be worth the frequent pain of a deeper self-awareness."[15]

Six

Self-Imagining

*I*n the clear surface of the pool, surrounded by the reflection of
cypress trees and distant clouds, I see my reflection: my face,
both familiar and strange to me, provides a sameness by which I
can identify myself, a sameness that nevertheless involves a strange-
ness, a reversal of right to left, of front to back, of reality to image.
On the basis of this image I build a sense of self; it is this body, this
image, that others see when they observe me, realizing that I am
more than the image, a displacement and double *for them* of the
image, both visible and invisible, present and absent. The reciprocity
between self and Other, then, is based on the image of the self. The
relationship between self and Other is mediated by the reflection
of the self in the mirror, such that the universe, like that of Narcis-
sus, becomes an echo of my own interiority.

In the last chapter I demonstrated that the imagination is not
usually a cause for pathological experience. It has been suggested,
however, that it may involve what one might call the neurosis of a
philosophy of the same. Could it not be the case that between the
self and the mirror is an unbridgeable gap that displaces all hope
for total self-reflection? Are we misled into thinking that the self is
the measure of all things, including the measure of the Other's
face? Merleau-Ponty's philosophy of imagination provides a way

104   Self-Imagining

to break the spell of narcissism in traditional philosophy that reduces the Other to the experience of the self. The bond between the self and the Other, he contends, is mediated by the image of the body as both present and absent, and as more the bearer of difference than the basis of sameness, as an alterity, in other words, within the image of the body. The imagination of the body does not lead to a philosophy of the same, but to the virtual embodiment of difference that grounds intersubjective experience.

At about the age of six months a break occurs in the narcissism of the child, a moment that Jacques Lacan has famously called the "mirror stage" of a child's psychogenesis. At this age, a child ceases to be merely amused by his mirror image and comes to identify with it as a true externalization of himself. "We have only to understand the mirror stage *as an identification*," says Lacan, "in the full sense that analysis gives to the term: namely, the transformation that takes place in the subject when he assumes an image."[1] By identifying with the image, the child is enabled to become aware of himself as seen by others, and ultimately to prepare himself for the role-playing and reciprocity one finds in the early and later stages of social existence. But the externalization of self characteristic of the mirror stage also establishes a division within the self that the child never manages to overcome. Lacan writes:

> The *mirror stage* is a drama whose internal thrust is precipitated from insufficiency to anticipation — and which manufactures for the subject, caught up in the lure of spatial identification, the succession of phantasies that extends from a fragmented body-image to a form of its totality that I shall call orthopaedic — and, lastly, to the assumption of the armour of an alienating identity, which will mark with its rigid structure the subject's entire mental development.[2]

By identifying with the image in the mirror, the subject comes to witness his subjectivity in external form. But in the process of this identification there is a split between the new spectral identity and the immediacy of the will — a split that the subject will attempt to

Self-Imagining   *105*

bridge for the rest of his life. It is on the basis of this split, and the subject's quest for a unified self, that neurosis is made possible.[3]

In contrast to Lacan's description of the mirror stage as involving a fundamental splitting of the self from its self-identity through the image in the mirror, Merleau-Ponty believes that the mirror stage is a step toward both self-identity and healthy social relations. Merleau-Ponty claims that prior to the mirror stage children exist within a medium of "anonymous collectivity" in which they observe and imitate the behavior of others with no sense of detachment (PrP 119, 116/ROF 33, 39. See also PP 352–53/PPF 405). If a child cries, the other children in the room experience the same general sadness that has not yet become for them the property of a particular person. Sympathy is based on an anonymous mode of existence that operates by means of the body as symbolic of others.[4] As the child matures, he comes to distinguish between the Other's mirror image and the Other's body and to relate the sound of the Other to her mirror image. Eventually, the child comes to realize that he is also the bearer of this mysterious reversibility between image and experience, between seeing and being seen. In particular, this reversibility is found in the experience of double sensation, when one hand touches the other and the roles of touching and being touched become blurred. The genesis of a sense of self and Other is based on the child's ability to recognize an anonymous reversibility in his own body and in the bodies of other people. If reversibility suggests the presence of virtual roles and alternative modes of embodiment, then it could be said that the child learns, at this stage, to imagine with his body both a sense of self as seen by other people, and of others as the bearers of the same reversibility (PrP 125–41/ROF 41–62).

The sympathy of an adult remains rooted in an anonymous relatedness to the Other that develops by means of reversible modes of embodiment. The reversibility of the body as an agent and recipient of touch, for example, mediates the social experience of a handshake as a form of exchange with the Other. We do not begin

106 Self-Imagining

with a self-certain interiority and infer the existence of the Other from her behavior. In the handshake, we revisit our original syncretism with the Other in an anonymous mode of reversible embodiment. It is only after developing this sense of sympathy that we are able to experience our separation from the Other and that we develop a sense of unity and identity that distinguishes us from other people. Such a separation, however, is never total; the I and Thou, writes Merleau-Ponty, "are like organs of one single intercorporeality" within which we discover ourselves and others, and from which we can never extricate ourselves (S 168/SF 213; see also PrP 154/ROF 79; VI 141/VIF 185).

Adult sympathy in Merleau-Ponty's analysis is illustrated by the lover's caress. The experience of the caress introduces a paradigmatic proximity to the Other. The reversibility of self and Other is expressed, for instance, in the subject's desire to exist for the freedom of the Other and to risk rejection or abuse (PrP 154–55/ROF 80). Such exposure allows for an intensification of sympathy in which the adult is able to relinquish his self-interest and to surrender himself to the command of the Other. In the caress, the "internal weakness" of a person's anonymous collectivity is developed into a reciprocal relation between two individuals (PP xii/PPF vii; see also PrP 155/ROF 81).[5]

There is a major difference between Merleau-Ponty's descriptions of the mirror stage and Lacan's description. For Lacan, the mirror stage is formative of the ego (*soi* and *moi*), suggesting that the self is based on an imaginary unity between the self as will and the self as visible — a unity that is never achieved and only approximated by the imagination in the form of the illusion of and quest for a unified sense of self. Merleau-Ponty does not believe that the mirror stage is formative of the ego, but rather of the super-ego (*sur-moi* and *je-idéal*) that comes to serve as a standard for the self and the Other, the anonymous subjec-tivity that is shared by both.[6] For this reason, Lacan accuses Merleau-Ponty of overlooking

the radical trauma at the heart of self-identity and social existence —
a trauma that, like the neuroses of Freud's patients mentioned earlier,
is clouded over by the imagination. Only psychoanalysis can uncover
these deeper secrets of human experience, suggests Lacan.[7] It is
begging the question, however, to require phenomenology to accept
and compensate for such a radical split in the subject. Merleau-
Ponty's observations of young children bring into question Lacan's
radical "suspicion" of the project of self-identity and sociality. In
defense of Merleau-Ponty's position, David Michael Levin argues
that "there is a schematism of mutual recognition already inscribed
in the flesh, and it implicates the achievement of an ideal
communicative situation."[8] Lacan does not take account of this
essential sociality by overstressing the alienation that occurs during
the mirror stage.

It has been suggested by some of Merleau-Ponty's recent critics
that both he and Lacan are at fault for giving priority to vision in
their analyses of psychogenesis. Might it not be the case, they
suggest, that sound or touch, for instance, are equally formative in
a child's development of a sense of self? We are reminded of the
formative tactile experience that one has in the womb, and of the
social bond that is developed between the fetus and the mother on
the basis of bodily rhythms and responses. Luce Irigaray claims
that this experience precedes the objectifying experiences of seeing
and being seen, and describes this primal experience as "nourishing"
and as occurring "before there are images." The illusion or image
that is suspect in Irigaray's analysis is not one of escape from one's
original perspectivalism, as we have discussed above, but the
illusion of a development from this intrauterine experience of touch
in which there are no boundaries between self and other but "only
this liquid that flows from the one into the other, and that is
nameless."[9] Irigaray suggests that there is no escape from this
experience, in spite of our efforts to name it and to confine it within
conceptual categories and rigid boundaries. Is the self's effort to

articulate and to visualize itself in the mirror based on a failed project to separate itself from its primal, tactile bond to the mother that was experienced in the womb?

This criticism consists of two main points, namely that Merleau-Ponty gives priority to vision over other formative experiences of selfhood, and that it attempts to reduce to a common and identifiable experience the intrauterine or what Irigaray calls the maternal-feminine. Dealing with the first point, it is certainly true that throughout his career Merleau-Ponty exhibited a fascination for vision, expressing a strong interest in the bold gestures of the great artists and in the curious experiments of Modern optometry. Does this suggest that he is guilty of "ocularcentrism" (to borrow a phrase from Martin Jay), of basing his philosophical claims about the self and world on a single experience, the experience of sight?[10] Martin Dillon would seem to agree. He argues that Merleau-Ponty's description of the mirror stage betrays an overemphasis of vision at the expense of the other senses and the affective domain —both of which are equally or more central to self-development than the experience of vision. "The total experience of the phenomenal body is not primarily a visual experience," says Dillon. Embodied experience "incorporates all the senses (not only the identifiable five, but the feelings for which our vocabulary has not yet developed adequate terms) and is synaesthetic."[11] Dillon is particularly interested in the affective domain, where a child first learns to treat the world as an object of desire that is separate from itself and that resists the child's wishes. An alternative perspective — an "I" that is "Other" — is made possible because of the affective relation between the child and significant others, the mother or father from whom the child seeks approval. The child comes to see the father as Other not merely by identifying him with the mirror image as a reversible visible/seer, but as the bearer of a strong affective significance for the child. Prior to "visible alienation" through the mirror, there is an alienation of will and desire. Dillon explains: "Syncretic sociability breaks down—not because the infant has developed a capacity for visual recognition — but because a significant other, by some set of behavioral cues (e.g., punishment, failure to respond approvingly to the creation of feces, etc.), forces the infant to recognize an alien perspective as such." Affective and synesthetic experiences are just as important for self-development as visual ones, in spite of the importance that our own culture places on vision. Besides, Dillon says, the mirror is a recent invention, one that follows rather than constitutes the experience of self and Other.[12]

The claim by Dillon that Merleau-Ponty places too great an emphasis on vision is exaggerated. Dillon's suggestion, for instance, that an emphasis on the mirror stage involves an unacceptable anachronism because mirrors are a recent invention overlooks the predominance of reflective surfaces: the placid surface of a quiet lake, reflecting the trees that guard its periphery, the glare of polished stone or metal, the glassy surface of the eye of the Other. To assume that the mirror stage could only take place in front of an actual mirror is to overlook the reflective capabilities of the visible world. The mirror stage should be understood in a broader sense, including such nonvisual experiences of self-externalization as imitation and role-playing, of hearing one's echo, and of touching one's flesh. The mirror stage must involve not only a crisscrossing of seer/visible, but also a crisscrossing of the senses, of sight and touch, of thought and feeling.

The visual experience of the mirror also incorporates other forms of "mirroring" that occur in a social context. Reflection is found in the caress, for example, where the roles of touching and being touched are blurred, and the Other becomes the center or the "subject" of the lover's world. This tactile experience serves as a figure or background for the other senses, such as vision, in which the Other is not reduced to a spectacle. "In a visual sense," says Glen Mazis, "the touch of the caress sparks a translucency of the flesh that allows the lived body to reveal within itself the glow of the attributes and possibilities of the consciousness of the other

110   Self-Imagining

that one is affirming."[13] Merleau-Ponty also admits that children learn to develop a sense of self and Other through the mirror-play of imitation in children's games, including especially the imitation of linguistic sounds, of the pronouns "I" and "Thou," until suddenly they expose the child to a new dimension of intersubjective experience that was only previously hinted at by the child's mimetic context. "The other's words make me speak and think because they create within me an other than myself" (VI 224/VIF 277). Merleau-Ponty's emphasis on language as a medium for intersubjective relations testifies to his belief that the mirror stage spills over from the visual domain of experience into the domains of feelings and mimetic action that eventually assume the form of discourse. The reflective experience referred to by the mirror stage is only an image or model for understanding the reflective roles and experiences that are formative for the self and its social relations.

The accusation of ocularcentrism, however, takes on a unique shape in Irigaray's analysis of Merleau-Ponty's philosophy. Irigaray suggests that Merleau-Ponty's concept of reversibility is reductionistic because it eliminates an essential difference between masculine and feminine experience as paradigmatically presented by a mother's relation to her unborn child, what she calls the "the intrauterine: irreducible darkness."[14] The significance of this relation, one holding within the body itself, is by nature not subject to visibility or to linguistic expression; it remains a relation of touch, of sound in the form of a heartbeat, an alterity that defines femininity and that defies the masculine desire to see and to control. Merleau-Ponty's suggestion that the roles of self and Other are reversible overlooks this difference, dissolving it within the light of vision and the precision of language. Irigaray writes: "Although he dismisses the subject and the object, Merleau-Ponty nevertheless retains this polarity: seer/visible, which presupposes, here in particular, that the visible, still invisible in its resting place, would have vision and could give it to or take it away from the seer." This means that the visible retains its place of prominence, reducing the meaning of what is hidden to what can be made visible, providing an "illusion of the flesh" in which all meaning is an invitation to observation and categorization, an entrance, in the words of Hegel, of the sensible into sense-certainty.[15] The duality of subject and object is maintained since the Other is reduced to an object, to a standard of the same. Merleau-Ponty's call to the feminine to visual exposure creates an absence, a "black hole" between the self and the Other, in the form of the loss of alterity, "[t]he black hole of that into which we disappear, each into the other, continually."[16] Such exposure to vision, inaugurated by the mirror stage, leaves no room for the Other (and especially for the feminine Other), and "has no spacing or interval for the freedom of questioning between two. No other or Other to keep the world open. No genesis. No grace."[17]

This "deeper" criticism of Merleau-Ponty's philosophy, however, fails to see the corresponding "deep" relationship in Merleau-Ponty's philosophy between vision and what Merleau-Ponty calls the *écart*. It was already shown above how vision in Merleau-Ponty's analysis spills over into synesthesis and how the visual can serve equally as figure or background for the other senses. Even the mirror stage itself involves more than a visual experience, expanding into the other senses to include sound, touch, feelings, and mimetic activity. It is also the case that the reversibility of intersubjective relations does not reduce the Other to the self. The reversibility of self and Other is a reversibility that is "always immanent and never realized in fact" (VI 147/VIF 194). It is a basic experience, claims Merleau-Ponty, that the Other always escapes me, and that I remain within my own perspective: "I am always on the same side of my body" (VI 148/VIF 194). Between subject and Other lies a radical difference or *écart* that is overcome only virtually by means of sympathy (VI 203/VIF 257).[18] Thus, even in the experience of the caress, the reversibility of self and Other remains a virtual project that is never completed. Since reversibility is only virtual, Merleau-Ponty cannot be accused of reducing the Other to the same, but only of seeing the self as constituted in relation to the Other within an event of co-constitution that preserves alterity. It is precisely by means of (and not in spite of) the *écart* of social relations that the subject becomes exposed to alterity. David Michael Levin explains that the *écart* reveals "the paradoxical truth that in the dialectic of reflection, our moment of narcissism is subject to reversal: seduced into openness, we find ourselves in each other and are slowly appropriated, by and for a more mature intersubjective life."[19] By contrast, in a desperate attempt to protect the alterity of the intrauterine from the manipulation of vision and linguistic expression, Irigaray approaches either an essentialism or mysticism of sexual differences, closing off the intrauterine from discourse and even from sentiment (in the sense that Dillon would say feelings can be articulated).[20] It remains possible, then, to see alterity as possibly revealed on the basis of the same, provided that the same, in Merleau-Ponty, remains an *écart*, a hollow or a difference, and not an image based exclusively on the experience of the subject.

Failure to appreciate the significance of the *écart* in the development of the self is also found in Iris Young's criticism of social and moral theories that emphasize reversibility as a basis for understanding the relationship between the self and others.[21] Young is particularly concerned for such feminist philosophers as Seyla Benhabib who construct an ethics on the basis of mutual respect and reciprocity. Young cites Benhabib as stating that "communicative action entails symmetry and reciprocity of normative expectations among group members."[22] This symmetry and reciprocity, Benhabib suggests, is made possible by the imagination which allows us to consider other perspectives and to include them within a universalizing framework for moral judgment. Young argues that the unique personal experiences of individuals render their perspectives irreversible with each other. "Individuals bring different life histories, emotional habits and life plans to a relationship," Young explains, "which makes their positions irreversible."[23] She mentions as an example the inability of able-bodied people to appreciate the value of the lives of people with disabilities, as found in a survey in which many able-bodied people reported a preference of death to being disabled. Such a perspective clearly shows, to Young, an inability to truly imagine the other's perspective and to thus respect their difference on the basis of reversibility. The only solution, according to Young, is to make the encounter with the Other a shattering experience for the self so that it produces not a mutual respect but wonder and awe at the Other's difference. "A respectful stance of wonder toward other people," she writes, "is one of openness across, awaiting new insight about their needs, interests, perceptions, or assumptions." Young concludes: "Thus we each must be open to learning about the other person's perspective, since we cannot take the other person's standpoint and imagine that perspective as our own."[24]

It is questionable whether or not Young's criticisms of Benhabib are accurate. Benhabib's insistence on embedding her universalizing discourse ethics in the embodied experiences and situations of the subjects involved, and her claim that she is concerned for an "interactive universalism" that serves only as "a regulative ideal that does not deny our embodied and embedded identity,"[25] suggests that Young's criticism may be too harsh. What is more important with respect to Merleau-Ponty's philosophy, however, is Young's rigid and narrow conception of reversibility. Consider, for instance, her claim that "the idea of reversing perspectives assumes that the perspectives brought to a situation are equally legitimate" and that "the image of reversibility of positions may assume an unfortunate binarism," a binarism between the self and an Other that is based on the same. Young is unwilling to explore the possibility that reversibility may, in fact, resist such a binarism, when it is expanded to involve something other than having perspectives merely "plucked from their contextualized relations and substituted for one another."[26] Reversibility can involve precisely a *respect* for difference and for boundaries between self and other when related

114   Self-Imagining

to Merleau-Ponty's concept of the *écart*. Gail Weiss explains: "Reversibility describes an ongoing interaction between the flesh of the body, the flesh of others, and the flesh of the world, a process in which corporeal boundaries are simultaneously erected and dismantled."[27] This view of reversibility is consistent with Young's own claim that "who we are is constituted to a considerable extent by the relations in which we stand to others, along with our past experience of our relations with others."[28] Young identifies the uniqueness of an individual's perspective with the nexus of relationships that he or she has with others, and of his or her past experiences of these relationships.[29] In this, Young is in line with other feminist philosophers who stress the irreducibility of, for them, feminist experience to "masculine" concepts of representations. Consider Judith Butler's claim, for instance, that "we must lose the perspective of a subject already formed in order to account for our own becoming," or Nancy Love's belief that "voice crosses, even while it respects, boundaries."[30] That an emphasis on open dialogue (Young and Benhabib), tactility (Irigaray), or the feminine voice (Love) can preserve the uniqueness of a particular woman's (or man's) perspective need not suggest that this uniqueness is *irreversible* in every respect with other perspectives. Merleau-Ponty's conception of reversibility does as much as these feminist models to preserve the mystery and difference of embodied perspectives from becoming reduced to objective images or representations. Even when considering vision, for instance, Merleau-Ponty explains that "our body commands the visible for us, but it does not explain it, does not clarify it, it only concentrates the mystery of its scattered visibility" (VI 136/VIF 127). Thus, while Young is correct to point out the uniqueness of an individual's experience, she does not consider the possibility that a form of reversibility might serve as a potential solution to bridging the gap between self and Other. Merleau-Ponty's concept of reversibility is sufficiently flexible to preserve the boundaries between self and Other, and indeed to place emphasis on the irreducible mystery of an individual's unique perspective, without making that perspective symmetrical with others and reducing all perspectives to an image of the same. Reversibility, when considered on the basis of the *écart*, is the very hinge that allows experiences to be shared and that thus makes social relations possible. Intercorporeality, as illustrated by Merleau-Ponty, occurs at a level that is deeper than Young or Benhabib's models, which focus on discourse, and is more encompassing than Love's suggestion of focusing on the feminine voice as the bridge between the self and Other. It is by means of the imagining body, as the site for the reversibility of perspectives and the preservation of difference, that different experiences can be shared without reducing social existence to symmetrical relationships.

It could still be suggested that Merleau-Ponty's analysis does not take into consideration the role of culturally defined boundaries in psychogenesis. This is suggested, for instance, in the examples used by Merleau-Ponty which some critics propose tend to favor a particular, male perspective over other potential perspectives. Although these criticisms concern more the *content* than the *form* of Merleau-Ponty's analysis, it would be instructive to take a moment to consider them. The suggestion is that the self is developed in part along socially and culturally defined lines, depending on the nature of the relationships between particular individuals. For example, young boys tend to be encouraged to engage in aggressive physical activities, leading to the incorporation of various skills into their body schema that young girls may not be encouraged to develop. Thus, what begins as a cultural difference comes to affect the abilities of the male and female body.[31] Such differences are begun even earlier, according to Carol Gilligan, as determined by the fact that both boys and girls usually spend most of their time with a female caregiver, creating a sense of self-identity between the caregiver and young girls that is absent in the relationship between the female caregiver and boys. As a result, claims Gilligan, boys become more concerned about independence and detachment while girls come to identify themselves in relation to others. "Women not only define themselves in a context of human relationship," writes Gilligan, "but also judge themselves in terms of their ability to care."[32] J. Lever suggests that these differences are portrayed in the way that children play games: while boys play long, competitive and strategic games in large, age-heterogeneous groups, girls tend to play shorter, simpler games in small, intimate groups. When a dispute develops, boys become more interested in its resolution than the game itself, while girls tend to stop the game immediately for fear of hurting people's feelings.[33] The various skills and activities of a young child contribute to his or her developing sense of self and Other.

Gender difference is also the result of the different ways that children experience the mirror stage. As a child comes to develop a sense of self and Other through the exchange of body images, he begins to recognize the differences as well as the similarities between himself and Others. These differences often become the basis for stereotypes that the child uses to make sense of his social experience. A young girl might come to feel that her body is essentially alien or Other, or as being deficient from the body image of her father. Men may come to identify the Other with personal traits they wish to ignore, such as weakness and sensitivity, so that they can think of themselves as dominant and self-assured; women may respond by subverting the traits of power and control into the negative characteristics of insecurity and brutality.[34] The result is a reciprocal exchange of shame or disapproval that eventually becomes an arena for the traditional "battle of the sexes" (PrP 103/ ROF 10). The same dynamic can be found along the fault lines of other bodily differences, such as race, and can be further transposed to nonbodily differences such as economic class or religious membership.

While Merleau-Ponty tends to treat this stage of self-development as a "tacit agreement" (PrP 104/ROF 11) between the sexes, Judith

Butler, Frantz Fanon, Gail Weiss and others argue that the white male body image often plays a dominant role in social relations. For women and nonwhite children, the development of social relations through the exchange of body images involves the experience of what Butler calls "an imaginary threat"[35] to their humanity, the threat of being reduced to the hateful and the subhuman, of living forever in the shadow of a privileged body image.[36] Within the exchange of body images, young children of a dominant group manipulate contingent differences between their bodies and those of minority groups as a means of diverting attention away from unwanted characteristics and attributing them to others around them. The social development of minority children, by contrast, may begin with a sense of inferiority and suppression, and with a feeling of not being invited into social exchanges, of being excluded from what counts as normal. The pathological becomes defined in terms of what is not privileged, what is not similar to the characteristics of the body of white men. While sympathizing with Merleau-Ponty's attempt to address feminism (a considerable feat, considering his own time and culture), Talia Welsh points out his difficulty in maintaining a norm between bodies of difference that does not privilege his own cultural group: "All groups in a society are defined by stereotypes which are not of their own making. However, the dominating group will inevitably give more weight to its own psychological possibilities and remain less defined, and define the other groups largely by their physical possibilities (which are relatively limited). The suppressed groups will thus be more determined and see fewer possibilities for themselves."[37] A similar criticism, with which I am inclined to agree, can be found in Young's suggestion that "when privileged people put themselves in the position of those who are less privileged, the assumptions derived from their privilege often allow them unknowingly to misrepresent the other's situation."[38] A proper philosophy of the self and of social relations should be conscious of the potential for bias; while preferring one form over another as a basis for one's personal experience, one's philosophy of the self must not become the basis by which one understands other races and genders.

Although it may be true that Merleau-Ponty does not address this problem to the extent that contemporary feminist philosophy does, it is not the case that his philosophy of the imagining body cannot account for sexual difference. Thomas Busch accepts the fact that "there is no sexual originary untouched by differences and that there are many ways to be sexual."[39] But he also believes that such difference can be compensated for by Merleau-Ponty's concept of the social *écart*. Busch recalls how, in *Signs*, Merleau-Ponty alludes to his later philosophy in his criticism of psychologists who claim that there is a causal relation between a person's infantile experience and his or her mature sexuality. One's sex, referred to as a "technique" of the body, "can never be reduced to simply one among possible techniques; for it is against the background of this privileged experience, where we learn to know the body as a 'structuring' principle, that we glimpse the other 'possibles,' no matter how different from it they may be" (S 101/SF 126–27). Neither my own sex nor that of the Other is reducible to the same because they are related by means of a dimension, an *écart*, a hinge between two levels of experience that join but never collapse into each other, like the relations between colors as figure and as background, like the very hinge between the pathological and normal behavior of the body. While it becomes imperative to ward against turning one's personal preferences into a universal standard, one's technique of the body provides the only access to the sex or race of the Other. And the mediation of the two occurs within the "imaginary variation" (S 100/SF 125) of body images, and involves the crisscrossing of the actual body with virtual possibilities of embodiment that occur at the threshold of the real and the imaginary.

Although the above does not provide an exhaustive analysis of the relation of Merleau-Ponty's philosophy of psychogenesis to feminist thought (or even to Lacanian psychoanalysis), it should

Self-Imagining   119

suffice to show that within his philosophy of the imagining body is a sense of alterity that is shared by the self and the Other, and that underlies the influences on one's self-development, including both the visual representation of the self in the mirror and the culturally defined roles of gender, race and class that are imposed upon the self by society. The imagining body, then, does not reduce the Other and the self to the same image, but ushers both into a reciprocal and reversible relation that neither the self nor the Other completely controls or understands. It is the virtuality of the body image that allows for difference, rather than reducing intersubjectivity to an inevitable narcissism. At the hinge between the self and the Other is the imagining body, articulating the real and the imaginary, and exposing the subject to the virtual bodies of others. It is also at this chiasm of the real and the imaginary that the self discovers itself through the body image of the Other and enters into an inter-corporeality that is replete with possible techniques of living one's body. That the subject makes use of his or her own body to make sense of the social world need not result in giving priority to only one technique of embodiment; the imagining body introduces a unity-in-difference that embraces without eliminating the alterity of the Other. The development of the self is not based on an illusion of sameness, but on the open and intertwining nexus of relationships between the self and its world that forms the medium of intercorporeality.

SEVEN

Elemental Imagining

*W*hile studying at college I often found myself on the week-
end peering out the window of a Greyhound bus as it drove
through the countryside toward home. The route followed a beau-
tiful river valley lined by ancient elms and closed in by colorful
rolling hills of hay and cattle. About halfway down the valley the
bus would take a sharp turn toward the river and ascend the tall
steel girder bridge that straddled the two banks of the river. As we
began our ascent, my attention was divided between the scenery
around me and the book that I had been reading, especially the
following paragraph, which seemed to leap off the page:

> The bridge swings over the stream "with ease and power." . . . It
> brings stream and bank and land into each other's neighbourhood,
> [and] guides and attends the stream through the meadows. Resting
> upright in the stream's bed, the bridge-piers bear the swing of the
> arches that leave the stream's waters to run their course . . . the bridge
> holds [their] flow up to the sky by taking it for a moment under the
> vaulted gateway and then setting it free once more. . . . Always and
> ever differently the bridge initiates the lingering and hastening ways
> of men to and fro, so that they may get to other banks and in the
> end, as mortals, to the other side. . . . The bridge *gathers*, as a passage
> that crosses, before the divinities [such as when] we explicitly think

122 Elemental Imagining

of, and visibly *give thanks for*, their presence, as in the figure of the saint of the bridge.

The bridge *gathers* to it itself *in its own way* earth and sky, divinities and mortals.[1]

These are, of course, the words of Martin Heidegger, and they assumed a particular meaning for me on this Friday evening journey toward home. Heidegger's description of the bridge suggests that it is more than simply steel and coil, but precisely the activity of the gathering of the river's banks, of the autumn sky overhead, of the spiritual mood punctuated by the spire of a church in the background, and of me, the traveling mortal, for whom the bridge is a passageway home. The gathering, as well, occurs in "its own way," in a way different from a hydroelectric dam or a small stone bridge over a country stream.

Like Heidegger, Merleau-Ponty sought to revive a sense of wonder concerning our experience with things, and in particular to renew the philosophical study of Nature. In a working note he reminds himself of the need to conduct "a psychoanalysis of Nature" (VI 267/VIF 321), a curious suggestion, for traditional psychoanalysis is applied to human beings who have minds and souls, things that are traditionally not attributed to rocks and rivers and trees. Behind Merleau-Ponty's suggestion, however, lies a radically new way of understanding our relation to Nature and the meaning that Nature offers to us.

Since there are only a few references to a psychoanalysis of Nature in Merleau-Ponty's work, we are left to piece together what it would involve by considering similar comments by his contemporaries. Two, in particular, are Jean-Paul Sartre and Gaston Bachelard. Sartre, for instance, describes what he calls the "material meanings" of things such as "the human sense of needles, snow, grained wood, of crowded, of greasy, *etc.*," and claims that they "are as real as the world, neither more nor less, and to come into the world means to rise up in the midst of these meanings." His proposed analysis is "to be concerned with establishing the way in which each thing is the *objective* symbol of being and of the relation of human reality to this being." He continues: "All this comes to pass as if we come to life in a universe where feelings and acts are all charged with something material, have a substantial stuff, are *really* soft, dull, slimy, low, elevated, *etc.*, and in which material substances have originally a psychic meaning which renders them repugnant, horrifying, alluring, *etc.* No explanation by projection or by analogy is acceptable here."[2] One of Sartre's examples is the symbolic nature of "the slimy." We readily see a metaphorical connection between the experience of physical slime and the smooth-talking of a used car salesman. This occurs naturally and not by means of explicit association or enculturation. In particular, the slimy "represents in itself a dawning triumph of the solid over the liquid — that is, a tendency of the indifferent in-itself, which is represented by the pure solid, to fix liquidity, to absorb the for-itself which ought to dissolve it." What is worse, this triumph is delayed indefinitely; a solid object sinks slowly into the sticky mass "like a retarded annihilation." In this quality, we witness our helplessness before the elements of nature, and we are threatened by a continual death, which is both horrific and alluring. We would not get the same meaning from water, which melts everything into the same, or from fire, which voraciously enraptures and consumes. Thus, each element has its own law that predates us. "The gluey, the sticky, the hazy, etc., holes in the sand and in the earth, . . . all reveal to [a child] modes of pre-psychic and pre-sexual being which he will spend the rest of his life explaining." In order to understand the extent of control that nature has over our experience, we must explore the meaning of these elemental images.[3]

The material meanings of things is a concept that Sartre borrows from Gaston Bachelard, who claims that they are the products of the unconscious that determine, to some extent, how we encounter the world around us. The natural world and our own affective predispositions toward it simultaneously establish a series of meaningful gestalts which allow the natural world to assume a vague, affective significance, like the fear of suffocation as symbolized by slimy objects. To detect these meanings we must elicit what Bachelard calls the material imagination: not the power to recast perceptual images in a new configuration, as the image of a centaur is gleaned from perceptions of men and horses, but the imagination that gives itself to the object in its singular presentation and materiality.[4] Bachelard discusses four primordial images that are the focus of the material imagination: earth, air, water and fire. These elements provide us with the most basic affective qualities that condition our openness to the world around us.

Bachelard is not alone in treating the four elements as a basis for understanding our relation to Nature. Examples of the meaning of the elements abound in both recent and ancient literature. The pre-Socratic philosophers discussed the elements as the fundamental basis for reality, while more recent philosophers, including especially Martin Heidegger, John Sallis and David Abram, have provided detailed illustrations of what these images mean. Consider, for instance, the following descriptions:

• *Earth* is usually treated as an image of ground and support. We stand on the earth at a particular point from which we can look around or dig beneath our feet into the ground. The earth beneath us hides its contents as an internal horizon without which our perception would be impossible. Even if we dig down, we simply alter our vantage point and conceal the sky from our view. From out of it grow the plants which provide us with sustenance, and springs the water that nourishes us. "Earth is the serving bearer," says Heidegger, "blossoming and fruiting, spreading out in rock and water, rising up into plant and animal."[5] Merleau-Ponty adds the image of the earth as protector in that it "lifts all particular beings out of nothingness, as Noah's Ark preserved the living creatures from the flood" (TFL 122/TFLF 169; see also S 180/SF 227).

• *Air* suggests a sense of openness and formlessness, as the wind that blows but is visible only in the flag or swaying branches; it provides the space for language and culture and provides access to the heavens. Air eludes us like a vapor that recedes without a surface, without a face. The earth allows us to graze upon its surface, but the sky *is* the immeasurable, it has no beginning and no end; it has no substance and no surface. Air is the space for human thought and imagination. John Sallis explains: "As opposed to the non-recessive, closed bearing of earth, its self-seclusion, sky is recessive and open, indeed to such an extent that, arching over the earth, it effects the very opening of the expanse where things come to pass and come to be manifest."[6]

• *Water* is cleansing and purifying. Unlike air, it retains a syrupy texture that can be either transparent or opaque, an elemental Proteus. Water is chaotic, cutting into the earth with its soft texture and exposing it to the air, or tossing the earth about as if in a stormy sea. Water suggests unity and homogeneity, the forgetting of differences, of boundaries, of particularity. Water provides an abyss as the formless void referred to by Anaximander's concept of the *Apeiron*. Water disrupts the order of earth, striating its surface, so that everything is said to be "floating in being" (VI 144/VIF 189).

• *Fire* is a replenishing lightning flash or "spark (*l'étincelle*)" (PrP 163/EMF 21) of energy that radiates throughout the other elements and brings them to life. Fire *is* the radiation of Being, allowing the other elements to be filled with Being, to radiate Nature's essence by the energy that flows through them like the electrical current that flows through live wires. Because of fire, the elements are "nervures" (VI 118–19, 215/VIF 158–59, 269), central nerves that bring energy to the sensible and the sensing, themselves described as "leaves" (VI 137/VIF 180) of Being.[7] Fire is not a static "thing" but lives by means of its own consumption.[8] It is the progenitor of the gathering of the elements and their medium of exchange between each other, from ice to water to steam.

In all of these descriptions, there is a sense in which our experience of earth, air, water and fire presents a mystery of the sensible that is

126 Elemental Imagining

never completely lost even in modern times. It remains to be seen exactly what this mystery involves, and to what extent it is Nature, and not our own subjective fantasies, that places that meaning out there for us to explore and to develop.

It is for this purpose that Merleau-Ponty, along with Sartre and Bachelard, calls for a psychoanalysis of Nature. They claim to be conducting a phenomenology of elemental experience, an analysis of the way that qualities appear to us at the root of experience, when scientific assumptions are put aside and the qualities are allowed to show themselves in their original affective meanings for consciousness. Bachelard in particular was determined to disclose the logic of elemental images, claiming that he was not concerned about subjective meanings but about the elemental laws of Nature.[9] These laws, he said, recall a time when physics and poetry were indistinguishable, such as the time of pre-Socratic philosophy. Bachelard claimed that the mystery that forms an essential part of this early "science" still enfolds our modern world of computer technology, but that we often fail to notice what is left unexplained by our contemporary theories and scientific models. A return to the mystery of the sensible, through the analysis of elemental images, is for Bachelard the aim of a phenomenology of the sensible.[10]

Merleau-Ponty also claims to have found a law of perception that is not placed there by the perceiver and that informs our perception according to elemental images. Even in the experience of color, says Merleau-Ponty, there is a particular law of appearing that the artist learns to recognize and follow in his art. He explains: "What is indefinable in the quale, in the colour, is nothing else than a brief, peremptory manner of giving in one sole something, in one sole tone of being" (VI 135/VIF 178). We come to understand this "something" by examining its texture and particularity as containing a depth or thickness that infiltrates the particular quality (or, if you will, its particularity) with inexhaustible meaning. The element is made manifest as "a general thing, midway between the spatiotemporal individual and the idea, a sort of incarnate principle that brings a style of being wherever there is a fragment of being" (VI 139/VIF 184). For example, when we are considering the elemental quality of yellow, "it is precisely within its particularity as yellow and through it that the yellow becomes a universe or an element" (VI 218). The elemental depth of sense qualities provides consciousness with a natural or sensible meaning that is provided by the natural world as perceived. This leads Merleau-Ponty to argue that "[p]erception is not first a perception of *things*, but a perception of *elements* (water, air . . .) of *rays of the world*, of things which are dimensions, which are worlds, I slip on these 'elements' and here I am in the *world*, I slip from the 'subjective' to Being" (VI 218/VIF 271). Each color partakes of elemental Being, allowing it to present the world in a unique way that defies exhaustive explanation and which continues to make Nature appear magical, as if possessing a life and meaning of its own — a life and meaning that we can analyze.

Elemental meanings prepattern our experience, interweaving with each other within a common fabric Merleau-Ponty calls the flesh of the world (*chair du monde*). This fabric provides the bridge between the subjective constitution of meaning and the appearing of Being, made manifest especially in the sensible world. Between subject and object, consciousness and Being, are vague meanings traced out beforehand within the various modes of elemental Being that the body interprets as general modes of relating to the world. Merleau-Ponty writes: "To designate [the flesh], we should need the old term 'element,' in the sense it was used to speak of water, air, earth, and fire. The flesh is in this sense an 'element' of Being" (VI 139/VIF 184). To illustrate this, Merleau-Ponty comments on how the element of water has its own laws, such as in what is revealed when we see tiles at the bottom of a pool. What to the modern eye would be distortions in color and size are in fact the very grammar of a logic of water, revealing the tiles as "straight-while-submerged" (rather than as "straight-while-in-open-air"). We do not see the tiles despite the distortions of the water, but precisely by means of the water and its own laws of delivering up the appearance of objects to our sentient bodies. Water has its own effects on the objects as they appear to us, distorting their sizes, muffling their sounds, and it also has a blurring effect on our senses so that we can decipher the appearance (PrP 182/EMF 70–71). These laws are neither given by the subject nor fixed in Nature, but occur in the encounter of eye and world as a momentary medium for experiencing the tiles. They also elicit a number of psychic meanings, like the values of homogeneity, purity and sustenance, so that we are reviled if the medium is murky or opaque to the extent that it approximates the texture of the slimy. Likewise, all of the elements provide general laws by means of which they can serve as a level or medium for the appearing of Being.[11]

Merleau-Ponty's description of the elements attempts to preserve a sense of sameness suggested by the pre-Socratic *Urstoff* while maintaining within the elements a sense of difference or *écart* that would avoid a reduction of Being to presence. The pre-Socratics correctly observed a reversibility of the elements by which they pass into each other: water, for example, when boiled becomes steam or air because water is in some way similar to air. Thus, one element can act as a measure or dimension of another so that, as Renaud Barbaras explains, "the element is a secret principle of equivalence, the carnal invisible of phenomena, concrete generality."[12] But the reversibility of water into air is always immanent and never actual. An element is essentially an act of differentiation, inaugurating a differential realm or a diacritical system like language. Barbaras explains, "the element is not subjective, nor is it *that which* is perceived, it is the dimension by means of which perception takes place." It is thus not simply a means for achieving unity but also for achieving difference, an "active producer of heterogeneity." We must conceive of elemental images, then, not simply in terms of a single matter that underlies

Elemental Imagining 129

all of Being, but as the potential differentiation and mediation of Being along a particular line or direction (*sens*) — a particular trace for the spacing and temporalizing of Being. An element does not offer a unity for the cosmos but what Barbaras calls "the identity of being and mediation."[13]

It is not immediately clear whether or not Merleau-Ponty gives priority to a particular set of elemental images, or whether every appearing of Being in Nature is equally elemental. Marc Richir interprets Merleau-Ponty as implying the latter: "The *cosmos* of Merleau-Ponty is not only constituted, like that of the Greeks, by the four elements — again in a sense that we can take back — because there are, within it, as many elements as there are apparent modulations of flesh, the appearing of *appearances* of the phenomenality of the phenomenon."[14] According to this interpretation there are not four elements but as many elements as there are qualities and experiences. Although we may focus on earth, air, water and fire as central images for our experience, they are no different in kind from other qualities as the pre-Socratics suggested. According to Richir, at least, the number of elements is limitless.

Marc Richir's comments help to protect Merleau-Ponty's philosophy from cultural relativism, in which the established number of elements of a particular tradition may be taken to be fundamental for all experience. It also keeps his philosophy open to the various ways that Being reveals itself to us in nature. But Richir's interpretation overlooks an elemental hierarchy that gives to the experience of nature a complexity, depth, and a sense of gravity. What is of interest to Merleau-Ponty is not only the fact that yellow, along with every other sense quality, can act as a dimension for the appearing of other qualities and thus, in that sense, can be seen to be like an elemental image, but also that the yellow is essentially *this* yellow, with a particular texture and quality that is unique from all other instances of yellow. The red of the carpet would not offer its color if it were not the fibrous and textured red

130 Elemental Imagining

of *this* carpet; what strikes me first is not the absolute shade but the rough strands and tufts of the carpet's material (PP 5). The fibers of the carpet recall the element of earth, in contrast with red blood or the red of fire. The four elements of earth, air, water and fire suggest a weight or texture to Being that mere sense qualities may not convey as general shades in a spectrum.

It is precisely the hierarchical structure of elemental flesh that preserves elemental images from becoming identical to both simulacra and signifiers. Consider simulacra. Jean Baudrillard describes simulacra as mere copies of images that bear no relation to the reality that they are supposed to signify. He suggests that the difference between image and reality, so important for establishing reference, has been called into question by the prevalence of simulacra. "The very definition of the real becomes: *that of which it is possible to give an equivalent reproduction.* . . . At the limit of this process of reproducibility, the real is not only what can be reproduced, but *that which is always already reproduced.* The hyperreal."[15] The challenge of Baudrillard to Merleau-Ponty is to determine in what way elemental images, with their reference to nature, can be said to signify nature and refer to something beyond themselves.

At first it seems that Merleau-Ponty agrees with Baudrillard that elemental images are mere simulacra. Elemental images, he claims, do not provide direct references to objects in the manner of a representational drawing of something that exists already. The only way to properly understand the logic of elemental images is to treat them as poetry or art. Merleau-Ponty writes that the painter "gives visible existence to what profane vision believes to be invisible" (PrP 166/EMF 29), namely, the creative emergence of perceptual meaning found in the elemental image.[16] A proper, direct relation between the elemental image and reality cannot be established because the elements provide a general affective meaning of experience that is only later developed into the determinate shape and structure of a particular sensible image. The elements do not concern a reality that is ready-made, but the originary possibility of meaning that the world presents to the body, what Merleau-Ponty at one point refers to as "the imaginary texture of the real" (PrP 165/EMF 24). Thus, the elemental image seems to assume the same form as a simulacrum that generates its meaning in the absence of a determinate reality.

So strong is the relation between elemental images and language that Barbaras explains them in terms of metaphor. As metaphors the elements are said to provide the "ontological doorway"[17] to the essence of Nature. Borrowing from Paul Ricoeur's understanding of metaphor as the creation of new meaning from clashing semantic structures (such as "man" and "wolf" to create the metaphor "man is a wolf"),[18] Barbaras argues that the elements, as well, involve a clash of meanings in the creation of new meaning. Traditional habits of perception are restructured by elemental images in order to provide new perspectives of reality. The elemental significance of sand, and thus earth, brings the familiar grainy texture of the shore into question, exposing the observer to the secret powers of perception that allow him to see the world as assuming a determinate structure. Barbaras argues that elemental images are the result of an "originary metaphoricity" of Nature in which various meanings are disseminated in an arbitrary fashion that are only later interpreted in terms of familiar and determinate objects. He concludes that "we must define being by a *fundamental metaphoricity* as the constitutive excess of the visible on itself."[19]

In contrast with Barbaras's interpretation of elemental images, Merleau-Ponty's discussion of metaphor in *The Visible and the Invisible* reveals a resistance to reducing elemental images to natural metaphors. Merleau-Ponty warns us that "[t]here is no *metaphor* between the visible and the invisible . . . *metaphor* is too much if the invisible is really invisible, too little if it lends itself to transposition" (VI 221–22/VIF 275). Too much, in other words, if elemental images are subjective and fanciful, since metaphors are entrenched in a diacritical system and attain a sense of stasis and materiality; too little if they simply refer to a fixed and static mode of being, since metaphors defer their ostensive references indefinitely. Merleau-Ponty is arguing that in saying that two things *are* and *are not* the same (that a man is like a wolf, while not being identical to a wolf), one is already dealing with two semantic fields (however "open" those fields might be to change). But elemental images are involved in the very creation of such fields. Before we can have a clash of meanings leading toward a new meaning (and thus a metaphor), there must already be meaning in the form of elemental images. Metaphors presuppose an order of meaning that is established by the affective meanings of elemental images.[20]

Rather than emphasizing the metaphorical structure of the four elements, Merleau-Ponty turns to the concept of "archetypes" (VI 116/VIF 156) that consist of "clusters" (VI 135/VIF 178) of meanings that are unified according to the particular logic of each element.[21] A good description of the logic of archetypes is provided by Edward Murray in *Imaginative Thinking and Human Existence*, where he shows how they differ from ordinary metaphors. He explains that while traditional metaphors contain a centrifugal force away from the original meanings of words and toward new meanings, the archetype involves a root metaphor that draws other metaphors toward it like a magnet. An archetype is described as "a ganglion of metaphors around which, indeed, families of metaphors might cluster."[22] Although Murray does not say what these meanings are, the four elements can be seen to perform a similar function. Even in the very sensual experience of water, earth, air and fire, clusters of meanings begin to emerge. If we consider water, for instance, the fluid and clear substance offers the tiles at the bottom of the pool to vision according to unique laws. When poetically expressed, these laws can lead to a series of associated images. It might suggest innocence and cleansing, or unity and homogeneity. These literary meanings are not subjective, but stem from a cluster of meanings that we discover when we consider the elemental image of water. By "element," Merleau-Ponty was not talking about an

Elemental Imagining 133

ancient myth or an abstract concept, but the "intentional tissue" (PP 53/PPF 65) that connects us to the sensible world. Within this tissue or texture of Being are elemental images that cluster around them a host of meanings that we spend the rest of our lives discovering and developing — the meaning of the images of earth, air, water and fire.

The archetypes stand apart from language precisely because, like the phenomenal body, they possess a "nameless weight" (S 56/SF 70) that anchors them in Nature from the free play of literary expression described by Baudrillard and others. The archetypes revolve "about the dimensions and the site of our own existence" (VI 116/VIF 156), itself anchored in the world according to the way that the body makes space and produces around it a world of significance. We cannot reduce the meanings of the elements to those of language, since without the elemental determination of the natural world language has no bearing and is an empty narcissism, a mere echo or double. Without the weight and depth and centripetal force of the elements, we would arrive at a level where all images are simulacra, where meaning would cease to "mean" and would simply copy itself, dropping its reference to a world of truth and ultimately imploding the sense of reference for an endless play of images. Not only would the elements be reduced to mere images, but the human body, as well, would be reduced to a copying of images (such as the genetic reproduction of DNA, to borrow an example from Baudrillard).[23] In order to avoid such a reduction of the elemental image and of the body, one must discover between elemental images and both simulacra and metaphors an essential difference, what Merleau-Ponty calls a "verticality" or "thickness" of Being (VI 127, 227, 271/VIF 169, 281, 325). Barbaras explains: "the known horizon in the manner of something horizontal, as a potentiality of consciousness, the opening of a halo of perception, rests on a horizon of an originary or vertical sense of a presentation of the world that is totally present."[24] Merleau-Ponty is not content to see the originary sense of Being reduced to a play of signifiers or simulacra, but insists on the fact that the world maintains a differentiation that is essentially vertical. By this he means that we cannot reduce all images to the level of the same, but rather find them scattered throughout an interchange of a series of diacritical systems, between which one can find yet another exchange of differences. Yellow is understood as being different from green, and both occur within a diacritical system of color that collides with that of touch in a diacritical system of sense experience, and all of them in turn are different from the world so that, between the sentient and the sensible, another "differential system" is established.[25] Though each of these systems provide for a Being that is in flux, a Being in the process of becoming, they do not, as Baudrillard would suggest, become reduced to a level of sameness. "Embodiment," says Thomas Busch, "is a sort of gravitational force on language so that, for Merleau-Ponty, language does not break free of sensibility in dissemination, but circulates within the levels of sensibility and embodied expression."[26] Being is essentially self-differentiation, and holds itself together not along lines of similarity, but along folds and divergences, in the joints of things which serve as "archetypes and variants of human life" (VI 116/VIF 156). There is inherent in Being an irreducible verticality that is held in place by elemental images and their affective meanings for consciousness. This verticality frees elemental images from being treated as simply another set of disseminations or simulacra.

The primordial role that elemental images play in our experience also allows Merleau-Ponty to provide a theory of truth in the sense of a "presence-in-the-making" to which the elements refer, not in a one-to-one relation with a reality that is already present, but in the sense of the meaning of an artwork or of history that is consistent with the past while remaining indeterminate in the future. Thus Gary Madison is correct to observe that an observation of the elements facilitates an ontology of *becoming* and a new theory of truth as event and perceptual history. He writes: "Strictly speaking, reality, like truth, *is not*; it becomes, it transpires, *elle s'écrit*, and the locus of its most eloquent (*parlante*) inscription is the human seeing/writing subject."[27] The elements bear a certain weight and centripetal energy that propel toward them whole clusters of meanings that we articulate when we attempt to understand our experience. Rooted in the earth and under the sky, we discover the particular sense of Nature that is expressed by the tree or by the river, and within that experience we come to see our difference from the signs that we create and the words that we speak on a silent level of embodied meaning where Nature, and Being, are first imagined.

The elements provide the "natal pact between our body and the world" (PrP 6/INF 404), a pact that we are committed to throughout our lives. They provide the source for our ability to perceive the world and to renew the imagination with fresh images from Nature. The elements thus involve more than poetic expressions and subjective fancies but reveal a rootedness in the truth of perceptual experience as the site for the appearing of Being. Merleau-Ponty believes that it is essential to expose any philosophical analysis of Nature to the elemental dimension of existence before proceeding too briskly to an ontology that would otherwise remain empty and ungrounded in the truth of elemental experience. The four elements of earth, air, water and fire, when gathered together in what Heidegger calls "World" and what Merleau-Ponty calls "flesh," provide the most general intertwining of affective meaning that shapes our perceptual experience in a certain way. Referring to "flesh," David Abram concludes, "this interplay of the different senses is what enables the chiasm between the body and the earth, the reciprocal participation — between one's own flesh and the encompassing flesh of the world — that we commonly call perception."[28] This means that an analysis of perception, of Nature and of truth must (to borrow a phrase from Ricoeur) take a detour not only through the signs provided by language and culture but also through those signs of Nature that we have come to call the elements of earth, air, water and fire.

EIGHT

Imagining Being

Beyond the elements, the lofty spaces of the air, the all-consuming energy of fire, can be found the traces of the meaning of Being as it allows itself to appear in the sensible world. Although they wait to be developed and articulated by the imagining body, the elements possess a brute and wild nature that already gives shape to our experience. To perform a psychoanalysis of Nature is to determine in what ways these natural images generate meanings for themselves, and to determine the effect that these meanings have on our bodies and on how we perceive the world.

When we turn to explore the meaning of Being itself, we begin to realize that to understand Being is as much an interpretation as a discovery. Being is involved in what Michael Yeo calls a "creative adequation" between the imagining body and the appearance of Being in the images of the sensible world.[1] In the philosophy of Merleau-Ponty, ontology is not simply the development of a concept, "Being," but an activity of imagining how Being appears by interpreting elemental images and creating new ones through which Being can be made manifest. Contrary to Hegel's warnings that images hinder our understanding, Merleau-Ponty suggests that it is precisely through the activity of imagining that we come closer to understanding the meaning of Being.

138 Imagining Being

Ontology becomes a major theme in Merleau-Ponty's later philosophy. Though there is no need to say, as some critics do,[2] that Merleau-Ponty's earlier works provide an insufficient ground for an ontology, it is at least fair to say that it is only in his later works that he began to focus on ontology in its own right. It is also in his later works that we see Merleau-Ponty beginning to explore the ontological implications of embodiment. By developing the concept of the lived body into what he calls the flesh of the world, Merleau-Ponty provides a fresh look at how we are to understand the meaning of Being.

To think of Being in a way that is true to how it appears requires a phenomenological analysis of the source for the appearing of things, of what makes it possible for Being to appear. This description of the "appearing" of appearances is what John Sallis calls a "proto-phenomenology," a study of what precedes the appearance of phenomena, and a "monstrology" in the sense that it is an analysis of "showing" (in Latin, *monstrare*) whose subject is "monstrous" in transcending what is actually seen.[3] Because ontology must make use of signs and symbols to break the silent spell of Being and render it intelligible, it assumes the paradoxical nature of a science of the ineffable, a reflection on what cannot be brought to reflection. A true ontology, according to Merleau-Ponty, must disclose "the brute or wild Being" (*L'être brut ou sauvage*, VI 170/VIF 223), "the vertical Being which none of the 'representations' exhaust and which all 'reach,' the wild Being" (VI 253/VIF 306). "One cannot make a direct ontology" (VI 179/ VIF 233), he claims, but rather one must resort to an "indirect" or "negative" approach to the appearing of Being.

The primary medium for the appearing of Being is what Merleau-Ponty calls "flesh." We have seen this flesh already at a simpler level: the level of the phenomenal body in the form of double sensation, and in perception where the body intertwines with the perceptual world. The flesh is the structure of transfer and reversibility between sensing and being sensed, between consciousness and world. It involves an engagement with the world and a distance from it as well, allowing us to be involved with beings while remaining separate from them. Regarding perception, Merleau-Ponty writes: "The act which draws together at the same time takes away and holds at a distance, so that I touch myself only by escaping from myself" (PP 408/PP 467). This unity-in-difference is made possible, we have seen, by the body schema. The body is the place for the "meeting of the inner and the outer" (PP 454/PPF 518), of the sensible world that can be handled and measured and the phenomenon of sensing that remains at a distance from the sensible. Another way of understanding this exchange of sensing and being sensed is to think of how the mind, or subjectivity, is totally outside of itself and engaged in projects, while at the same time external objects become transformed into possibilities for the phenomenal body, a mountain as an obstacle to be climbed and overcome, or a hammer as a means of equipment for a particular project (PP 408/PPF 467). In each case, the meaning of consciousness is to be involved with the world, and the meaning of the object is to be a piece of equipment for my use and to be understood primarily in terms of what my body can do. "Inside and outside are inseparable. The world is wholly inside and I am wholly outside myself" (PP 407/PPF 466–67). Double sensation and the phenomenon of perception both provide examples of the structure of flesh.

Merleau-Ponty provides a more complex description of flesh in *Eye and Mind*. Between the body and the world is a common fabric, the fabric of flesh, by which the world becomes intelligible and the body is enabled to engage with the world. "[T]he world," he explains, "is made of the same stuff as the body" (PrP 163/EMF 19). This stuff is neither matter, as is suggested by empiricism, nor ideas as found in the idealism of Bishop Berkeley, but is the very blending of roles that we have already discovered in double sensation. The body emerges at the point of convergence of activity and passivity, of sensing and being sensed. "There is a human body

140 Imagining Being

when, between the seeing and the seen, between touching and the touched, between one eye and the other, between hand and hand, a blending of some sort takes place" (PrP 163/EMF 21). This blending or chiasm of the sensible is made possible because the body that senses is also part of the sensible world. "Visible and mobile, my body is a thing among things; it is caught in the fabric of the world, and its cohesion is that of a thing" (PrP 163/EMF 19). I cannot escape this exteriorization of my being; I am literally in the world, transcending myself toward things. And things resemble my own visibility. The body "holds things in a circle around itself. Things are an annex or prolongation of itself; they are encrusted into its flesh, they are part of its full definition" (ibid.). The first meaning we have of things is not their Euclidean form or their pragmatic value, but their "carnal formula" (PrP 164/EMF 22), which determines the ways that my body can relate to them. A thing is tactile or visible insofar as it allows me to grasp it or to see it. My body interprets the thing by grasping it or by observing it. "Everything I see is in principle within my reach, at least within reach of my sight, and is marked upon the map of the 'I can'" (PrP 162/EMF 17). The result is that the body and the thing are virtually the same, in terms of the "I can" of the body. "The visible world and the world of my motor projects are each total parts of the same Being" (ibid.).[4] One of these "total parts," that of the body, establishes a field in which everything can be seen in terms of a possibility of embodiment. The other, that of things, makes it so that I can observe objects at a distance and recognize myself as the object of another person's observation. "That which looks at all things can also look at itself and recognize, in what it sees, the 'other side' of its power of looking" (PrP 162/EMF 18). If we could not see ourselves as visible, we would not realize ourselves as being in contact with the world but rather, like ghosts, like an "adamantine body" (PrP 163/EMF 17), would see the world as an extended idea; indeed, for Merleau-Ponty, the world would completely lose its meaning for consciousness if we were not also visible ourselves, for even numbers and logical concepts make sense only in relation to the world. Perception, he concludes, involves an "overlapping (*empiétement*)" (PrP 162/EMF 17) of the two orders of sensing and being sensed—of the visible and the invisible. And this overlapping is mediated by the fabric of flesh that is common to both orders.

Brute Being occurs within the fabric of the flesh of the world, between the generality of concepts and universal principles that we think about in abstraction and the particularity of sense qualities that we discover in our dealings with the sensible world. Brute Being is both "higher than the 'facts,' lower than the 'essences'" (VI 121/VIF 162); it does not allow itself to be reduced to a concept that is understood, but only to resonate within the sensible with what Heidegger at one point called the "shining,"[5] the power to appear that subtends and thus conceals itself from the appearing of things. But Being is not a mystical entity, a hidden deity behind all things, that is ontologically different from beings and their appearances as things. Marc Richir highlights an essential difference between Heidegger and Merleau-Ponty in that the latter does not commit the error of an "ontological difference," of hiding Being from phenomena (as he suggests occurs in the later Heidegger), but rather acknowledges the impossibility of separating Being from beings. Richir explains: "The division which, in our opinion, *must* be thought between the phenomenological and the symbolic [or between Being and appearances] is architectonic and by no means ontological, and this insofar as, if we borrow Husserl's language, there is not a single *Gebilde*, or rather not a single *Sinngebilde* (that we human beings encounter), which is not penetrated simultaneously, exactly as it appears, by the phenomenological dimension and the symbolic dimension."[6] A phenomenology of Being can and must occur on the same level as the symbolic meanings of its expression and manifestation in the form of the flesh of the world. Being, in all of its mystery and splendor, is available in the very showing of the thing, or as Sallis comments,

142   Imagining Being

"it is the thing itself that shines."[7] To understand the meaning of Being, we need to look no further than to the appearances themselves, the primary form of which involves the flesh of the world.

What does flesh reveal to us about brute Being? That it is the coming-to-appearance of all things, their manner of appearing, both general and particular, the concrete universal found in the experience of the elements. Being's most general expression is in the fabric of flesh, forming the reversal of roles between sensing and sensed, touching and the visible, self and other, mind and Nature. Being is circulation and chiasm, proliferating itself in many different dimensions while maintaining a unity or oneness that holds these levels (of mind and Nature, of sensing and sensed) together. Thomas Busch, inspired by the following quote from *The Visible and the Invisible*, describes "Being" as the movement of "circulation" between the different levels of flesh: "There is a circle of the touched and the touching, the touched takes hold of the touching; there is a circle of the visible and the seeing, the seeing is not without visible existence; there is even an inscription of the touching in the visible, of the seeing in the tangible — and the converse; there is finally a propagation of these exchanges to all the bodies of the same type and of the same style which I see and touch" (VI 143/VIF 188).[8] Essential to flesh is the characteristic of circulation and oneness, of the continuous thread that binds sensing to sensed, mind to Nature, while allowing for the proliferation of appearances through which Being can appear in different ways.

Another essential characteristic of flesh is that of divergence or separation, of providing an openness or *écart* by which it is broken into an expressive medium, like the myriad words in a language or colors in a spectrum, complete with punctuation and gaps, letters and blank spaces, figures and backgrounds that proliferate the many forms that Being can assume. In order to appear, Being must divide itself, must inaugurate a dehiscence of itself so that it can provide the distance and externalization required to have sense. Flesh, then, suggests that Being is always deferred, is always separated from itself. Flesh must be understood as "segregation, dimensionality, continuation, latency, encroachment" (VI 248/VIF 302). This does not make of flesh a simple negation of Being, but the opening and development of Being into a series of dimensions in which it can appear. Perhaps the best description of flesh is that provided by David Abram: "The flesh is the mysterious tissue or matrix that underlies and gives rise to both the perceiver and the perceived as interdependent aspects of its own spontaneous activity. It is the reciprocal presence of the sentient in the sensible and of the sensible in the sentient, a mystery of which we have always, at least tacitly, been aware, since we have never been able to affirm one of these phenomena, the perceivable world or the perceiving self, without implicitly affirming the existence of the other."[9] We experience the roles of sensing and being sensed simultaneously and cannot imagine having one without the other. Rather than reducing one mode of being to the other, Merleau-Ponty sets out to understand their mysterious union as a primordial dimension of the appearing of Being.

While the self and Being are in a sense reversible with each other in the form of flesh, they cannot be reduced to a level of the same. Being is not a mind behind the showing of things, as if it arrived on the scene (itself ready-made) to provide it with a determinate meaning that we merely imitate in our expressions. Although it does not hide completely from the showing of things, Being cannot be reduced to that showing or to the eye that perceives it.

There is a sense, no doubt, in which Being seems to see us, whether it be in the form of the glassy stare of an animal or the ominous feeling of being watched by nature. Merleau-Ponty refers to Paul Klee's illustration of a walk that he once took in a forest. Klee recounted the experience: "I have felt many times over that it was not I who looked at the forest. Some days, I felt that the trees were looking at me, were speaking to me" (PrP 167/EMF 31). Merleau-Ponty himself admits that on many occasions, "I feel myself looked at by things" (VI 139/VIF 183). There is, he adds,

144 Imagining Being

an "emigration" of my consciousness to the realm of things where I am "to be seen by the outside, to exist within it, to emigrate into it, to be seduced, captivated . . . so that the seer and the visible reciprocate one another and we no longer know which sees and which is seen" (VI 139/VIF 183). At the heart of perception is a remarkable blending of seeing and being seen providing a virtual identification of consciousness with Nature. But we should not think that this identification involves a kind of "animism" or "psychism" of Nature; Merleau-Ponty makes it clear that this is not his intention. We are not talking about "that absurdity: color that sees itself, surface that touches itself" but the paradox of "a set of colors and surfaces inhabited by a touch, a vision" (VI 135/VIF 178–79). To be seen by the world cannot be explained in terms of animism or psychism. A better interpretation is provided by Martin Dillon, who claims that "we are speaking here in similes" and should not read the passages literally.[10] He explains that the tree, like a mirror, allows me to experience my externality and visibility — my inability to escape the fact that I am, in some ways, like the trees (in being visible). The mirror provides an external image of myself that reminds me of my being among the objects that I see. The tree, obviously, does not "reflect" my visibility in the same manner as the mirror, but the mere fact that it shares with me the possibility of being seen provides me with the opportunity to see that my visibility is as embedded in the world as that of the tree. Dillon explains that Merleau-Ponty "wants to give consciousness an outside which limits it and makes it visible as a body which can be seen from external points of view." The tree, far from assuming an experience and a reflexivity like my own, is a reminder of the fact that even my own vision is grounded in the possibility of being seen. Thus there is no identification of consciousness with Nature, but a radical asymmetry between my body and Nature. "The plain fact," writes Dillon, "is that the table is neither part of my body nor sentient in the way my body is. There is an asymmetry in the reversibility thesis emerging here that needs to be investigated."[11]

The asymmetry between the body and Being revolves around the concept of reflexivity. In stark contrast to modern philosophy, which stresses a reflection of the self based on thought, Merleau-Ponty suggests that it is the body, and not the mind, that allows for self-reflection; he writes: "There is vision, touch, when a certain visible, a certain tangible, turns back upon the whole of the visible, the whole of the tangible, of which it is a part, or when suddenly it finds itself surrounded by them, or when between it and them, and through their commerce, is formed a Visibility, a Tangibility in itself" (VI 139/VIF 183). What Merleau-Ponty is trying to explain is that reflective awareness occurs not in a thought about self, but in embodied experience. And this experience, in turn, is an event that occurs within the flesh of Being, a Visibility or a Tangibility inaugurated in the very separation or *écart* between sensing and sensed. The body, then, has a unique role in the appearing of Being. It is an "exemplar sensible, which offers to him who inhabits it and senses it the wherewithal to sense everything that resembles himself on the outside, such that, caught up in the tissue of the things, it draws it entirely to itself, incorporates it, and, with the same movement, communicates to the things upon which it closes over that identity without superposition, that difference without contradiction, that divergence (*écart*) between the within and the without that constitutes its natal secret" (VI 135–36/VIF 178–79). "The human body," explains Dillon, "is that particular kind of flesh that allows the flesh of the world to double back on itself and be seen."[12] There is an asymmetry between my embodied experience and Nature because while Nature can serve as the site for such an intertwining of vision and the visible, the spectacle can only be seen from my side of the divide.

An important distinction that emerges in *The Visible and the Invisible* is that between sentient and nonsentient flesh: "The flesh of the world is not explained by the flesh of the body. . . . The flesh of the world is not self-sensing as is my flesh — *It is sensible and not sentient (sensible et non sentant)*" (VI 250/VIF 304; emphasis

146 Imagining Being

added). We see here an obvious support for Dillon's claim that the reversibility between my body and Nature is asymmetrical, and that the way that I experience my own flesh is not the same way that flesh appears in Nature. But the flesh is neither the sensing nor the sensed; it is the crisscrossing or chiasm that exists between them. Michael B. Smith suggests that a clue to what Merleau-Ponty means by this mysterious medium is in considering the way he describes transcendence.[13] Transcendence for Merleau-Ponty is the ability of consciousness to be outside of itself and focused on projects within the world. In order to do that, one need not be a Sartrean "for-itself," a pure negation with no content. Merleau-Ponty writes, "the for itself is *a hollow and not a void*, not absolute non-being."[14] This invisible hollow, further, is not absolutely different from the world (as an "in-itself," for Sartre), but is visible like other beings — it is the sensible flesh. Smith explains: "While traditional transcendence was a movement from self to what is outside of self, Merleau-Ponty's transcendence of perception does not stop at the exteriority of the outer world, but loops back: that movement is but one strand of a '*chiasme*,' an '*Ineinander*' or crossing, a Husserlian '*Überschreitung*' that moves from self to world and from world to self, via the mediating elemental flesh."[15] This suggests a blending of self and Being, an intertwining in which the self externalizes itself and becomes visible while the visible infects the self with visibility, is taken back up into the interiority of consciousness. "To say that there is transcendence, being at a distance, is to say that Being (in the Sartrean sense) is thus inflated with non-being or with the possible, that it is not only what it is" (VI 181/VIF 234). No longer can the self hide behind its absolute difference from Being, or within its ivory tower of indubitable existence, since it is the inner of the outer and is the sensible turned inside out. The for-itself and Nature blend with each other, within the medium of flesh. Flesh must be like both of them in some way, and not explained exclusively in terms of consciousness.

To go one step further, Merleau-Ponty decenters the for-itself or transcendence from the self altogether. He argues that transcendence is not a "possession of the object" but a "divergence" or a "separation (*écart*)" (VI 198, 197/VIF 251, 250) within Being, a dimensionality, an ability to reflect all of being not as consciousness but as the tree mentioned above (VI 218/VIF 271–72). In other words, the reflexivity of flesh need not be *self*-reflection, but can take the form of the tree or of the color as a dimension of the sensible, reflecting our own dimensionality, which is for us in terms of the reversibility of sensing and being sensed. That reversibility is a unique mode of the same transcendence that is found within Being itself.[16] Transcendence is not the outward movement of an inner self, but is the *écart* or differentiation of Being itself. "*Écart* is not nothing," writes Claude Lefort; "it is being as transcendence."[17] We must take Merleau-Ponty seriously when he says that he is going to replace a philosophy of the subject with one of Being (VI 167/VIF 221). He is not only asking about the nature of subjectivity, but exploring the possibility of a for-itself that is prior to the distinction of sentience from the sensible, that is the inner lining of the sensible before the sentient emerges, that is the imaginative aspect of Being underlying human imagining and perception.

The decentering of consciousness also applies, in a sense, to the imagining body. Merleau-Ponty's ontology of the flesh gives priority not to the body as a center of consciousness but to Being itself as it manifests itself in the transcendence of the flesh. Merleau-Ponty argues that "to perceive a part of my body is also to perceive it as visible, i.e. for the other" (VI 244–45/VIF 298). This suggests that the transcendence of the body depends on its ability to be seen, on its very *inherence* in the flesh. My body "assumes this character because in fact someone does look at it — But this *fact* of the other's presence would not itself be possible if antecedently the part of the body in question were not *visible*, if there were not, around each part of the body, a halo of *visibility*" (VI 245/VIF 298). The transcendence of the body is nothing more than this instance of flesh folding back on itself, creating a foreground and a background, in this ontological gestalt of reciprocal roles. For this reason, Lefort is correct to say of the *écart* that "we must think of it with the Gestalt."[18] The flesh of the body, in spite of its unique role in the expression of Being, is still only an instance of a transcendence of Being within the general medium of the flesh.

The transcendence of flesh from the phenomenal body also frees the flesh from being reduced to an instance of visibility at the expense of other dimensions of experience. Drew Leder suggests, for example, that Merleau-Ponty's analysis of flesh requires an additional concern for the "deeper blood relation with the world" in the form of the visceral body. Leder writes: "I am not just a gazing upon the world, but one who breathes, feeds and drinks of it, such that inner and outer corporeality intertwine."[19] A proper description of flesh, says Leder, must also include a consideration of how Being conceals itself in our visceral relations with the world: how Being, for instance, can be found in the background provided by the functioning of vital organs which make vision possible. The visceral, he claims, introduces "another sort of depth, another sort of invisibility," a "vertical synergy," to complement the horizontal nature of fleshly transcendence.[20] At one point in *The Visible and the Invisible*, Merleau-Ponty seems to overlook the "visceral" dimension of flesh. He argues that "we say therefore that our body is a being of two leaves, from one side a thing among things and otherwise what sees them and touches them" (VI 137/VIF 180). Thus it sounds as if he ignores the visceral body and focuses only on the body as an object that is sensed (especially as "seen" by a physician) and the body as sentience. But he immediately rejects this description for another: "each of the two beings is an archetype for the other, because the body belongs to the order of the things as the world is universal flesh. . . . There are not in it two leaves or two layers; fundamentally it is neither thing seen only nor seer only, it is Visibility sometimes wandering and sometimes

reassembled" (VI 137–38/VIF 181). The actual visibility of the
flesh is not important, but only its virtual visibility, its inherence in
the visible (VI 244–45/VIF 298). This means that the visceral, like
all other aspects of embodiment, is equally "available to the gaze"
as well as "hidden." To the extent that the visceral is proprioceptive,
it enters the domain of the phenomenal body; to the extent that it
conceals itself from internal observation, it becomes an organ
capable of being seen from the outside (by a physician, for instance).
There is not, then, a radical difference between the visceral body
and either the objective or phenomenal body, but a single mass
that is both visible and vision, a single tissue or flesh.[21] There is
also no priority here given to visibility, but only to the view that all
being is virtually visible, is virtually an appearing or a becoming,
and that nothing remains inherently in-itself as an absolute plenum.
As surely as it is the vehicle for perceiving presences, the body is
also the locus for absence. The body and its distances or differences
(such as that holding between the visceral and the exteroceptive),
"participate in one same corporeity or visibility in general, which
reigns between them and it, and even beyond the horizon, beneath [its] skin, unto the depths of being" (VI 149/VIF 195). It
must not be said, then, that Merleau-Ponty's concept of the flesh
is a philosophy of the surface or the skin at the expense of
the visceral.[22]

The flesh, then, is neither subject nor object, and forms a medium
between the two for the appearing of Being. Merleau-Ponty often
illustrates flesh in terms of a dynamic energy grounded in an abyss.
The flesh involves "one sole explosion of Being (*éclatement d'Être*)
that is forever" (VI 265/VIF 318), "one sole vortex (*tourbillon*)"
(VI 151/VIF 199) — what Jacques Garelli calls "the turbulent
metastability"[23] of Being. Ontology requires a "return to *Sigè*, the
Abyss (*L'abîme*)" (VI 179/VIF 233). But this metastability, the
abysmal ground of stability, is not without order. Flesh, he writes,
"is not contingency, chaos (*chaos*), but a texture that returns to
itself and conforms to itself" (VI 146/VIF 192). As shown above,
there is a radical asymmetry between the reversibility of double

150   Imagining Being

sensation and of the body's relation to the world, so that one could not reduce the nature of the world to a single homogeneous relational structure. Within these asymmetries, the body is also able to make sense of the world, to discern regularities and develop universals in the medium of language. "What there is," writes Merleau-Ponty, "is a whole architecture, a whole complex of phenomena 'in tiers,' a whole series of 'levels of being'" (VI 114/ VIF 153).[24] Flesh is not a chaotic structure based solely on chance, but is rather grounded in a series of divergences and levels that already partially determine what the world can mean for consciousness. Flesh involves an open and dynamic medium for the appearing of Being, that is neither subjective nor objective, organic nor chaotic, but a system of levels and dimensions in which Being can become meaningful.[25]

The dynamic nature of flesh suggests that Being cannot be understood strictly in terms of actual reality. The mediation of Being in the form of flesh precedes any real/virtual distinction, as well as any actuality/possibility distinction. The reversibility of the real and the virtual can be seen in the fact that the flesh, while being immersed in the real experience of the sensible, contains the possibility of the sentient as the sensible's inner lining. Flesh, in other words, is the medium for the possible without which possibilities could never be taken up by the sensing body. Without the virtuality of the flesh, it would also be impossible to interpret the various meanings of the sensible world, all of which become translatable into various modes of embodiment. Merleau-Ponty explains this in terms of Leibniz's discussion of possible worlds: "I call it flesh, nonetheless . . . in order to say that it is a pregnancy of possibles, *Weltmöglichkeit* (the possible worlds variants of this world, the world beneath the singular and the plural)" (VI 250/VIF 304). Merleau-Ponty is suggesting, like Heidegger, a primacy of the possible over the actual. Before the actual experience of the reflexivity of Being within the human body, there must be a possibility for sentience. The flesh is essentially the first layer of imagining, the "virtual focus" (VI 215/VIF 269) of Being that is taken up and creatively developed by the human body.

To explain the imagining of Being, Merleau-Ponty uses the metaphor of pregnancy and "embryonic development" (VI 147/ VIF 193). He discusses birth as deriving not from anything actual but from a virtuality at the heart of the mother's flesh that develops its own visibility and actuality. "It can be said that a human is born at the instant when something that was only virtually visible, inside the mother's body, becomes at one and the same time visible for itself and for us" (PrP 168–69/EMF 32). He later explains that "through a labor upon itself the visible body provides for the hollow whence a vision will come, inaugurates the long maturation at whose term suddenly it will see" (VI 147/VIF 193). The flesh, "this worked-over mass," inaugurates an "invagination" in which visibility emerges (VI 152/VIF 199; see also VI 233–34/VIF 287). But this is possible only because the fetus (within the mother's flesh) contains within itself the ability to explore itself and divide itself, to develop its possibilizing nature to the point where an actual imaginer is born. Before we can explore possibilities within our own bodies, there must have already been an exploration of Being that established the possibility of our bodies as flesh. The flesh is essentially the pure imagination, pure possibility, that does not await actualization but rather bears it as a mother bears her child. The flesh exists in latency and virtuality, an imagination before all self-perception and at the heart of perception, which gives birth to the very imagining body (that is, the human body) in which it is able to realize itself.

We can see this more clearly by means of a contrast with the imagination theories of Casey and Sartre. Both argue that the imagination has a fundamental role in human existence as the source for possibility. The imagination, says Casey, is the locus of "possibilizing" my existence, of developing and exploring alternatives to my present situation. And for Sartre, the imagination is the essence of human freedom as the power to negate reality. The

152 *Imagining Being*

imagination rests on an existential ability to be open to the actual world while being able to negate it and transcend it either by changing it according to imagined plans or by living in a fanciful alternative world.

The possibility that is most important in *The Visible and the Invisible* is not a negation of the world that is already there, but the possibility of flesh to fold on itself, to become sensible and to inaugurate the original appearing of a world. The presence of a world upon which the imagination theory of Casey and Sartre depends is itself grounded in another possibility that is provided not by our own being but by Being itself. Merleau-Ponty explains that "the unicity of the world means not that it is actual and that every other world is imaginary, not that it is in itself and every other world for us only, but that it is at the root of every thought of possibles, that it even is surrounded with a halo of possibilities" (VI 228/VIF 282).[26] This means that, unlike the possibility discussed by Sartre and Casey, the possibility here is not of consciousness being open to the world but of the world being open to itself in the matrix of flesh. The imagination that is primary is not that of consciousness, elaborating on a situation that is already given, but the virtual beginning of flesh in the moment of the fold, before any consciousness, and before any reality.[27]

What form does such a pure possibility take? Is it completely indeterminate? At the end of *Merleau-Ponty's Ontology*, Martin Dillon recalls the pre-Socratic story of chaos as the origin of earth and sky, the first differentiation and order of Being. "Beneath this story," writes Dillon, "there is chaos, as there is beneath all such stories; because all stories, all the *logoi*, impart all the meaning and order there is to be had."[28] Dillon also alludes to Anaximander's concept of *apeiron*, a neutral element out of which are born the four elements and everything in the world.[29] Being, as abyss, is pure potentiality, the initial energy or heartbeat of the entire universe. Being, in this state, is pure virtuality, pure imagination, a dream that dreams itself with no real awareness of itself, a pure interiority that lacks an outer and thus dissolves its interiority in a moment of immanence. It is out of this virtuality that Being is made actual, that it comes to divide itself in the moment of sensing and being sensed, and as ultimately actualized and reflected on itself within embodied existence.

A brief return to the four elements can help to clarify what is meant by this imagining of Being. The four elements are not the earth, water, air and fire studied by geologists, chemists, meteorologists and pyrotechnicians. Each suggests a vague and general sense in which Being is already partially determined and conversant with itself. Before there is a child to play in the sand and the waves there is a silent logos of the seashore that the child takes up and makes his own in the activities of swimming or building sand castles, as if guided by forces over which he has only a limited amount of control. These forces already assume a certain shape before they become the sensible fragments of qualities, such as the green-blue hue of the ocean or the graininess of the sand. We find, in Merleau-Ponty, a hint of water as a universal mode of relating to the world. Earth provides the ground for the openness of air and the possibility of determinate spaces (S 180/SF 227).[30] Fire is a consuming and energizing force that enlivens the other elements and alters their immediate composition. Each of the four elements, as we have already seen in the previous chapter, provides a general sense or meaning that the body interprets and makes determinate. They are, in a sense, Being's original images, the first traces of a possibility and imagination that is as much discovered by the body as it is interpreted. "The ontology of Merleau-Ponty," concludes Barbaras, "can be characterized as an ontology of the elements."[31]

The imagining of flesh is not pure indeterminacy, an abstract neutral substance like the *apeiron* of the Greeks, but the very phenomenality of phenomena: the invisibility that makes phenomena visible. This self-inscription[32] of Being, the laying out of the possible meanings, takes the form of what Merleau-Ponty calls a "brute essence (*essence brute*)" (VI 115/VIF 155). These "essences" are neither intuited presences nor ideas;[33] they involve a generality of meaning that assumes "a cohesion without concepts, which is of the same type as the cohesion of the parts of my body, or the cohesion of my body with the world" (VI 152/VIF 199). Each essence marks the place of a certain "excess" of Being, an overlapping or cantilever of flesh that assumes a general and repeatable form, such as the graininess of sand that predisposes my body to react to the world in a particular manner.[34] The "form" of these essences is like a musical style that is developed and transposed without losing a sense of unity and identity. Another way to illustrate this unity-in-process is to imagine the genetic cohesion of the body that continues to give to it a sense of identity despite the many changes caused by the body's maturation. Thus, Garelli defines the development of brute essences as "a transductional progress of the character of a differential and amplified variation, which invests its wild rhythm in the metastable system [that is, the flesh] in which it is inscribed."[35]

The analysis of brute essences in terms of their virtuality recalls the imaginative variation of Husserl. Imaginative variation is used to vary the essence of an object in order to develop it along the lines of its diverse appearances, such as changing one's overall concept of a perceptual object as one explores its various sides. By neutralizing any concern for the reality of a given object, the imagination allows one to synthesize the presentations of an object into a single, generative essence that remains flexible throughout the process.[36] But for Merleau-Ponty, the method of phenomenology becomes not a neutralizing imagination, negating the belief in the world to study its meaning, but a productive one, an aesthetic imagination more in line with Ricoeur and Bachelard than Husserl and Sartre. There is, according to Merleau-Ponty, no intuition of essences but rather an encroachment upon them through the inexhaustible divergences of flesh — a sort of "auscultation or palpation in depth" (VI 128/VIF 170). We are reminded, at this point, of Bachelard's theory of the resonance of Being found in elemental images that the philosopher responds to and already interprets in terms of a particular affective situation. This means that there is no direct ontology, and that philosophy, rather than obtaining a bird's-eye view of the dehiscence of Being in the flesh, is merely its interpretation and expression or, better, its production and actualization at the level of the symbolic behavior of the body.

Marc Richir helps to clarify the meaning of "brute essences" by claiming that surrounding each essence is a halo of fiction. The essence, he explains, appears by virtue of two illusions: the illusion of centering, that there is a universal and primordial sense behind the appearance, and the illusion of decentering, that the appearance is only a sign of a universal idea.[37] This suggests that essences emerge out of the imaginary, creating a faith in the world when originally there is no actual world to base our claims on, when the world, in other words, is as much interpreted as discovered. In order to reflect on this production of reality, we must consider flesh as a "poetic and oneiric power."[38] This means that the artist, and not the scientist or even the philosopher, is perhaps closest to these brute essences. Jocelyn Lebrun explains: "Art becomes the only means of restoring a sense of the world of Being as a world of phenomena, in that the artist is this sublime illusionist who makes us believe in the reality of this world of phenomena."[39] Though Lebrun's position is extreme (for certainly other forms of expression also encroach upon brute essences), it does show that art assumes a prominent role in the expression and understanding of the meaning of Being. The imagination expresses and reflects the poetic power of flesh when it is engaged in aesthetic production, carrying forward a potency and productivity that has already begun at the level of elemental images. All other instances of the imagination, be they fanciful thinking or perception, are modes of this productivity of flesh that is exemplified in the work of the artist and the interpretation of elements found in poetry.

What remains to be seen by most scholars of Merleau-Ponty's work, and what I have tried to show throughout this chapter, is that the meaning of Being is based on the imagining body. It is in the human body, Merleau-Ponty claims, that Being is able to express itself and to reflect on itself. The body is the site for the institution of a meaning of Being, albeit an indirect meaning as it is mediated within the flesh of the world. Referring to Husserl, Merleau-Ponty writes that, "since we are at the junction of Nature, body, soul, and philosophical consciousness, since we live that juncture, no problem can be conceived of whose solution is not sketched out within us and in the world's spectacle" (S 177/SF 223–24). Being, he later says, is "realized through man" (S 181/SF 228). Gary Madison explains: "It is in man, who is an opening in Being, that the question about Being arises; it is therefore in man that Being makes its advent or puts itself into question."[40] The question of Being is its latency and virtuality, its call to the body to become articulated and expressed within the medium of the flesh that connects the body to the world and to other people. It is the body that makes actual and determinate the general traces of meaning laid out for it within the metastable tissue of flesh. John Russon explains that, "in the absence of bodily contact, the world remains only indeterminate possibility. . . . Embodied existence, then, is something which is performed, and its performance is a motivated creation of meaningfulness in which an indeterminate situation is resolved into a determinate relation of a determinate subject and a determinate object."[41] It is the body that "sings the world" (PP 187/ PPF 218), that makes specific the general traces of Being. Without the body, Being would be held, as it were, in suspense, would be bracketed by its own indeterminacy from expressing itself in the form of language and gesture.[42]

There is, in Being, a sense of its own imagining, its own emergence out of the plenum of immediacy into the rich and varied polymorphous flesh that supplies the asymmetrical dimensions for its own appearance. On their own, these dimensions are still vague and indeterminate, waiting to become the qualities of a Visibility or a Tangibility — the blue of the sea, the grainy texture of the sand. They await the advent of the imagining body that will develop them into determinate meanings, like the animals mentioned in Genesis that waited for Adam to give them a name. The imagining of Being awaits its actualization in the imagining body that develops these traces into a situation and a life. Just as Cézanne found in his own situation a life to live and a creative profession (SNS 20/SNSF 35), so we all find ourselves, by means of the imagining body, with a particular trace of Being that we are called to express in our own way. The direction and meaning of these traces contain the illusion or faith in a reality to which we can compare our interpretations and establish a ground for truth and knowledge. But this sense of reality is created by the imagination as a dream folded onto itself, the product of an oneiric substance that, like a work of art, never ceases to be reinterpreted and, in the words of Merleau-Ponty, to have its whole life before it (PrP 190/EMF 92–93).

The imagination assumes a prominent role in Merleau-Ponty's ontology. We have seen throughout how the imagination of the body, captured by the expressivity and creativity of mime, forms the basis of all forms of imagination. The imagining body is also a basic structure of our existence, providing an openness and flexibility to our embodied encounter with the world. It has been shown, finally, how the imagining of the body is related to the appearing of Being. We have found within the concept of flesh a transcendence that is not an explicit reflection but a kernel of potency and virtuality that precedes the imagination of the body. There is a sense, as Bachelard once wrote, of a narcissism of Being: "The cosmos, in some way, has a touch of narcissism. The world wants to see itself."[43] I suggest that this narcissism is a form of imagining, the imagining of Being that remains a potential or *unthought* thought at the heart of Merleau-Ponty's later ontology (VI 119/VIF 159). The imagining body completes the work of Being by bringing its virtuality to fruition, proliferating its meaning in

158 Imagining Being

the form of words and gestures while remaining open to new ways of seeing and expressing the world.

* * *

In *On the Way to Language*, Martin Heidegger cites a poem by Stefan George on the relationship between linguistic expression and the world that words are said to express. The poem ends with the line: "Where word breaks off, no thing may be."[44] Heidegger takes the poem to mean that where word breaks off, Being no longer appears; outside of language Being is pure possibility and unable to disclose itself in a word or image. But in this silence, we are also open to the essence of linguistic expression as transcending all words and as providing the possibility for the appearing of Being. With the last line, one arrives at a paradoxical moment of closure and opening, of the twilight of a philosophy that makes use of language to understand Being, and the dawning of a silent appearing of Being.

Merleau-Ponty, like Heidegger, believes that philosophy must end in silence. At the end of *Phenomenology of Perception*, he admits that when all is said and done, we return to our lives and live through our bodies, immersing ourselves in everyday concerns. But this does not mean that we cease from imagining new possibilities of existence and of the appearing of Being, or that we become locked up in a silent and private state of solipsism. "Man is but a network of relationships, and these alone matter to him."[45] Even when one returns to silent existence, one is still related to Nature by means of elemental images, and related to others in a silent but meaningful intercorporeality.

We see this especially in the life of the mime. Throughout the festival she communicates to her audience with gestures that speak louder than words. But even when the festival is over and the mime returns to her ordinary life, the imagining of the body continues. She continues to imagine new ways to be aware of her body, new ways to perceive the world around her, new ways to explore the

Imagining Being 159

elasticity of space and time, and new ways to endow a personal significance on her surroundings. When word breaks off, we do not return to a meaningless silence, but to the silent language and open future of the imagining body.

Notes

Notes to Introduction

1. For a good introduction to mime, see Maravene Sheppard Loeschke, *All About Mime* (Englewood Cliffs, N.J.: Prentice-Hall, 1982).

2. We notice the importance of gesture for ordinary discourse in situations where this level of communication is no longer possible, such as when we talk on the telephone. Unable to reinforce our statements with gesture, we distort and exaggerate our voice, tone and even the content of our statements in order to ensure that communication is achieved. The telephone reduces the communicative experience to sound, causing us to draw from this medium much more than usual. A similar hypersensitivity is developed by people lacking one of the main senses, such as a blind person with an acute sense of smell or sound, or a deaf person with an acute sense of sight in lip and sign reading.

3. See, for instance, John Bannan, *The Philosophy of Merleau-Ponty* (New York: Harcourt, Brace and World, 1967); Mary Rose Barral, *Merleau-Ponty: The Role of the Body-Subject in Interpersonal Relations* (Pittsburgh: Duquesne University Press, 1965); Remi Kwant, *The Phenomenological Philosophy of Merleau-Ponty* (Pittsburgh: Duquesne University Press, 1963); Richard Zaner, *The Problem of Embodiment* (The Hague: Martinus Nijhoff, 1964).

4. Mary Warnock, *Imagination* (London: Faber & Faber, 1976), writes that Merleau-Ponty's early philosophy "has the relatively limited aim of expounding and elaborating Husserl's theory specifically as it concerns perception" (144). Glen Mazis argues that Merleau-Ponty's theory of imagination involves a radical turn from the early to the later works in "*La Chair et l'Imaginaire*: The Developing Role of Imagination in Merleau-Ponty's Philosophy," *Philosophy Today* 32 (1988): 30–42. See also Françoise Dastur, "Perceptual Faith and the Invisible," *Journal of the British Society for Phenomenology* 25 (1994): 44–52.

162   Notes to Pages 3–18

5. Gary Madison, "Did Merleau-Ponty Have a Theory of Perception?" in *Merleau-Ponty, Hermeneutics, and Postmodernism*, ed. Thomas Busch and Shaun Gallagher (Albany: State University of New York Press, 1992), 85.

6. Peter Strawson, "Imagination and Perception," *Freedom and Resentment and Other Essays* (London: Methuen, 1974), 45, 64.

7. Warnock, *Imagination*, 10.

8. Richard Kearney, *The Wake of Imagination* (Minneapolis: University of Minnesota Press, 1988), 15; Ludwig Wittgenstein, *Philosophical Investigations*, trans. G. E. M. Anscombe (Oxford: Basil Blackwell, 1958), para. 67.

Notes to Chapter One

1. Etienne Decroux, cited in Thomas Leabhart, *Modern and Post-modern Mime* (New York: St. Martin's Press, 1989), 27–28.

2. Paul Bellugue, cited in ibid., 10.

3. Marcel Carné, *Les enfants du paradis* (Paris: Pathe Cinema, 1945).

4. Edmund Husserl, *Ideas: General Introduction to Pure Phenomenology*, trans. W. R. Boyce Gibson (New York: Collier, 1962), 98, 160. Merleau-Ponty discusses phenomenological reduction and description in PP viii–xiv/PPF ii–ix.

5. See also Seymour Fisher, *Body Consciousness* (Englewood Cliffs, N.J.: Prentice-Hall, 1973), 3.

6. Rudolph Arnheim, *Visual Thinking* (Berkeley and Los Angeles: University of California Press, 1969), 22–23, observes that a frog will try to capture with its tongue not just flies but any small object that behaves like a fly; he also noticed that when the same frog is surrounded by dead flies, it will starve to death. Arnheim concludes that the frog responds to a general stimulus within a general context in which other objects will appear as food, and in which even flies, when dormant, will be overlooked. His conclusion suggests that the frog does not respond to a particular stimulus, as behaviorism would suggest, but to a general context that the frog interprets according to what Merleau-Ponty calls a "descriptive norm" of what will serve as food (SB 28/SBF 28).

7. Henry Head, cited in PP 140/PPF 163. The example of calculating the required space to get through a tunnel is also provided by Head (PP 143/PPF 167). Merleau-Ponty's objection is that even though Head does not think that these judgments are explicit, they are still judgments based on an awareness of the body as an object. This gives precedence to an objective view of the body and its parts. See also PP 103–4/PPF 119–20.

8. The French reads *schéma corporel* (PP 98/PPF 114). Colin Smith's translation is "body image" rather than "body schema." By contrast, John O'Neill translates the term as "body schema" (TFL 129/TFLF 177).

9. Understanding the body in terms of the body schema is not the only alternative to behaviorism and intellectualism. Another alternative is to focus on the

body as a conglomerate of drives and urges. Inspired by Sigmund Freud and the Marquis de Sade, Michel Foucault and Gilles Deleuze have developed this alternative. For a comparison between Merleau-Ponty's philosophy of the body and that of Foucault, see Richard Cohen, "Merleau-Ponty, the Flesh and Foucault," *Philosophy Today* 28 (1984): 329–37. Cohen argues that Foucault focuses on specific modes of embodiment rather than on an enveloping flesh of the world (to be discussed in chapter 8), and concludes that the difference between the two philosophers is only "a difference in tone" (335). For a discussion concerning the relation of Merleau-Ponty's philosophy of the body to that of Deleuze, see John Mullarkey, "Duplicity in the Flesh: Bergson and Current Philosophy of the Body," *Philosophy Today* 38, no. 4 (1994): 339–55. Mullarkey asserts that Bergson provides a bridge between the two poles of unity and disunity that can be found in the body; he suggests that the pole of unity is emphasized in the work of Merleau-Ponty, and the pole of disunity is stressed in Deleuze's theory of the body. A problem with Mullarkey's analysis is that these poles are drawn at the expense of the complexity of Merleau-Ponty's analysis of the body, in which the body is shown to be not simply a moment of unity but an opening and exposure which is similar, in some ways, to Mullarkey's "Deleuzian" pole. See especially 342–44 and 348–51.

10. This confusion is discussed by Shaun Gallagher, "Body Schema and Intentionality," in *The Body and the Self*, ed. José Bermudéz et al. (Cambridge: Massachusetts Institute of Technology Press, 1995), 227.

11. Seymour Fisher and Sidney E. Cleveland, *Body Image and Personality*, 2nd rev. ed. (New York: Dover, 1968), for example, describe the "body image" as "a term which refers to the body as a psychological experience, and focuses on the individual's feelings and attitudes toward his own body. It is concerned with the individual's subjective experiences with his body and the manner in which he has organized these experiences" (x). This definition suggests that the body schema is a representation in the mind, and not an immediate sense of the body and its abilities.

12. He also would include under the general concept of the body schema what have come to be called proprioceptive and kinesthetic awareness: a person's ability to see the parts of her body as her own (proprioception), and her ability to sense the movement of her body "from within" (kinesthesis). A discussion of kinesthesis is reserved for chapter 2.

13. A good summary of the psychological literature on the body schema prior to the publication of *Phenomenology of Perception* is found in Douwe Tiemersma, "'Body-Image' and 'Body-Schema' in the Existential Phenomenology of Merleau-Ponty," *Journal of the British Society for Phenomenology* 13 (1982): 246–55. Tiemersma traces the concept as far back as 1905.

14. Merleau-Ponty cites several examples from the research of Schilder and J. Lhermitte. He criticizes a similar theory by I. P. Pavlov in chapter 2 of *The Structure of Behavior*.

164 Notes to Pages 20–26

15. Seymour Fisher and Sidney E. Cleveland, *Body Image and Personality*, 2nd rev. ed. (New York: Dover, 1968), 7.

16. The first test was conducted by Teuber on thirty-eight men who had had their knees amputated, and the second was conducted by Haber on twenty-five men who had had their arms amputated. The tests are cited in ibid., 11.

17. Ibid., 11.

18. Hubert Dreyfus, "The Current Relevance of Merleau-Ponty's Phenomenology of Embodiment," *The Electronic Journal of Analytic Philosophy* 4 (1996), n.p. Edward Casey, "Habitual Body and Memory in Merleau-Ponty," *Man and World* 17 (1984): 279–97, provides a good description of how the acquisition of habits provides the body with a form of memory.

19. Merleau-Ponty adds that "[t]he subject does not weld together individual movements and individual stimuli but acquires the power to respond with a certain type of solution to situations of a certain general form. The situations may differ widely from case to case, and the response movements may be entrusted sometimes to one operative organ, sometimes to another, both situations and responses in the various cases having in common not so much a partial identity of elements as a shared significance" (PP 142/PPF 166). See also John Bannan, *The Philosophy of Merleau-Ponty* (New York: Harcourt, Brace and World, 1967), who writes, "Each situation is the analogue of many others, and what our experience with them generates are global aptitudes, not repeatable gestures" (39).

20. The example of using the mirror to shave is given by Richard McCleary, *Imagination's Body* (Washington: University Press of America, 1986), 65. Another example, given by Merleau-Ponty, is of the geometer who studies objective laws by relating them to the body's motility, an operation that involves describing geometrical laws "at least virtually with his body" (PP 387/PPF 443). Colin Smith translates *virtuellement* as "potentially."

21. We use the same method to learn how to use machines and instruments such as typewriters and pianos. In each case, learning to use the instrument does not involve focusing on particular actions such as the pressing of specific keys; it consists, instead, in "taking possession with our body of a type of 'artificial' behavior in the image of which the object was made" (SB 120 n. 198/SBF 131 n. 2). The image referred to is the virtual body that must be appropriated in order to learn to play the instrument. Thus when learning to use a new instrument, an organist attempts to assume the virtual body for which it was intended and not to learn where all of the keys are first.

22. A good description of the body as "absent" is provided by Drew Leder, *The Absent Body* (Chicago: University of Chicago Press, 1990). See especially chapter 1.

23. Leder uses the example of sense organs that are experienced as "absent" so that sense qualities can appear. He writes: "Insofar as I perceive through an organ it necessarily recedes from the perceptual field it discloses" (ibid., 14).

24. The French text reads *situations verbales et fictives*, which I have

Notes to Pages 26–27   165

translated as "verbal and fictional situations"; Colin Smith translates *fictives* as "imaginary."

25. The French text reads *des situations imaginaires* and *dans l'imaginaire* which Colin Smith translates as "imaginary situations" and "in the realm of the imagination." It seems in this context that the words *fictives* and *imaginaires* are interchangeable.

26. The fact that Schneider's world remains more symbolic and general than that of the primate suggests that the virtual body is never completely lost and is always available for development.

27. There is some controversy concerning Merleau-Ponty's interpretation of the genesis of the body schema. He claims that infants are primarily interested only in particular regions of the body, and that they only begin to develop their body schemas at the age of about four months (PrP 123/ROF 39). Recent studies, however, suggest that the body schema is present from birth. In an experiment by Andrew Meltzoff and M. Keith Moore, "Infant's Understanding of People and Things: From Body Imitation to Folk Psychology," in *The Body and the Self*, ed. José Bermudéz, Anthony Marcel and Naomi Eilan (Cambridge: Massachusetts Institute of Technology Press, 1995), 48–58, infants were shown to be able to imitate gestures, recognize faces according to previous gestures, and return the same gestures when unsolicited; the infants were also able to frequently develop and simplify the gestures to suit their preferences. Although, as Shaun Gallagher and Andrew Meltzoff, "The Earliest Sense of Self and Others: Merleau-Ponty and Recent Developmental Studies," *Philosophical Psychology* 9 (1996): 224–29, show, Merleau-Ponty's analysis overlooks the extent to which the body is functional at birth, it is consistent with Merleau-Ponty's analysis to say that there is a vague and general body schema at birth that undergoes radical development after the age of four months. See PrP 122–23/ROF 37–39.

28. While some psychologists do not distinguish between the body schema and the body image (such as Paul Schilder and Seymour Fisher), Shaun Gallagher argues that the two concepts refer to two different experiences. In an experiment conducted by Gallagher and Jonathan Cole, a patient who has lost all propriocep- tive awareness from below the neck is able to construct a body image and recog- nize it as representative of his own body (Gallagher and Cole, ibid., 374–76). In another experiment by D. Denny-Brown, J. S. Meyer and S. Horenstein, "The Significance of Perceptual Rivalry Resulting from Parietal Lesion," *Brain* 75 (1952): 463, a patient is reported to have lost all awareness of the left side of her body but is able to perform ordinary activities such as walking. She can comb her hair with her left hand, for example, but forgets to comb the left side of her head. In the first experiment, a body schema that has become deficient is supplemented by an explicit body image. In the second experiment, the body schema continues to function as usual even though the body image has become impaired. These experiments suggest to Gallagher and Meltzoff, "The Earliest Sense of Self and Others," 214–17, that the body schema and the body image are different

experiences. For a more detailed analysis of this distinction, see Gallagher, "Body Schema and Intentionality," in *The Body and the Self*, ed. José Bermudéz, Anthony Marcel and Naomi Eilan (Cambridge: MIT Press, 1995), 227–31. Because of the consistency with which Merleau-Ponty uses the term "body schema" throughout his writings on the body and the fact that he distinguishes the term from the "specular image," Merleau-Ponty's analysis seems to be in agreement with Gallagher's distinction.

29. The mirror image, however, can play an essential role in learning about one's body image. This discovery by Jacques Lacan is further developed in chapter 6.

30. This is not to say, however, that physiological factors are not considered. I am only suggesting that the imagination can be used as an aid to physiotherapy.

31. Shaun Gallagher and Jonathan Cole, "Body Image and Body Schema in a Deafferented Subject," *The Journal of Mind and Behavior* 16 (1995): 374–76. Although they do not make reference to the imagination in the article, Gallagher reported the comments of the patient in a private interview with the author.

32. Ullica Segerstrale and Peter Molnar, "Nonverbal Communication: Crossing the Boundary between Culture and Nature," in *Nonverbal Communication: Where Nature Meets Nurture*, ed. Segerstrale and Molnar (New Jersey: Lawrence Erlbaum, 1997), 9–10, for example, refer to studies that show how body language reveals the intentions of a person who is lying. See also Ronald Riggio, "Social Interaction Skills and Nonverbal Behavior," in *Applications of Nonverbal Behavioral Theories and Research*, ed. Robert Feldman (New Jersey: Lawrence Erlbaum, 1992), 14.

33. Julias Fast, *Body Language* (Richmond Hill: Simon and Schuster, 1971), tells the story of a psychologist who decided to host a party where only body language could be used by the guests throughout the evening. After an initial period of awkwardness, all of the guests eventually found that their bodies allowed them to communicate as much to each other as if they had resorted to language (24–25).

34. Loeschke, Maravene Sheppard, *All About Mime* (Englewood Cliffs, N.J.: Prentice-Hall, 1982), 31–32, 43–45.

35. Mark Johnson, *The Body in the Mind* (Chicago: University of Chicago Press, 1987), 31, argues that embodied experience is based on metaphor. He claims, for example, that a child first learns basic meanings such as the relation of inside to outside on the basis of embodied experience, and later extends that experience metaphorically into other modes of existence. The use of "into" and "out" in such phrases as "entering *into* a conversation" and "speaking *out* on some topic," for instance, is an extension of an original bodily experience of being inside or outside something.

36. See, for example, Segerstrale and Molnar, "Nonverbal Communication," 5–10. They conclude that "[o]verall, we seem to have an inborn and very rapid encoding and decoding capacity for facial emotional messages; that is, we are naturally capable senders and receivers" (9).

Notes to Pages 30–31 167

37. Merleau-Ponty proceeds to adopt Saussure's belief that the meaning of a word is based on its relation to other words, and not on the word's relation to an object in the world that the word is supposed to represent. Linguistic signs should be seen "not as representations of certain significations but as the means of differentiation in the verbal chain and of 'oppositive, relative and negative entities' in speech" (POW 31/POWF 45). For example, the meaning of the word "blue" is not determined by an absolute shade in nature but by its meaning in relation to the other colors of the spectrum. Merleau-Ponty's understanding of perception will be discussed in chapter 2.

38. See TFL 9/TFLF 18, where Merleau-Ponty writes: "The body is the vehicle of an indefinite number of symbolic systems whose intrinsic development definitely surpasses the signification in 'natural' gestures, but would collapse if ever the body ceases to prompt their operation and install them in the world and our life." Merleau-Ponty's claim is verified by more recent research on the relationship between natural and cultural expression. Paul Ekman and Dacher Keltner, "Universal Facial Expressions of Emotion: An Old Controversy and New Findings," in Segerstrale and Molnar, *Nonverbal Communication*, 31, for example, found in many studies that general natural expressions are given more specific differentiations of meaning depending on a person's culture. Social influences, for instance, allow certain gestures to serve as conversational cues, such as when a reply is expected or when a conversation has begun or ended. Such meanings would not be possible if the person did not already possess the natural gestures that are modified. (See also Riggio, "Social Interaction Skills," 12.) Other studies have shown that treating language as either natural or cultural overlooks the complexity of language acquisition. Hanus Papousek and Mechthild Papousek, "Preverbal Communication in Humans and the Genesis of Culture," in Segerstrale and Molnar, *Nonverbal Communication*, 87–107, even suggest that parents intuitively respond to particular cues in their children's behavior that are revealed when the child is ready to learn a new aspect of speech; parents will instinctively begin to stress vowels, for example, when children are ready to learn to voice them. Mothers were also shown to respond to their children's hand cues when they claimed, instead, to be responding to their children's facial gestures. Thus between child and parent, the acquisition of language involves a complex development of natural gestures into cultural expressions.

39. In a blurb for his video, *The Art of Mime* (Colorado Springs: Meriwether, 1991), E. Reid Gilbert comments: "When I performed as a mime in an Indian Theatre Festival, I was the only one understood by the entire audience, because my language of Mime was more basic and universal than the various regional languages of India." For a good summary of the mime techniques practiced by Marcel Marceau, see Ben Martin, *Marcel Marceau: Master of Mime* (Ottawa: Optimum Publishing Co. Ltd., 1978).

40. Katherine Sorley Walker, *Eyes on Mime* (New York: John Day, 1969), 169. The examples mentioned can be found on 162–64.

168   Notes to Pages 33–40

Notes to Chapter Two

1. Merleau-Ponty was especially interested in René Descartes's pioneering studies on optics, published as *Dioptrique*, translated by Paul Olscamp as "Optics" in *Discourse on Method, Optics, Geometry, and Meteorology* (New York: Bobbs-Merrill, 1965). Merleau-Ponty makes several references to this work throughout his career, including a detailed criticism in *Eye and Mind*. Claude Lefort, *Sur une colonne absente: Écrits autour de Merleau-Ponty* (Paris: Gallimard, 1978), 140, reports that at the time of Merleau-Ponty's death, a copy of *Dioptrique* was found open on his desk, showing the commitment that Merleau-Ponty had for understanding the mysteries of perception.

2. Merleau-Ponty does not reject science as an adequate description of experience. Without reflection, the unreflected life that is the theme of phenomenology would never be accessible because "this unreflective experience is known to us only after reflection" (PP 43/PPF 53). He is critical of science only when it claims to provide a complete explanation of perceptual experience: "Reflection never lifts itself out of any situation, nor does the analysis of perception do away with the fact of perception, the thisness of the percept or the inherence of perceptual consciousness in some temporality and some locality. Reflection is not absolutely transparent for itself, it is always given to itself in an *experience*, . . . it always springs up without itself knowing whence it springs and offers itself to me as a gift of nature" (PP 42–43/PPF 53). There is a two-way relation between the meaning of perceptual experience and scientific reflection. While experience requires a theory to be explained, all scientific theories remain rooted in experience. Merleau-Ponty concludes by saying: "Experience anticipates a philosophy and philosophy is merely an elucidated experience" (PP 63/PPF 77).

3. Merleau-Ponty also explains the contextual nature of perception in terms of tactile experience. A prick on the skin is distinguishable only in relation to other moments during which the point of skin is not pricked. If the same spot is repeatedly pricked by a pin, the awareness of the pricks will eventually blend into a single burning sensation (PP 74–75/PPF 88–90). Rudolph Arnheim, *Visual Thinking* (Berkeley and Los Angeles: University of California Press, 1969), 20, explains that we need to have an experience of difference (between the prick and other moments of rest) in order to have sensation in the first place.

4. PP 306/PPF 353. Merleau-Ponty uses the technical terms *Flächenfarben* (colored area) and *Oberflächenfarbe* (surface color) to illustrate his point.

5. Merleau-Ponty describes the essence of the perceptual object by saying: "The unity of the thing beyond all its fixed properties is not a substratum, a vacant X, an inherent subject, but that unique accent which is to be found in each one of them, that unique manner of existing of which they are a second order expression" (PP 319/PPF 368). The essence is also subject to continual revision: it "disintegrates and reforms ceaselessly" (PP 38/PPF 48).

6. It is for this reason that Gary Madison, "Did Merleau-Ponty Have a Theory of Perception?" in *Merleau-Ponty, Hermeneutics, and Postmodernism*, ed. Thomas Busch and Shaun Gallagher (Albany: State University of New York Press, 1992), 83–85, claims that Merleau-Ponty had no theory of perception. The kind of "theory" that Madison is referring to would reduce perception to explainable causes and overlook the structure of synesthesis described above. But Madison's claim that *Phenomenology of Perception* is thus an "anti-text" with "no positive thesis" (85) is too strong. My reference to *The Visible and the Invisible* is only to articulate a theory of perception that is already latent in the earlier text.

7. Samuel Mallin, *Merleau-Ponty's Philosophy* (New Haven, Conn.: Yale University Press, 1979), 146–47, provides a detailed interpretation of Merleau-Ponty's theory of synesthesis. He observes that the difference between two colors, red and green for instance, will show up more or less clearly depending on whether the objects involved are lights themselves, transparent or opaque. For example, red and green are distinguished to a high degree when they take the form of traffic lights and to a lesser degree in the form of stained glass or carpet. A numerical value can thus be attributed to the differentiation of colors as they appear in various textures, with red and green glass assuming a high numerical value and red and green carpet a lower value. In this way, when a person sees a particular degree of clarity between the colors, he can also determine what texture is involved.

8. Jacques Garelli, "Voir ceci et voir selon," in *Merleau-Ponty: Phénoménologie et expériences*, ed. Marc Richir and Etienne Tassin (Grenoble: Jerôme Millon, 1992), 79–99.

9. VI 218/VIF 271, cited in ibid., 87–88. This chapter will be focusing on qualities as dimensions or rays of Being. A discussion of what Merleau-Ponty means by the elements is reserved for chapter 7.

10. Renaud Barbaras, *Le tournant de l'expérience: Recherches sur la philosophie de Merleau-Ponty* (Paris: J. Vrin, 1998), 279.

11. Merleau-Ponty highlights the difference between his own philosophy of perception and that of traditional Gestalt psychology: "But although the Gestalt may be expressible in terms of some internal law, this law must not be considered as a model on which the phenomena of structure are built up. Their appearance is not the external unfolding of a pre-existing reason" (PP 60/PPF 74).

12. Edmund Husserl, *The Crisis of European Sciences and Transcendental Phenomenology*, ed. David Carr (Evanston, Ill.: Northwestern University Press, 1970), 121.

13. Another example given by Merleau-Ponty is when a hexagon is camouflaged in a series of lines (PP 17–19/PPF 25–27).

14. PrP 162/EMF 17. See also S 66/SF 82, where he says, "the spirit of the world is ourselves, as soon as we know how to move ourselves and look."

15. TFL 8/TFLF 17. This point echoes Heidegger's observation that objects are primarily understood in terms of their use-value as "ready-to-hand." See

170   Notes to Pages 44–53

Heidegger, *Being and Time*, trans. John Macquarrie and Edward Robinson (San Francisco: Harper Collins, 1962), 98.

16. Barbaras, *Le tournant de l'expérience*, 228.

17. See Yorihiro Yamagata, "The Self or the Cogito in Kinaesthesis," in *Self-Awareness, Temporality, and Alterity*, ed. Dan Zahavi (Netherlands: Kluwer Academic Pubishers, 1998), 12. The text that forms the basis for Yamagata's criticism is provided here in full:

> *Wahrnehmung* [perception] and *Sich bewegen* [self-movement] are synonymous: it is for this reason that the *Wahrnehmung* never rejoins the *Sich bewegen* it wishes to apprehend; it is another of the same. But this failure, this invisible, precisely attests that *Wahrnehmung* is *Sich bewegen*, there is here a success in the failure. *Wahrnehmung* fails to apprehend *Sich bewegen* (and I am for myself a zero of movement even during movement, I do not move away from myself) precisely because they are homogeneous, and this failure is the proof of this homogeneity: *Wahrnehmung* and *Sich bewegen* emerge from one another. A sort of reflection by Ec-stacy, they are the same tuft. (VI 255/VIF 308)

Yamagata's analysis relies on the interpretation of *Wahrnehmung* as perception and *Sich bewegen* as kinesthesis. The latter term, however, could mean simply "self-movement" and not the more narrow and technical sense that Yamagata attributes to Merleau-Ponty. The fact that Merleau-Ponty uses German words in this context rather than the French term *kinesthésique* (as he does elsewhere, PP 303/PPF 349) suggests that he is criticizing the traditional use of the terms and not using them as his own. He is not subject, then, to Yamagata's criticism because he is not equating self-movement with the kind of kinesthesis that Yamagata is concerned with. See also Barbaras's comments on kinesthesis in *Le tournant de l'expérience*, 228–31.

18. Barbaras, *Le tournant de l'expérience*, 231.

19. The meaning of the object is not subjective, however. Madison, *The Phenomenology of Merleau-Ponty*, explains: "As an overflowing fullness the thing reveals to us the existence of a depth of being which transcends us" (32). The similarity between the order of perception and the order of the body need not be seen as an identification of the two.

20. Madison, "Did Merleau-Ponty Have a Theory of Perception," 84.

Notes to Chapter Three

1. André Malraux, "Museum without Walls," in *The Voices of Silence*, trans. Stuart Gilbert (Garden City, N.Y.: Doubleday, 1953), 13–14. This is a later edition (and translation) of Malraux's *Musée Imaginaire* (Paris: Gallimard, 1965).

2. See Giorgio Vasari's description of the doors in *The Lives of the Artists*,

Notes to Page 53–59   171

trans. George Bull (Harmondsworth: Penguin Books, 1965), 118. Michelangelo's reference to the doors as being fit for "the entrance to Paradise" can be found on page 120.

3. René Descartes, "Optics," in *Discourse on Method, Optics, Geometry, and Meteorology*, trans. Paul Olscamp (Indianapolis: Bobbs-Merrill, 1965), 65–66; Edmund Husserl, *The Crisis of European Sciences and Transcendental Phenomenology*, Trans. David Carr (Evanston, Ill.: Northwestern University Press, 1970), 23.

4. Malraux argues that the change from representation to expression need not be seen as an intentional change on the part of the artist. "The theoreticians of Impressionism asserted that the function of painting was a direct appeal to the eye," he explains, "but the new painting appealed far more to the eye *qua* picture than *qua* landscape" (Malraux, "Museum without Walls," 120).

5. Malraux, "The Creative Process," in *The Voices of Silence*, 347. See also PrP 169/EMF 35.

6. Leo Tolstoy, *What Is Art?* trans. A. Maude (Oxford: Oxford University Press, 1955), 123.

7. Kasimir Malevich, "Suprematism," in *Modern Artists on Art: Ten Unabridged Essays*, ed. Robert Herbert, trans. Howard Dearstyne (Englewood Cliffs, N.J.: Prentice-Hall, 1964), 94, 96.

8. Jean-Paul Sartre, *What Is Literature?* trans. Steven Ungar (Cambridge, Mass.: Harvard University Press, 1988), 27; Malraux, "The Creative Process," 466.

9. Freud argued that there is a causal connection between Leonardo da Vinci's paintings and sexual attitudes developed during his childhood. Leonardo was an illegitimate child and spent the first three to five years with his mother in the absence of his father, leading to a premature infatuation with his mother and an identification with feminine figures, shaping his later "ideal" (or, better, "Platonic") homosexuality. As a result, the discovery of his mother's femininity in the face of a young woman led to the "fixed" desire to create a unique feminine smile found in the *Mona Lisa* and *St. Anne*. It also gave to his art the significance of being "an outlet to his sexual desire." See Sigmund Freud, *Leonardo da Vinci: A Study in Psychosexuality*, trans. A. A. Brill (New York: Vintage, 1947), 25, 48, 113. For a good critique of Freud, see S 63–64/SF 79–80, SNS 22–25/SNSF 38–43, and Malraux, "The Creative Process," where he writes: "The idea is, they say, to get down to the man beneath the artist. So we scrape away ruthlessly at the fresco till finally we reach the plaster, and what is the result? The fresco is ruined and in hunting for the secret of the man we have lost the genius" (420).

10. Malraux, "The Creative Process," 420.

11. "Private universe" from Malraux, "Museum without Walls," 120. For a good discussion concerning the aesthetic significance of style, see Linda Singer, "Merleau-Ponty on the Concept of Style," *Man and World* 14 (1981): 153–63.

12. Alan Munchow, "Seeing Otherwise: Merleau-Ponty's Line," *Journal of the British Society for Phenomenology* 25 (1994): 68.

172 Notes to Pages 60–62

13. Maravene Sheppard Loeschke, *All about Mime* (Englewood Cliffs, N.J.: Prentice-Hall, 1982), 28–29.

14. Maxine Sheets-Johnstone, *The Phenomenology of Dance* (Madison: University of Wisconsin Press, 1966), 121, 124. Hereafter cited in the text by page number.

15. That Sheets-Johnstone agrees with the view that the prereflective awareness is the body schema is shown when she writes that the pattern for the movement "is already a part of the global bodily schema" (ibid., 118).

16. Ibid., 118. Sheets-Johnstone's analysis is based on Sartre's philosophy of the imagination, in which the imagination and perception are mutually exclusive. It is not possible, according to Sartre, to simultaneously imagine the idea of the dance sequence and perceive the sequence with the body. The audience imagines the sequence, while the dancer performs it with her body. For example, when Sartre, in *The Psychology of Imagination*, 4th ed. (New York: The Citadel Press, 1965), describes the mime, Franconay, he emphasizes her technique for making the absent person, the painter Maurice Chevalier, present: "The artist appears. She wears a straw hat; she protrudes the lower lip, she bends her head forward. I cease to perceive, I read, that is, I make a significant synthesis" (36). According to Sartre, a successful mime manages to turn her material, "the human body" (36), into an effective and simplified sign for the absent person. "An imitation," writes Sartre, "is already a studied model, a simplified representation. It is into these simplified representations that consciousness wants to slip an imaginative intuition" (37). A criticism of Sartre's understanding of the relation between the imagination and perception is provided in chapter 4.

17. Sheets-Johnstone refers to the difference between drawing a circle in the air and imagining it to illustrate the difference between the experience of the audience and the experience of the dancer. The dancer is like a person who can draw perfect circles in the air, closing them off without imagining them, while the audience requires the working of the imagination in order to see the completed circle (116). The illustration, however, does not suggest that there is a difference between kinesthetic experience and the imagination. We can imagine the circle while experiencing it kinesthetically, and indeed borrow from the imagination in order to develop our skill. What this illustrates is not a difference and incommensurability between kinesthetic experience and imagination, but the irreducibility of tactile to visual space. Visual space allows us to see the figure all at once, and to be more precise and thus more able to close the circle properly, while in tactile space we experience the parts of a figure over a period of time. Concerning the relationship between tactile and visual space, see PP 223–24/PPF 257–59.

18. SNS 20/SNSF 25. Merleau-Ponty sometimes refers to the artist's life in general, and not specifically to the artist's "embodiment." Thus in the case of Cézanne, Merleau-Ponty claims that his art "called for this life" (ibid.) and required that it be created in "the wretchedness of his empirical life" (SNS 25/SNSF 43). But following from his other works on the body, it is clear that this life called for by Cézanne's art was one of embodiment within a world.

Notes to Pages 62–69   173

19. PrP 184/EMF 76. Carleton Dallery translates the French "nervures" as "structural filaments," which is an unfortunate choice because it overlooks the connotation of "life" and "energy" found in the French word. Merleau-Ponty uses the same word elsewhere (VI 118–19/VIF 158–59), translated as "nervure," such as one finds in the central vein of a leaf. I have chosen "vein" here to stress the organic quality of the line and its relation to the body schema of the artist.

20. Some theorists such as Jean Mitry and George Wilson argue that the perspective of the film is the actual position of the camera. Gregory Currie, *Image and Mind: Film, Philosophy and Cognitive Science* (Cambridge: Cambridge University Press, 1995), cites several examples that challenge this view, in which the dramatic tension is developed by several shifts of perspective, and especially when these shifts alternate between the viewpoint of a character and the viewpoint of an observer. He concludes: "My imagining is not that I see the characters and the events of the movie; it is simply that there are these characters and that these events *occur*" (179). Since the perspective for Merleau-Ponty is an extended, virtual body, his theory can be shown to agree with Currie's analysis. See also Kendall Walton, *Mimesis as Make-Believe: On the Foundations of the Representational Arts* (Cambridge, Mass.: Harvard University Press, 1990), 294.

21. In *Thirty-two Short Films about Glenn Gould*, one of the scenes has Gould sitting in a diner listening to the customers talk, and shows how Gould could hear the rise, fall and harmony of the conversations as parts of an elaborate symphony of sound. See the screenplay by François Girard and Don McKellar (Toronto: Coach House Press, 1995), 83–89.

Notes to Chapter Four

1. Jerome Singer, cited in Albert Gilgen, "The Nature, Function, and Description of Sensation, Perception, Feeling, and Imagery," in *Imagery: Theoretical and Clinical Applications*, vol. 3, ed. Joseph Shorr, Gail Sobel-Whittington, Penee Robin and Jack Connella (New York: Plenum, 1983), 53. Gilgen proceeds to criticize Singer's description, showing that it is too general to suffice as a definition of imagination.

2. David Hume, *A Treatise of Human Nature*, ed. L. A. Selby-Bigge (Oxford: Clarendon Press, 1888), 19.

3. Immanuel Kant, *Critique of Pure Reason*, trans. J. M. D. Meiklejohn (Rutland, VT: Everyman's Library, 1991), 119. For a good discussion concerning Kant's theory of imagination, see Rudolf Makkreel, *Imagination and Interpretation in Kant* (Chicago: University of Chicago Press, 1990).

4. Kant, *Critique of Judgment*, trans. J. M. Bernard (New York: Hafner, 1951), 1.10.

5. Jerome Singer, *Daydreaming: An Introduction to the Experimental Study of Inner Experience* (New York: Random House, 1966), 187.

174   Notes to Pages 70–73

6. Casey, *Imagining: A Phenomenological Study* (Bloomington: Indiana University Press, 1976), 232. See also 198.

7. Jean-Paul Sartre, *The Psychology of Imagination*, 4th ed. (New York: The Citadel Press, 1965), 5, 270.

8. Gilbert Ryle, *The Concept of Mind* (Harmondsworth, Middlesex: Penguin Books, 1963), 234, 235, 239.

9. See, for instance, Casey, *Imagining*, 92.

10. The test is cited in Penelope Qualls, "On the Physiological Measurement of Imagery: An Overview," in *Imagery: Theoretical and Clinical Applications,* vol. 3, ed. Joseph Shorr et al. (New York: Plenum, 1983), 39.

11. Ibid., 43.

12. Ryle, *The Concept of Mind*, 244.

13. Kendall Walton, *Mimesis as Make-Believe: On the Foundations of the Representational Arts* (Cambridge, Mass.: Harvard University Press, 1990), 21–24, 35–43, 54–57.

14. Sartre, *Being and Nothingness*, 40–42.

15. The test is cited in Ned Block, "Introduction: What Is the Issue?" in *Imagery*, ed. Ned Block (Cambridge, Mass.: MIT Press, 1981), 9–10.

16. Stephen Kosslyn, Steven Pinker, George Smith and Steven Schwartz, "On the Demystification of Mental Imagery," in *Imagery*, ibid., 140. Another test by R. A. Finke and M. J. Schmidt showed that the "McCollough Effect" characteristic of perception also occurs in imagination. O. E. Favreau and M. C. Corballis demonstrated the effect in an experiment in which a subject was asked to study two sets of lines, one having alternating black and red vertical lines and the other black and green horizontal lines. When the subject looked away and then focused on similar sets of lines in black and white, they saw the white vertical lines as green and the white horizontal lines as red. Finke and Schmidt asked subjects to imagine the sets and found that the phenomenon was repeated in the imagination. The tests are summarized in Block, *Imagery*, 9–10.

17. Kosslyn et al., "On the Demystification of Mental Imagery," 135–38. R. N. Shepard has also tested mental rotation in imagination. In one test, he presented subjects with a series of pictures of pairs of geometrical figures. The pairs were either similar and rotated in two-dimensional space, similar and rotated in three-dimensional space, or dissimilar. When subjects were asked which of these three groups the pairs belonged to, they took longer to reply concerning the pairs that required the most rotation. The conclusion was that they were imagining the rotation of the figures in an imaginary three-dimensional space. The tests are cited in Roger Brown and Richard Herrnstein, "Icons and Images," in Block, *Imagery*, 30–32.

18. Daniel Dennett, "The Nature of Images and the Introspective Trap," in Block, *Imagery*, writes: "Consider the Tiger and his Stripes. I can dream, imagine or see a striped tiger, but must the tiger I experience have a particular number of stripes? If seeing or imagining is having a mental image, then the image of the

tiger *must* — obeying the rules of images in general — reveal a definite number of stripes showing, and one should be able to pin this down with such questions as 'more than ten?' 'less than twenty?'" (55). The controversy involved here is between the view that images are pictures and the concept that images are simply descriptions of perception (what Dennett, "Two Approaches to Mental Images" in Block, *Imagery*, 88, refers to as the "iconophiles," those who believe that images are pictures, and the "iconophobes," those who believe that images are descriptions). Dennett argues that images are merely descriptions, while Jerry Fodor, "Imagistic Representation," in Block, *Imagery*, 75–79, believes that images are more like pictures.

19. Block, *Imagery*, 11.

20. Fodor, "Imagistic Representation," 78–79, also thinks that images can simultaneously serve as both a description and a picture. He gives as an example a geographical map that represents the terrain pictorially while signifying population density by means of color or shading. Thus, it is too simplistic to reduce all images to mere descriptions, as Dennett suggests.

21. C. W. Perky, "An Experimental Study of Imagination," *American Journal of Psychology* 21 (1910): 422–52.

22. Sartre, *The Psychology of Imagination*, 97.

23. Casey, *Imagining*, 148–50; Sartre, *The Psychology of Imagination*, 75.

24. He even refers to Sartre's *l'Imaginaire* in this context. See also PP 296/PPF 343, where Merleau-Ponty says, "the illusion, like the image, is not observable."

25. Françoise Dastur, "Perceptual Faith and the Invisible," *Journal of the British Society for Phenomenology* 25 (1994), agrees with this reading of Merleau-Ponty: "there is a difference of nature and not just of degree between perception and imagination" (47). See also SB 196/SBF 211–12.

26. Sartre, *The Psychology of Imagination*, 54; his italics.

27. See Glen Mazis, "*La Chair et l'Imaginaire*: The Developing Role of Imagination in Merleau-Ponty's Philosophy," *Philosophy Today* 32 (1988): 30–42, and Dastur, "Perceptual Faith and the Invisible," 47.

28. Edmund Husserl, *Ideas: General Introduction to Pure Phenomenology*, trans. W. R. Boyce Gibson (New York: Collier, 1962), 98.

29. Ibid., 118, 119. This does not mean, however, that the imagination synthesizes distinct images or that every aspect of an object must be included in order to arrive at an intuition of the essence (see 181).

30. Mazis, "*La Chair et l'Imaginaire*," argues that "without the playing of the imaginary, it is the perceptual which becomes thin, loses its possibilities for *sens*" (36). But he attributes this view of the imagination only to Merleau-Ponty's later work.

31. Casey, *Imagining*, 92, 54, 53.

32. It is less cumbersome to say, with Merleau-Ponty, that imagination involves a different kind of space than to argue that its space is a "quasi" space with no depth. In other words, while Casey radically separates the imagination and

176 *Notes to Pages 80–84*

perception in order to maintain a particular notion of space, Merleau-Ponty allows space to assume a variety of meanings for the imagination and perception which need not be mutually exclusive. See PP 293/PPF 339.

33. Sartre, *The Psychology of Imagination*, 23, 70, 23, 77.

34. Sartre's reason for attempting to find material for mental images was to distinguish the imagination from eidetic analysis. He claims that Husserl confuses two functions of the imagination as a neutral domain for the analysis of essences and as a faculty that is diametrically opposed to perception. He writes, "the distinction between mental images and perceptions cannot derive from intentionality alone. A difference in intention is necessary but not sufficient. The matter must also be different" (ibid., 143). Mary Warnock, "The Imagination in Sartre," in *Existentialist Ontology and Human Consciousness*, ed. William McBride (New York: Garland Press, 1997), 107.

35. Thomas Flynn, "The Role of the Image in Sartre's Aesthetic," *Journal of Aesthetics and Art Criticism* 33 (1975): 433.

36. John Sallis, *Force of Imagination: The Sense of the Elemental* (Bloomington: Indiana University Press, 2000), shares my reserved acceptance of Sartre's discussion of the analogue and concludes his analysis of Sartre's theory with the poignant question: "in order to conceive properly the consciousness of images, is it required that one think without reference to space, or is it not perhaps that one needs to think more rigorously the spacing of the image?" (9). I suggest that Merleau-Ponty's analysis of the virtual body provides an example of such thinking.

37. Martin Heidegger, *Being and Time*, trans. John Macquarrie and Edward Robinson (San Francisco: Harper Collins, 1962), 98, 119.

38. Not only is orientation experienced prior to the thinking that would be involved in the coordination of tactile and visual experience; it has also been shown that prereflective orientation is more convenient than orientation based on thought. K. Machover discovered that people who tend to rely more on kinesthetic information for determining orientation adjust more quickly to new situations (like the Stratton experiment) than people who tend to rely more on the actual position of objects within their field. See Machover, cited in Seymour Fisher and Sidney E. Cleveland, *Body Image and Personality* (Princeton: Van Nostrand, 1958, 25–34.

39. A case where the actual body (rather than the virtual body) does in fact provide us with spatial orientation is when we are walking in the dark and have recourse only to the spatial relation of the actual parts of the body. In this case, if I tilt my head and extend my hand, I will extend my hand at an oblique angle. But this orientation occurs only when the virtual body called for by the situation happens to be the actual orientation of the body itself. Usually, the virtual body called for is not identical and reducible to the actual body (PP 249–50/PPF 288–89).

40. Samuel Mallin, *Merleau-Ponty's Philosophy* (New Haven, Conn.: Yale University Press, 1979), describes the spatial level as "the unique equilibrium and balance among all these capacities [of the body] which yields the maximum

grasp the body-subject as a whole is able to achieve on this particular field" (44).

41. Gilgen, "The Nature, Function, and Description," 60. Gilgen does not include dreaming or being overwhelmed by emotion in the list of experiences that remain connected to the everyday world. In the chapters that follow, I will show that all modes of human experience — including dreaming and hallucination — are grounded in the spatiality of the virtual body.

42. James Morley, "The Private Theatre: A Phenomenological Investigation of Daydreaming," *Journal of Phenomenological Psychology* 29, no. 1 (1998): 116–34.

43. Ibid., 23–24.

44. Concerning the illusion of seeing a spot of light as a flat stone, he writes: "I cannot say that I ever see the flat stone in the sense in which I am to see, as I draw nearer, the patch of sunlight. The flat stone, like all things at a distance, appears only in a field of confused structure in which connections are not yet clearly articulated. In this sense, the illusion, like the image, is not yet observable. . . . I cannot unfold it before me by an exploratory action" (PP 296/PPF 343). The flat stone is like a phantom that exists only in the particular experience; when we attempt to see it more clearly, it vanishes into the background and becomes the visible speck of light.

45. Casey, "Sartre on Imagination," in *The Philosophy of Jean-Paul Sartre*, ed. Paul Arthur Schlipp (La Salle, Ill.: Open Court, 1981), 156. Though Casey admits that some blurring occurs between imagination and perception, he claims that the imagination and perception are radically separate modes of consciousness. See his *Imagining*, 127–39, 146–76.

46. A major problem at the heart of the debate concerning the nature of imagination is a confusion between fanciful thinking and imagination in general. While Casey correctly argues, with Sartre, that there is no confusion between fancy and perception, Richard McCleary, *Imagination's Body* (Washington, D.C.: University Press of America, 1986), shows that the imagination in general still plays a central role in perception. This confusion is overcome by separating the two, so that while fanciful thinking could be said to be more or less opposed to perception, the imagination in general could be shown to be consistent with it. See Casey, *Imagining*, 146–50, and McCleary, 53–55.

47. Ludwig Wittgenstein, *Philosophical Investigations*, ed. G. E. M. Anscombe (Oxford: Basil Blackwell, 1958), 194–97, 213.

48. See, for instance, Sartre's discussion of seeing a face in the fire in *The Psychology of Imagination*, 49–52.

49. Mary Warnock, *Imagination* (London: Faber & Faber, 1976), 186, argues: "*All* perception is seeing as," thus radicalizing Wittgenstein's theory that only *some* perception is "seeing as"; Casey agrees that aspect-seeing is an instance of perception that is "intrinsically imaginative," although he sees it as a rare occurrence of imaginative perception and not as a regular perceptual experience (*Imagining*, 142–45).

178   Notes to Pages 92–98

Notes to Chapter Five

1.   Sigmund Freud, *Civilization and Its Discontents*, ed. James Strachey, trans. Joan Riviere (London: Hogarth Press, 1963), 11–20.

2.   Sigmund Freud and Josef Breuer, *Studies on Hysteria*, ed. and trans. James Strachey and Alix Strachey (Harmondsworth: Penguin Books, 1974), 376.

3.   Ibid., 368–79.

4.   Edward Casey, "The Unconscious Mind and the Prereflective Body," in *Merleau-Ponty, Interiority and Exteriority, Psychic Life and the World*, ed. Dorothea Olkowski and James Morley (Albany: State University of New York Press, 1999), 49.

5.   David Pettigrew, "Merleau-Ponty and the Unconscious," ibid., shows how the unconscious for Merleau-Ponty rests on the ambiguity of expression (60–61).

6.   M. C. Dillon, "The Unconscious: Language and World," in *Merleau-Ponty in Contemporary Perspective*, ed. Patrick Burke and Jan van der Veken (Boston: Kluwer Academic Publishers, 1993), 76.

7.   Merleau-Ponty attacks Sartre's endorsement of a politics that is based on individual will and intention by arguing that "the conception of communism that Sartre proposes is a denunciation of the dialectic and the philosophy of history and substitutes for them a philosophy of absolute creation amidst the unknown." According to such a theory, communism "is an undetermined enterprise of which one knows only that it is absolutely other, that, like duty, it is not subject to discussion, nor is it subject to rational proof or rational control" (AD 101/ADF 138).

8.   Merold Westphal, "Situation and Suspicion in the Thought of Merleau-Ponty: The Question of Politics and Phenomenology," in *Ontology and Alterity in Merleau-Ponty*, ed. Galen Johnson and Michael B. Smith (Evanston, Ill.: Northwestern University Press, 1990), 176, claims that Merleau-Ponty's analysis of the Moscow Trials involves a superior explanation of repression than is found in *Phenomenology of Perception*. She bases much of her argument on a quote from the latter in which Merleau-Ponty describes the subject of political history as "the living subject, man as creativity, as a person trying to endow his life with form" (PP 171/PPF 200). Although Merleau-Ponty refuses to accept an unconscious level of existence, he stresses that in the attempt to "endow our lives with form" (a seemingly Sartrean expression), the subject of history exists within an ambiguous context that she neither understands nor controls. Thus the analysis of repression found in *Phenomenology of Perception* considers the same ambiguity of history as that found in Merleau-Ponty's later works.

9.   In the second quote, Merleau-Ponty is citing L. Binswanger.

10.   Jerome Singer, *Daydreaming: An Introduction to the Experimental Study of Inner Experience* (New York: Random House, 1966), 202.

11.   J. H. van den Berg, "An Existential Explanation of the Guided Daydream in Psychotherapy," *Review of Existential Psychology and Psychiatry* 2 (1962): 30.

12. In this respect, the traditional attribution of "light" to consciousness and "dark" to the unconscious can be reinterpreted to mean that psychosis, like walking in the dark, assumes a rigid spatiality like that of walking in the dark.

13. James Morley, "The Imaginary Texture of the Real: Merleau-Ponty on Imagination and Psychopathology," in *Imagination and Its Pathologies*, ed. James Phillips and James Morley (Cambridge, Mass.: MIT Press, 2003), 134–39. Morley adds that the problem is not that the patient has placed faith in the imaginary rather than in the real, but that the patient is unable to place faith in any world at all. He also argues that the cause of this loss in faith is an obsessive determination to strive "for some absolute ontological certainty in a manner that makes one unable to function on the most rudimentary levels of social life" (139).

14. Research conducted by Jerome Singer confirms this. In the majority of cases of schizophrenia and hallucinations, for example, Singer finds that there is a distinct loss of imagination rather than wild imaginings as some theorists have suggested. "Instead of bizarre, imaginative tales of strange happenings, events, or places," argues Singer, "one usually gets from a schizophrenic a fragmentary account of suspicions, misinterpretations or recent occurrences, or repetitive accounts of assumed injustices." He also noticed that children with a vivid imagination were less likely to develop such symptoms than other children (*Daydreaming*, 196–97). See also Morley, "The Imaginary Texture of the Real," 139.

15. Singer, *Daydreaming*, 214.

Notes to Chapter Six

1. Jacques Lacan, "The Mirror Stage as Formative of the Function of the I as Revealed in Psychoanalytic Experience," in *Écrits: A Selection*, ed. and trans. Alan Sheridan (New York: W. W. Norton, 1977), 2.

2. Ibid., 4.

3. Ibid., 6–7.

4. Merleau-Ponty explains: "My life must have a significance which I do not constitute; there must strictly speaking be an intersubjectivity; each one of us must be both anonymous in the sense of absolutely individual, and anonymous in the sense of absolutely general. Our being in the world, is the concrete bearer of this double anonymity" (PP 448/PPF 512). The double anonymity is that of the subject's body in relation to personal existence, and the shared anonymity with Others.

5. It is unclear whether sympathy or reversibility grounds social relations. While in some places, such as in "The Child's Relations with Others" and VI 221/VIF 274, Merleau-Ponty stresses the role of sympathy in intersubjectivity, in other places (S 168–69/SF 212–14; VI 141, 233/VIF 185–86, 286) he bases intersubjectivity on the reversibility of the flesh as found in double sensation.

180 Notes to Pages 106–11

This suggests that both sympathy and reversibility provide the same anonymous level of existence out of which emerges a sense of self and Other. It also identifies sympathy with reversibility, so that just as the roles of sensing and being sensed are never actually simultaneous with each other, so the self and the Other remain actually distinct and are only virtually reversible. It would be wrong, then, to assume either a primacy of self or of difference. Merleau-Ponty explains that "there is here no problem of the alter ego because it is not I who sees, not he who sees, because an anonymous visibility inhabits both of us, a vision in general" (VI 142/VIF 187–88).

6. See PrP 136/ROF 56, and Lacan, "The Mirror Stage," 1–7. Martin Jay makes this observation in "Sartre, Merleau-Ponty, and the Search for a New Ontology of Sight," in *Modernity and the Hegemony of Vision*, ed. David Michael Levin (Berkeley and Los Angeles: University of California Press, 1993), 174.

7. Jacques Lacan, "Maurice Merleau-Ponty," *Les Temps Modernes*, nos. 184–85 (1961): 250.

8. David Michael Levin, "Visions of Narcissism: Intersubjectivity and the Reversals of Reflection," in *Merleau-Ponty Vivant*, ed. M. C. Dillon (Albany: State University of New York Press, 1991), 53. See also Helen Fielding, "Envisioning the Other: Lacan and Merleau-Ponty on Intersubjectivity," in *Merleau-Ponty, Interiority and Exteriority, Psychic Life and the World*, ed. Dorothea Olkowski and James Morley (Albany: State University of New York Press, 1999), 194–95.

9. Luce Irigaray, "And the One Doesn't Stir without the Other," *Signs* 7, no. 1 (1981): 63.

10. Jay, "Sartre, Merleau-Ponty, and the Search for a New Ontology of Sight," 144.

11. Martin Dillon, "Merleau-Ponty and the Psychogenesis of the Self," *Journal of Phenomenological Psychology* 9 (1978): 90.

12. Ibid., 91, 89.

13. Glen A. Mazis, "Touch and Vision: Rethinking with Merleau-Ponty Sartre on the Caress," in *The Debate between Sartre and Merleau-Ponty*, edited by Jon Stewart (Evanston: Northwestern University Press, 1998), 151.

14. Luce Irigaray, "The Invisible of the Flesh," in *An Ethics of Sexual Difference*, trans. Carolyn Burke and Gillian Gill (Ithaca, N.Y.: Cornell University Press, 1993), 171.

15. Ibid., 153, 182. G. W. F. Hegel, *Phenomenology of Spirit*, trans. A. V. Miller (Oxford: Oxford University Press, 1977), 58–66.

16. Irigaray, "The Invisible of the Flesh," 171. Irigaray's comments on the mirror stage : "Between the other in the mirror and the other who inverts me, there is also the other of the same, at once closer and more distant. Also a phenomenon of visibility, given that without realizing it, the other detains my look as it sees him, and that he sees that which I cannot see of myself. A mutual dereliction in which we constitute, each for the other, holes in the invisible other than

intrauterine life or carnal relations in the strict sense. The black hole of that into which we disappear, each into the other, continually" (170–71).

17. Ibid., 183.

18. Martin Dillon, "Écart: Reply to Claude Lefort's 'Flesh and Otherness,'" in *Ontology and Alterity in Merleau-Ponty*, ed. Galen Johnson and Michael B. Smith (Evanston, Ill.: Northwestern University Press, 1990), explains that otherness is "grounded in an originary difference, which is the écart across which the various forms of reversibility operate" (23).

19. Levin, "Visions of Narcissism," 47. For an alternative view, see Claude Lefort, "Flesh and Otherness," in Johnson and Smith, *Ontology and Alterity in Merleau-Ponty*, chapter 1, in which he claims that Merleau-Ponty's analysis of self-development overlooks the alterity found in the relationship between the child and the father that names the child. See also Dillon's response to Lefort, "Écart: Reply to Claude Lefort's 'Flesh and Otherness,'" which stresses the difference between self and Other.

20. Gail Weiss, *Body Images: Embodiment as Intercorporeality* (New York: Routledge & Kegan Paul, 1999), 122.

21. Iris Young, "Asymmetrical Reciprocity: On Moral Respect, Wonder, and Enlarged Thought," *Constellations* 3, no. 3 (1996): 340–63.

22. Seyla Benhabib, *Situating the Self: Gender, Community, and Postmodernism in Contemporary Ethics* (New York: Routledge, 1991), 32.

23. Young, "Asymmetrical Reciprocity," 347.

24. Ibid., 343, 358, 354.

25. Benbabib, *Situating the Self*, 157.

26. Young, "Asymmetrical Reciprocity," 350, 354, 353.

27. Weiss, *Body Images*, 113.

28. Young, "Asymmetrical Reciprocity," 348.

29. Here Young, ibid., and Weiss, *Body Images*, 123, are in agreement.

30. Judith Butler, *Bodies That Matter: On the Discursive Limits of "Sex"* (New York: Routledge, 1993), 30; Nancy Love, "Politics and Voice(s): An Empowerment Knowledge Regime," *Differences* 3, no. 1 (1991): 96.

31. For a good description of this process, see Iris Young, *Throwing Like a Girl and Other Essays in Feminist Philosophy and Social Theory* (Bloomington: Indiana University Press, 1990), 141–59.

32. Carol Gilligan, "Woman's Place in Man's Life Cycle," in *The Hidden Curriculum and Moral Education*, ed. Henry Giroux and David Purpel (Berkeley: McCutchan, 1983), 220. See also 211–12.

33. J. Lever, cited in ibid., 213–14.

34. Merleau-Ponty explains: "For example, men who, by virtue of the established myths as well as certain tendencies of their own physiological constitutions, do not want to be weak and sensitive and want to be self-sufficient, decisive, and energetic, project on women exactly those personality traits they do not themselves want to have. Women, who are accomplices in this masquerade, from their

182 Notes to Pages 117–25

side project on men the personality traits they wish to be rid of or are unable to assume. There is thus a mutual disparagement which is at the same time the basis of a pact concluded between the two sexes" (PrP 104/ROF 11).

35. Butler, *Bodies That Matter*, 100. See also Weiss, *Body Images*, 26–29. For a good feminist reading of Merleau-Ponty, see also 117–28.

36. Frantz Fanon illustrates the development of a black child within a social context in which white bodies are seen as superior in *Black Skin White Masks*, trans. Charles Lam Markmann (New York: Grove Weidenfeld, 1967).

37. Talia Welsh, "The Logic of the Observed: Merleau-Ponty's Conception of Women as Outlined in His 1951–1952 Sorbonne Lecture 'The Question of Method in Child Psychology,'" *Symposium* 5, no. 1 (2001): 92.

38. Young, *Throwing Like a Girl*, 349.

39. Thomas Busch, *Circulating Being: From Embodiment to Incorporation* (New York: Fordham University Press, 1999), 99.

Notes to Chapter Seven

1. Martin Heidegger, *Basic Writings*, ed. David Farrell Krell (San Francisco: Harper Collins, 1993), 354–55.

2. Jean-Paul Satre, *Being and Nothingness*, trans. Hazel Barnes (New York: Washington Square Press, 1956), 765, 768, 770–71.

3. Ibid., 774, 775, 780, 767. In order to maintain his radical separation of imagination from perception, Sartre stresses that the imagination is not involved in the perception of these qualities. Mary Warnock, "The Imagination in Sartre," in *Existentialist Ontology and Human Consciousness*, ed. William McBride (New York: Garland Press, 1997), however, argues that Sartre's description of elemental images betrays a powerful "concrete imagination" that undermines Sartre's actual comments concerning the imagination (110).

4. Gaston Bachelard, *On Poetic Imagination and Reverie*, ed. and trans. Colette Gaudin (Indianapolis: Bobbs-Merrill, 1971), refers to the other form of imagination — that of manipulating percepts to create new images — as the formal imagination (37).

5. Heidegger, *Basic Writings*, 351.

6. John Sallis, *Force of Imagination: The Sense of the Elemental* (Bloomington: Indiana University Press, 2000), 181.

7. See especially VI 147/VIF 183, where Merleau-Ponty refers to the elements as "channels" and "circuits." For a discussion on what he means by "rays of Being," see VI 241–42/VIF 294–95. Compare this discussion to the innate "net" in the preface to *Phenomenology of Perception* that allows the phenomenologist to bring back "all of the living relationships of experience, as the fisherman's net draws up from the depths of the ocean quivering fish and sea-

weed" (PP xv/PPF x). Now the "net" is the fabric of elemental Nature that energizes itself and from which we draw our sense of Nature.

8. T. M. Robinson, *Heraclitus: Fragments* (Toronto: University of Toronto Press, 1987), especially fragment 49a. See also G. Vlastos, "On Heraclitus," *American Journal of Philology* 76 (1955): 365–67; and Merrill Ring, *Beginning with the Presocratics* (Mountain View, Calif.: Mayfield, 1987), 14–17.

9. Bachelard writes: "If meanings become too profuse, [the image] can fall into *word play*. If it restricts itself to a single meaning, it can fall into didacticism" (*On Poetic Imagination and Reverie*, 28). He later writes that these poetical laws of interpreting images "are as positive as experimental laws" (37).

10. Unfortunately, Bachelard's poetics was drawn too closely in line with psychoanalysis. He claimed that his phenomenology of our oneiric ties to the universe had nothing to do with natural science (ibid., 3–4). Bachelard, *The Poetics of Space*, trans. Maria Jolas (Boston: Beacon Press, 1964), xiv.

11. Even as early as *Phenomenology of Perception*, Merleau-Ponty suggests that there are dynamic laws of perception that we do not control. In spite of his occasionally calling them "natural signs" (PP 61), he stresses the fact that they do not involve a "natural geometry" (PP 205/PPF 237), but, rather, are similar in nature to the dynamic unity of the body schema. For a good description of the dynamic nature of perceptual laws, see his description of perceptual foreshadowing in PP 17/PPF 24–25. This distinguishes Merleau-Ponty from Bachelard, who saw elemental laws as laws of nature.

12. Renaud Barbaras, *Le tournant de l'expérience: Recherches sur la philosophie de Merleau-Ponty* (Paris: J. Vrin, 1998), 222.

13. Ibid., 220, 223.

14. Marc Richir, *Phénomènes, temps et êtres: Ontologie et phénoménologie* (Grenoble: Jerôme Millon, 1987), 90.

15. Jean Baudrillard, *Simulations,* trans. Paul Foss, Paul Patton and Philip Beitchman (New York: Semiotext(e), 1983), 146.

16. David Pettigrew elaborates on how art expresses this elemental relation to Being in "Merleau-Ponty and the Unconscious," in *Merleau-Ponty, Interiority and Exteriority, Psychic Life and the World*, ed. Dorothea Olkowski and James Morley (Albany: State University of New York Press, 1999), 60–65.

17. Barbaras, *Le tournant de l'expérience*, 267.

18. Paul Ricoeur, *Hermeneutics and the Human Sciences*, ed. and trans. John Thompson (Cambridge: Cambridge University Press, 1981), 169–70, 190. The example, "man is a wolf," is from Gary Madison, *The Hermeneutics of Postmodernity: Figures and Themes* (Bloomington: Indiana University Press, 1993), 189.

19. Barbaras, *Le tournant de l'expérience*, 281, 284.

20. Barbaras admits that this reference in Merleau-Ponty's work might bring his own theory of the element as a metaphor into question, but responds to such

184 Notes to Pages 132–35

opposition by claiming that Merleau-Ponty overlooks another kind of metaphor: that of originary meaning. Thus, according to Barbaras, "it is not metaphor that is the concern here, but *a certain conception of metaphor*" (ibid., 284). And had Merleau-Ponty given metaphor more thought, he would have conceived of elemental images in this way. While Barbaras's theory is reasonable, it stretches the value of metaphor to a breaking point. It is true that the elements provide a proliferation of meaning on what might be called a horizontal plane, where images collide with other images to form new meanings and new expressions of Nature. But there is also a verticality or a weight to elemental images that sets them apart from the usual sense of metaphor. Though Barbaras distinguishes the ontological sense of metaphor to account for this verticality, it might be better to refer to elements in a different way altogether (as Merleau-Ponty does).

21. See also VI 137/VIF 181 and VI 158/VIF 210. In the latter case, Merleau-Ponty treats perception itself as an archetype for all other experiences.

22. Edward Murray, *Imaginative Thinking and Human Existence* (Pittsburgh: Duquesne University Press, 1986), 143. George Lakoff and Mark Johnson, *Metaphors We Live By* (Chicago: University of Chicago Press, 1980), describe the logic of metaphorical systems, showing how different metaphors combine to provide a single meaning. Arguments, for instance, are seen both as war (needing reinforcement and buttressing), and also as containers (as being empty or dense). The result is a complex structure of metaphors. This is not, however, the same thing that Murray and Barbaras are talking about. Lakoff and Johnson's metaphorical system presupposes a level of meaning that is already articulated (98–99).

23. For this example, see Baudrillard, *Simulations*, 56–75.

24. Barbaras, *Le tournant de l'expérience*, 250.

25. A good description of this layering of diacritical systems is provided by John Barry, "The Textual Body: Incorporating Writing and Flesh," *Philosophy Today* 30 (1986): 16–31, who writes that "it is only our difference from that other flesh [of the world] that makes the open dialectic of flesh" (24). In this case, it is the relation between the flesh of the world and of the imagining body that is being discussed.

26. Thomas Busch, *Circulating Being: From Embodiment to Incorporation* (New York: Fordham University Press, 1999), 121.

27. Gary Madison, "Merleau-Ponty and Derrida: La différence," in *Écart & Différance: Merleau-Ponty and Derrida on Seeing and Writing*, ed. M. C. Dillon (Atlantic Highlands, N.J.: Humanities Press, 1997), 106.

28. David Abram, *The Spell of the Sensuous: Perception and Language in a More-Than-Human World* (New York: Pantheon, 1996), 128.

Notes to Chapter Eight

1. Michael Yeo uses this expression in "Creative Adequation: Merleau-Ponty's Philosophy of Philosophy" (Ph.D. diss., McMaster University, 1987), 275. He bases the expression on the following quote: "[Philosophy] is hence a creation in a radical sense: a creation that is at the same time an adequation, the only way to obtain an adequation" (VI 197/VIF 251).

2. See Claude Lefort, *Sur une colonne absente: Écrits autour de Merleau-Ponty* (Paris: Gallimard, 1978), 152–54.

3. John Sallis, *Force of Imagination: The Sense of the Elemental* (Bloomington: Indiana University Press, 2000), 104.

4. "Total parts" does not mean two distinct parts within a common whole. It would be better to think of these "total parts" or "leaves" as different aspects of a whole, much as sexuality is explained as a mode of existence that encompasses all of existence while not being identical to it (PP 169/PPF 197).

5. Martin Heidegger, *Basic Writings*, ed. David Farrell Krell (San Francisco: Harper Collins, 1993), 181.

6. Marc Richir, "Merleau-Ponty and the Question of Phenomenological Architectonics," in *Merleau-Ponty in Contemporary Perspective*, ed. Patrick Burke and Jan Van der Veken (Boston: Kluwer Academic Publishers, 1993), 49.

7. Sallis, *Force of Imagination*, 119.

8. Thomas Busch, *Circulating Being: From Embodiment to Incorporation* (New York: Fordham University Press, 1999), 122.

9. David Abram, *The Spell of the Sensuous: Perception and Language in a More-Than-Human World* (New York: Pantheon, 1996), 66.

10. Martin Dillon, *Merleau-Ponty's Ontology* (Bloomington: Indiana University Press, 1988), 162.

11. Ibid., 162, 159.

12. Ibid., 169.

13. Michael B. Smith, "Transcendence in Merleau-Ponty," in *Merleau-Ponty, Interiority and Exteriority, Psychic Life and the World*, ed. Dorothea Olkowski and James Morley (Albany: State University of New York Press, 1999), 40.

14. VI 233/VIF 286; see also VI 191, 196, 200/VIF 244–45, 249–50, 253–54 and PP 215/PPF 249. Renaud Barbaras, *Le tournant de l'expérience: Recherches sur la philosophie de Merleau-Ponty* (Paris: J. Vrin, 1998), explains this by saying that "transcendence is not a modality of negativity . . . it is rather negativity that is a modality of transcendence" (251). In other words, a priority is given to flesh's own transcendence and not to nothingness (or the for-itself) as the ground for meaning.

15. Smith, "Transcendence in Merleau-Ponty," 40.

16. Of course, even the reversibility occurring within us is also within Being, for we are a part of Being. My concern here is to stress a difference that is found between Being's transcendence and that found specifically in the thinking subject.

186   Notes to Pages 147–49

17. Lefort, *Sur une colonne absente*, 144.

18. Ibid., 144.

19. Drew Leder, "Flesh and Blood: A Proposed Supplement to Merleau-Ponty," *Human Studies* 13, no. 3 (1990): 214, 215; see also Leder, *The Absent Body* (Chicago: University of Chicago Press, 1990), 66.

20. Leder, "Flesh and Blood," 216, 213. An emphasis on the visceral at the expense of the exteroceptive aspect of the flesh has led some commentators to resort to Eastern philosophy in order to make sense of Merleau-Ponty's concept of flesh. Leder himself compares flesh to *Ch'i*, a vital force or energy that permeates the universe. "Forming one body with the universe," writes Leder, "can literally mean that since all modalities of being are made of *Ch'i*, human life is part of a continuous flow of the blood and breath that constitutes the cosmic process" (Leder, *The Absent Body*, 157). But Leder does not explicitly connect these ideas to Merleau-Ponty, nor could he. Despite his sympathy for the value of Oriental thought, Merleau-Ponty would never attempt to understand it in terms of Western concepts, nor vice versa. The Orient, indeed, has something to teach us, but this includes only the rediscovery of "the existential field that [our own ideas] were born in and that their success has led us to forget" (S 139/SF 175). "Hence the full meaning of a language is never translatable into another. We may speak several languages, but one of them always remains the one in which we live. In order completely to assimilate a language [or concept], it would be necessary to make the world which it expresses one's own, and one never does belong to two worlds at once" (PP 187/PPF 218). Although the attempt to understand Merleau-Ponty's concept of flesh in terms of Oriental concepts may, indeed, prove to be fruitful in other contexts, it would not involve a proper reading of the concept as Merleau-Ponty would have understood it himself.

21. Leder, "Flesh and Blood," refers to the maternal/fetal relation as an internal relation based on blood and inherence rather than on the "surface" functioning of the flesh that we would see in mature intersubjectivity (215). In a similar fashion, Luce Irigaray, *An Ethics of Sexual Difference*, trans. Carolyn Burke and Gillian Gill (Ithaca, N.Y.: Cornell University Press, 1993), claims that Merleau-Ponty attempts to reduce the maternal-feminine to the masculine gaze of perception rather than preserve it in its hiddenness and immediacy (152–53, 159, 184). To the extent that Irigaray wishes to preserve the feminine as an absolute mystery, Merleau-Ponty would certainly give priority to visibility over mystery. But as I have just shown, he is not attempting to reduce everything to the gaze of perception, but only to the common medium of flesh in which all things are potentially visible.

22. Leder, *The Absent Body*, does admit that the two levels of the body, the exteroceptive and visceral, are not opposed to each other but occur within a "chiasmatic identity-in-difference of perceptual and visceral life" (65). The absences of the visceral, he adds, "always remain depths of a surface, adhering to the esthesiological and expressive body" (67).

Notes to Pages 149–52 187

23. Garelli, "Voir ceci et voir selon," in *Merleau-Ponty: Phénoménologie et experiences*, ed. Marc Richir and Etienne Tassin (Grenoble: Jerôme Millon, 1992), 94; see also 97, and *Rhythmes et mondes: Au revers de l'identité et de l'alterité* (Grenoble: Jerôme Millon, 1991), 358.

24. See also Richir, "Merleau-Ponty and the Question of Phenomenological Architectonics," esp. 46–47.

25. Some commentators have suggested that flesh can be understood in terms of chaos theory. Glen Mazis, "Chaos Theory and Merleau-Ponty's Ontology: Beyond the Dead Father's Paralysis toward a Dynamic and Fragile Materiality," in *Merleau-Ponty, Interiority and Exteriority, Psychic Life and the World*, ed. Dorothea Olkowski and James Morley (Albany: State University of New York Press, 1999), for instance, argues that the flesh, with all of its openings and dimensions, is similar to a chaotic structure that is open, dynamic, and yet extremely fragile. A small change in the system can cause a radical change in the whole, such as when a decrease in temperature can cause ice to form on the wing of a DC-9 and ultimately cause the plane to crash. He writes: "Both Merleau-Ponty's ontology and chaos theory not only face the implications of mortality that undoing the dualistic retreat from matter entails, but both conceive of matter as itself part of a dynamic, unfolding open system of forces. Thus, they reveal, for the first time, the authentic fragility of both human and nonhuman existence" (237). Just as a simple change in the environment can cause an airplane to crash, so Being, it is claimed, can become radically different from its present condition by means of a simple shift in the way that it divides itself and creates a world for us. But chaos theory suggests that order follows contingency in the form of arbitrariness; it is totally arbitrary that ice begins to build on the wing, or that pressure mounts when exchanged in a feedback loop. By contrast, there is an interiority to flesh that is lacking in a chaotic structure, suggesting that Being does not simply happen to be structured a certain way, but imagines that structure from within (VI 151/VIF 198).

26. Merleau-Ponty is here commenting on Husserl's use of Leibniz's notion of possible worlds. Elsewhere, he writes: "Every evocation of possible worlds refers to a way of seeing our own world (*Weltanschauung*). Every possibility is a variant of our reality, an effective possibility of reality (*Möglichkeit an Wirklichkeit*)" (S 180/SF 227–28).

27. The essentially virtual character of flesh as the "sensible" is particularly shown in the following: "There are certainly more things in the world and in us than what is perceptible in the narrow sense of the term. . . . Sensible being is not only things but also everything sketched out there, even virtually, everything which leaves its trace there, everything which figures there, even as divergence and a certain absence" (S 171–72/SF 216–17); see also PrP 7/INF 405.

28. Dillon, *Merleau-Ponty's Ontology*, 241. It is more accurate, however, to say "abyss" than "chaos" in this context.

29. See also Marc Richir, *Phénomènes, temps et êtres: Ontologie et phénoménologie* (Grenoble: Jerôme Millon, 1987), 84–85.

188   Notes to Pages 153–58

30. See also Madison, *The Phenomenology of Merleau-Ponty* (Athens: Ohio State University Press, 1981), 212.

31. Barbaras, *Le tournant de l'expérience*, 221.

32. Barbaras calls it an "originary inscription of being" (ibid., 258).

33. Richir describes them as being "'upstream' from concepts and ideas" (ibid., 47).

34. Barbaras, *Le tournant de l'expérience*, 251.

35. Jacques Garelli, *Rhythmes et mondes: Au revers de l'identité et de l'alterité* (Grenoble: Jerôme Millon, 1991), 359–60. One is reminded here of Baudrillard's simulacra as an implosion of being to the level of DNA where everything is simply doubled (see the previous chapter). This is clearly not what Garelli has in mind. See esp. 358, where he explains that there is an essential gravity to metastability that is reminiscent of the verticality that was discussed in the last chapter.

36. See Richir, *Phénomènes*, 67–103; Garelli, *Rhythmes et mondes*, 359–72; VI 105–29/VIF 142–71.

37. Richir, *Phénomènes*, 78–79.

38. Ibid., 102.

39. Jocelyn Lebrun, "Pour une phénoménologie de l'imagination poétique," *Archives de Philosophie* 51 (1988): 207.

40. Madison, *The Phenomenology of Merleau-Ponty*, 265.

41. John Russon, "Embodiment and Responsibility: Merleau-Ponty and the Ontology of Nature," *Man and World* 27, no. 3 (1994): 294–95.

42. This does not make ontology anthropocentric, because it is not man who first poses the question of Being. Merleau-Ponty reminds us that "it is indeed a paradox of Being, not a paradox of man, that we are dealing with here" (VI 136/ VIF 180). Thus, even though humanity, in the form of embodied consciousness, has a privileged position as the site for Being's indirect reflection on itself (through the medium of flesh and its reversibilities), it remains an interrogation that is begun by Being — a problem posed, and a domain imagined, from the heart of Being itself.

43. Gaston Bachelard, *On Poetic Imagination and Reverie*, ed. and trans. Colette Gaudin (Indianapolis: Bobbs-Merrill, 1971), 77.

44. Stefan George, "Words," in Heidegger, *On The Way to Language*, trans. Peter D. Hertz (New York: Harper & Row, 1971), 140.

45. A. de Saint-Exupery, quoted in PP 456.

Bibliography

Abram, David. *The Spell of the Sensuous: Perception and Language in a More-Than-Human World*. New York: Pantheon, 1996.

Arnheim, Rudolf. *Visual Thinking*. Berkeley and Los Angeles: University of California Press, 1969.

Bachelard, Gaston. *On Poetic Imagination and Reverie*. Edited and translated by Colette Gaudin. Indianapolis: Bobbs-Merrill, 1971.

———. *The Poetics of Space*. Translated by Maria Jolas. Boston: Beacon Press, 1964.

Bannan. John. *The Philosophy of Merleau-Ponty*. New York: Harcourt, Brace and World, 1967.

Barbaras, Renaud. *Le tournant de l'expérience: Recherches sur la philosophie de Merleau-Ponty*. Paris: J. Vrin, 1998.

Barral, Mary Rose. *Merleau-Ponty: The Role of the Body-Subject in Interpersonal Relations*. Pittsburgh: Duquesne University Press, 1965.

Barry, John. "The Textual Body: Incorporating Writing and Flesh," *Philosophy Today* 30 (1986): 16–31.

Baudrillard, Jean. *Simulations*. Translated by Paul Foss, Paul Patton and Philip Beitchman. New York: Semiotext(e), 1983.

Benhabib, Seyla. *Situating the Self: Gender, Community, and Post-modernism in Contemporary Ethics*. New York: Routledge, 1991.

Bermudéz, José, Anthony Marcel and Naomi Eilan, eds. *The Body and the Self*. Cambridge, Mass.: MIT Press, 1995.

190 Bibliography

Block, Ned. "Introduction: What Is the Issue?" In *Imagery*, edited by Ned Block, 1–18. Cambridge, Mass.: MIT Press, 1981.

Block, Ned, ed. *Imagery*. Cambridge, Mass.: MIT Press, 1981.

Brown, Roger, and Richard Herrnstein. "Icons and Images." In *Imagery*, edited by Ned Block, 19–50. Cambridge, Mass.: MIT Press, 1981.

Burke, Patrick, and Jan Van Der Veken, eds. *Merleau-Ponty in Contemporary Perspective*. Boston: Kluwer Academic Publishers, 1993.

Busch, Thomas. *Circulating Being: From Embodiment to Incorporation*. New York: Fordham University Press, 1999.

Busch, Thomas, and Shaun Gallagher, eds. *Merleau-Ponty, Hermeneutics and Postmodernism*. Albany: State University of New York Press, 1992.

Butler, Judith. *Bodies That Matter: On the Discursive Limits of "Sex."* New York: Routledge, 1993.

―――. *The Psychic Life of Power: Theories of Subjection*. Stanford, Calif.: Stanford University Press, 1997.

Carné, Marcel, director. *Les enfants du paradis*. Paris: Pathe Cinema, 1945.

Casey, Edward. "Habitual Body and Memory in Merleau-Ponty." *Man and World* 17 (1984): 279–97.

―――. *Imagining: A Phenomenological Study*. Bloomington: Indiana University Press, 1976.

―――. "Sartre on Imagination." In *The Philosophy of Jean-Paul Sartre*, edited by Paul Arthur Schlipp. Vol. 16. The Library of Living Philosophers. La Salle, Ill.: Open Court Publishers, 1981.

―――. "The Unconscious Mind and the Prereflective Body." In *Merleau-Ponty, Interiority and Exteriority, Psychic Life and the World*, edited by Dorothea Olkowski and James Morley. Albany: State University of New York Press, 1999.

Cocking, J. M. *Imagination: A Study in the History of Ideas*. New York: Routledge, 1991.

Cohen, Richard. "Merleau-Ponty, the Flesh and Foucault." *Philosophy Today* 28 (1984): 329–38.

Coleridge, Samuel Taylor. *Biographia literaria*. Vol. 1. Edited by J. Shawcross. Oxford: Oxford University Press, 1973.

Currie, Gregory. *Image and Mind: Film, Philosophy and Cognitive Science*. Cambridge: Cambridge University Press, 1995.

Dastur, Françoise. "Perceptual Faith and the Invisible." *Journal of the British Society for Phenomenology* 25 (1994): 44–52.

Dennett, Daniel. "The Nature of Images and the Introspective Trap." In *Imagery,* edited by Ned Block, 51–62. Cambridge, Mass.: MIT Press, 1981.

———. "Two Approaches to Mental Images." In *Imagery*, edited by Ned Block, 87–108. Cambridge, Mass.: MIT Press, 1981.

Denny-Brown, D., J. S. Meyer and S. Horenstein. "The Significance of Perceptual Rivalry Resulting from Parietal Lesion." *Brain* 75 (1952): 433–71.

Derrida, Jacques. *Dissemination.* Translated by Barbara Johnson. Chicago: University of Chicago Press, 1981.

Descartes, René. *Discourse on Method, Optics, Geometry, and Meteorology.* Translated by Paul Olscamp. Indianapolis: Bobbs-Merrill, 1965.

Dillon, Martin. "Écart: A Reply to Claude Lefort's 'Flesh and Otherness.' " In *Ontology and Alterity in Merleau-Ponty*, edited by Galen Johnson and Michael B. Smith, 14–26. Evanston, Ill.: Northwestern University Press, 1990.

———. "Merleau-Ponty and the Psychogenesis of the Self." *Journal of Phenomenological Psychology* 9 (1978): 84–98.

———. *Merleau-Ponty's Ontology.* Bloomington: Indiana University Press, 1988.

———. "The Unconscious: Language and World." In *Merleau-Ponty in Contemporary Perspective,* edited by Patrick Burke and Jan van der Veken, 69–83. Boston: Kluwer Academic Publishers, 1993.

Dillon, M. C., ed. *Écart & Différance: Merleau-Ponty and Derrida on Seeing and Writing.* Atlantic Highlands, N.J.: Humanities Press, 1997.

———. *Merleau-Ponty Vivant.* Albany: State University of New York Press, 1991.

Dreyfus, Hubert. "The Current Relevance of Merleau-Ponty's Phenomenology of Embodiment." *The Electronic Journal of Analytic Philosophy* 4 (1996).

Ekman, Paul, and Dacher Keltner. "Universal Facial Expressions of Emotions: An Old Controversy and New Findings." In *Nonverbal Communication: Where Nature Meets Nurture*, edited by Ullica Segerstrale and Peter Molnar, 27–46. Mahwah, N.J.: Lawrence Erlbaum Associates, 1997.

Fanon, Frantz. *Black Skin White Masks*. Translated by Charles Lam Markmann. New York: Grove Weidenfeld, 1967.

Fast, Julias. *Body Language*. Richmond Hill, Ontario: Simon & Schuster, 1971.

Fielding, Helen. "Envisioning the Other: Lacan and Merleau-Ponty on Intersubjectivity." In *Merleau-Ponty, Interiority and Exteriority, Psychic Life and the World*, edited by Dorothea Olkowski and James Morley. Albany: State University of New York Press, 1999.

Finke, Ronald, and Marty Schmidt. "Orientation-Specific Color After-effects Following Imagination." *Journal of Experimental Psychology: Human Perception and Performance* 3, no. 4 (1977): 599–606.

Fisher, Seymour. *Body Consciousness*. Englewood Cliffs, N.J.: Prentice-Hall, 1973.

Fisher, Seymour, and Sidney E. Cleveland. *Body Image and Personality*. 2nd rev. ed. New York: Dover, 1968.

Flynn, Bernard. "Textuality and the Flesh: Derrida and Merleau-Ponty." *Journal of the British Society for Phenomenology* 15, no. 2 (1984): 164–79.

Flynn, Thomas. "The Role of the Image in Sartre's Aesthetic." *Journal of Aesthetics and Art Criticism* 33 (1975): 431–42.

Fodor, Jerry. "Imagistic Representation." In *Imagery*, edited by Ned Block, 63–86. Cambridge, Mass.: MIT Press, 1981.

Freud, Sigmund. *Civilization and Its Discontents*. Edited by James Strachey. Translated by Joan Riviere. London: Hogarth Press, 1963.

———. *Leonardo da Vinci: A Study in Psychosexuality*. Translated by A. A. Brill. New York: Vintage, 1947.

Freud, Sigmund, and Josef Breuer. *Studies on Hysteria*. Edited and translated by James Strachey and Alix Strachey. Harmondsworth: Penguin Books, 1974.

Gallagher, Shaun. "Body Schema and Intentionality." In *The Body and the Self*. Edited by José Bermudéz et al. Cambridge, Mass.: MIT Press, 1995.

Gallagher, Shaun, and Jonathan Cole. "Body Image and Body Schema in a Deafferented Subject." *The Journal of Mind and Behavior* 16 (1995): 369–80.

Gallagher, Shaun, and Andrew Meltzoff. "The Earliest Sense of Self and Others: Merleau-Ponty and Recent Developmental Studies." *Philosophical Psychology* 9 (1996): 211–33.

Garelli, Jacques. *Rhythmes et mondes: Au revers de l'identité et de l'alterité*. Grenoble: Jerôme Millon, 1991.

———. "Voir ceci et voir selon." In *Merleau-Ponty: Phénoménologie et expériences*. Edited by Marc Richir and Etienne Tassin. Grenoble: Jerôme Millon, 1992.

George, Stefan. "Words." In Heidegger, *On the Way to Language*, translated by Peter D. Hertz. New York: Harper & Row, 1971.

Gilbert, E. Reid. *The Art of Mime*. Video. Colorado Springs: Meriwether, 1991.

Gilgen, Albert. "The Nature, Function, and Description of Sensation, Perception, Feeling, and Imagery." In *Imagery: Theoretical and Clinical Applications*. Vol. 3. Edited by Joseph Shorr, Gail Sobel-Whittington, Penee Robin and Jack Connella, 53–62. New York: Plenum, 1983.

Gill, Jerry. *Merleau-Ponty and Metaphor*. Atlantic Highlands, N.J.: Humanities Press, 1991.

Gilligan, Carol. "Woman's Place in Man's Life Cycle." In *The Hidden Curriculum and Moral Education*, edited by Henry Giroux and David Purpel, 209–28. Berkeley: McCutchan, 1983.

Girard, François, and Don McKellar. *Thirty-Two Short Films about Glenn Gould*. Toronto: Coach House Press, 1995.

Hegel, G. W. F. *Phenomenology of Spirit*. Translated by A. V. Miller. Oxford: Oxford University Press, 1977.

Heidegger, Martin. *Basic Writings*. Edited by David Farrell Krell. San Francisco: Harper Collins, 1993.

———. *Being and Time*. Translated by John Macquarrie and Edward Robinson. San Francisco: Harper Collins, 1962.

———. *On the Way to Language*. Translated by Peter D. Hertz. New York: Harper & Row, 1971.

Holland, Nancy. "Merleau-Ponty on Presence: A Derridian Reading." *Research in Phenomenology* 16 (1986): 111–20.

Hume, David. *A Treatise of Human Nature*. Edited by L. A. Selby-Bigge. Oxford: Clarendon Press, 1975.

Husserl, Edmund. *The Crisis of European Sciences and Transcendental Phenomenology*. Translated by David Carr. Evanston, Ill.: Northwestern University Press, 1970.

———. *Ideas: General Introduction to Pure Phenomenology*. Translated by W. R. Boyce Gibson. New York: Collier, 1962.

Irigaray, Luce. "And the One Doesn't Stir without the Other." *Signs* 7, no. 1 (1981): 60–67.

———. "The Invisible of the Flesh." In *An Ethics of Sexual Difference,* translated by Carolyn Burke and Gillian Gill. Ithaca, N.Y.: Cornell University Press, 1993.

Jay, Martin. "Sartre, Merleau-Ponty, and the Search for a New Ontology of Sight." In *Modernity and the Hegemony of Vision*, edited by David Michael Levin. Berkeley and Los Angeles: University of California Press, 1993.

Johnson, Galen, ed. *The Merleau-Ponty Aesthetics Reader: Philosophy and Painting*. Evanston, Ill.: Northwestern University Press, 1993.

Johnson, Galen, and Michael B. Smith, eds. *Ontology and Alterity in Merleau-Ponty*. Evanston, Ill.: Northwestern University Press, 1990.

Johnson, Mark. *The Body in the Mind*. Chicago: University of Chicago Press, 1987.

Kant, Immanuel, *Critique of Judgment*. Translated by J. M. Bernard. New York: Hafner, 1951.

———. *Critique of Pure Reason*. Translated by J. M. D. Meiklejohn. Rutland, Vt.: Charles E. Tuttle, 1991.

Kearney, Richard. *Poetics of Imagining: Modern to Postmodern*. New York: Fordham University Press, 1998.

———. *The Wake of Imagination*. Minneapolis: University of Minnesota Press, 1988.

Kosslyn, Stephen, Steven Pinker, George Smith and Steven Schwartz. "On the Demystification of Mental Imagery." In *Imagery*, edited by Ned Block, 131–50. Cambridge, Mass.: MIT Press, 1981.

Kwant, Remi C. *The Phenomenological Philosophy of Merleau-Ponty*. Pittsburgh: Duquesne University Press, 1963.

Lacan, Jacques. "Maurice Merleau-Ponty." *Les Temps Modernes*, nos. 184–85 (1961): 245–54.

———. "The Mirror Stage as Formative of the Function of the I as Revealed in Psychoanalytic Experience." In *Écrits: A Selection,* edited and translated by Alan Sheridan. New York: W. W. Norton, 1977.

Lakoff, George, and Mark Johnson. *Metaphors We Live By.* Chicago: University of Chicago Press, 1980.

Leabhart, Thomas. *Modern and Post-modern Mime.* New York: St. Martin's Press, 1989.

Lebrun, Jocelyn. "Pour une phénoménologie de l'imagination poétique." *Archives de Philosophie* 51 (1988): 195–211.

Leder, Drew. *The Absent Body.* Chicago: University of Chicago Press, 1990.

———. "Flesh and Blood: A Proposed Supplement to Merleau-Ponty." *Human Studies* 13, no. 3 (1990): 209–19.

Lefort, Claude. "Flesh and Otherness." In *Ontology and Alterity in Merleau-Ponty,* edited by Galen Johnson and Michael B. Smith, 3–13. Evanston, Ill.: Northwestern University Press, 1990.

———. *Sur une colonne absente: Écrits autour de Merleau-Ponty.* Paris: Gallimard, 1978.

Levin, David Michael. "Visions of Narcissism: Intersubjectivity and the Reversals of Vision." In *Merleau-Ponty Vivant,* edited by M. C. Dillon. Albany: State University of New York Press, 1991.

Loeschke, Maravene Sheppard. *All about Mime.* Englewood Cliffs, N.J.: Prentice-Hall, 1982.

Love, Nancy. "Politics and Voice(s): An Empowerment Knowledge Regime." *Differences* 3, no. 1 (1991): 92–102.

Madison, Gary. "Did Merleau-Ponty Have a Theory of Perception?" In *Merleau-Ponty, Hermeneutics, and Postmodernism,* edited by Thomas Busch and Shaun Gallagher. Albany: State University of New York Press, 1992.

———. *The Hermeneutics of Postmodernity: Figures and Themes.* Bloomington: Indiana University Press, 1993.

———. "Merleau-Ponty and Derrida: *La différence.*" In *Écart & Différance: Merleau-Ponty and Derrida on Seeing and Writing,* edited by M. C. Dillon. Atlantic Highlands, N.J.: Humanities Press, 1997.

———. *The Phenomenology of Merleau-Ponty.* Athens: Ohio State University Press, 1981.

Makkreel, Rudolf. *Imagination and Interpretation in Kant*. Chicago: University of Chicago Press, 1990.

Malevich, Kasimir. "Suprematism." In *Modern Artists on Art: Ten Unabridged Essays*, edited by Robert Herbert. Englewood Cliffs, N.J.: Prentice-Hall, 1964.

Mallin, Samuel. *Merleau-Ponty's Philosophy*. New Haven, Conn.: Yale University Press, 1979.

Malraux, André. *The Voices of Silence*. Translated by Stuart Gilbert. Garden City, N.Y.: Doubleday, 1953.

Manser, Anthony. *Sartre: A Philosophical Study*. New York: Oxford University Press, 1966.

Martin, Ben. *Marcel Marceau: Master of Mime*. Ottawa: Optimum Publishing Co. Ltd., 1978.

Mazis, Glen A. "Chaos Theory and Merleau-Ponty's Ontology: Beyond the Dead Father's Paralysis toward a Dynamic and Fragile Materiality." In *Merleau-Ponty, Interiority and Exteriority, Psychic Life and the World*, edited by Dorothea Olkowski and James Morley, 219–41. Albany: State University of New York Press, 1999.

———. "*La Chair et L'Imaginaire*: The Developing Role of Imagination in Merleau-Ponty's Philosophy." *Philosophy Today* 32 (1988): 30–42.

———. "Touch and Vision: Rethinking with Merleau-Ponty Sartre on the Caress." In *The Debate between Sartre and Merleau-Ponty*, edited by Jon Stewart, 144–53. Evanston, Ill.: Northwestern University Press, 1998.

McCleary, Richard. *Imagination's Body*. Washington, D.C.: University Press of America, 1986.

Meltzoff, Andrew, and Keith M. Moore. "Infant's Understanding of People and Things: From Body Imitation to Folk Psychology." In *The Body and the Self*, edited by José Bermudéz, Anthony Marcel and Naomi Eilan, 43–65. Cambridge, Mass.: MIT Press, 1995.

Morley, James. "The Imaginary Texture of the Real: Merleau-Ponty on Imagination and Psychopathology." In *Imagination and Its Pathologies*, edited by James Phillips and James Morley. Cambridge, Mass.: MIT Press, 2003.

———. "The Private Theater: A Phenomenological Investigation of Daydreaming." *Journal of Phenomenological Psychology* 29, no. 1 (1998): 116–34.

―――. "The Sleeping Subject: Merleau-Ponty on Dreaming." *Theory & Psychology* 9, no. 1 (1999): 89–101.

Mullarkey, John. "Duplicity in the Flesh: Bergson and Current Philosophy of the Body." *Philosophy Today* 38, no. 4 (1994): 339–55.

Munchow, Alan. "Seeing Otherwise: Merleau-Ponty's Line." *Journal of the British Society for Phenomenology* 25 (1994): 64–73.

Murray, Edward. *Imaginative Thinking and Human Existence*. Pittsburgh: Duquesne University Press, 1986.

Olkowski, Dorothea, and James Morley, eds. *Merleau-Ponty, Interiority and Exteriority, Psychic Life and the World*. Albany: State University of New York Press, 1999.

Papousek, Hanus, and Mechthild Papousek. "Preverbal Communication in Humans and the Genesis of Culture." In *Nonverbal Communication: Where Nature Meets Nurture*, edited by Ullica Segerstrale and Peter Molnar, 87–107. New Jersey: Lawrence Erlbaum, 1997.

Perky, C. W. "An Experimental Study of Imagination." *American Journal of Psychology* 21 (1910): 422–52.

Pettigrew, David. "Merleau-Ponty and the Unconscious." In *Merleau-Ponty, Interiority and Exteriority, Psychic Life and the World*, edited by Dorothea Olkowski and James Morley, 57–68. Albany: State University of New York Press, 1999.

Qualls, Penelope. "On the Physiological Measurement of Imagery: An Overview." In *Imagery: Theoretical and Clinical Applications*, vol. 3, edited by Joseph Shorr et al., 39–51. New York: Plenum, 1983.

Richir, Marc. "Merleau-Ponty and the Question of Phenomenological Architectonics." In *Merleau-Ponty in Contemporary Perspective*, edited by Patrick Burke and Jan Van der Veken, 37–50. Boston: Kluwer Academic Publishers, 1993.

―――. *Phénomènes, temps et êtres: Ontologie et phénoménologie*. Grenoble: Jerôme Millon, 1987.

Richir, Marc, and Etienne Tassin, eds. *Merleau-Ponty, phénoménologie et expériences*. Grenoble: Jerôme Millon, 1992.

Ricoeur, Paul. *Hermeneutics and the Human Sciences*. Edited and translated by John Thompson. Cambridge: Cambridge University Press, 1981.

―――. "Hommage a Merleau-Ponty." *Esprit*, no. 296 (1961): 1115–20.

198 Bibliography

————. "Imagination in Discourse and Action." In *From Text to Action,* translated by Kathleen Blamey and John Thompson, 168–87. Evanston, Ill.: Northwestern University Press, 1991.

————. "On Interpretation." In *Philosophy in France Today*, edited by Alan Montefiore, translated by Kathleen McLaughlin, 175–96. Cambridge: Cambridge University Press, 1983.

————. "Sartre and Ryle on the Imagination." In *The Philosophy of Jean-Paul Sartre*, vol. 16, The Library of Living Philosophers, edited by Paul Arthur Schlipp, translated by R. Bradley Deford, 167–78. La Salle, Ill.: Open Court, 1981.

Riggio, Ronald. "Social Interaction Skills and Nonverbal Behavior." In *Applications of Nonverbal Behavioral Theories*, edited by Robert Feldman, 3–19. New Jersey: Lawrence Erlbaum, 1992.

Ring, Merrill. *Beginning with the Presocratics*. Mountain View, Calif.: Mayfield, 1987.

Robinson, T. M. *Heraclitus: Fragments*. Toronto: University of Toronto Press, 1987.

Russon, John. "Embodiment and Responsibility: Merleau-Ponty and the Ontology of Nature." *Man and World* 27, no. 3 (1994): 291–308.

Ryle, Gilbert. *The Concept of Mind*. Harmondsworth, Middlesex: Penguin Books, 1963.

Sallis, John. *Force of Imagination: The Sense of the Elemental*. Bloomington: Indiana University Press, 2000.

Sartre, Jean-Paul. *Being and Nothingness*. Translated by Hazel Barnes. New York: Washington Square Press, 1956.

————. *Imagination*. Translated by Forrest Williams. Ann Arbor: University of Michigan Press, 1972.

————. *The Psychology of Imagination*. 4th ed. New York: The Citadel Press, 1965.

————. *What Is Literature?* Translated by Steven Ungar. Cambridge, Mass.: Harvard University Press, 1988.

Schlipp, Paul Arthur, ed. *The Philosophy of Jean-Paul Sartre*. Vol. 16, The Library of Living Philosophers. La Salle, Ill.: Open Court, 1981.

Segerstrale, Ullica, and Peter Molnar. "Nonverbal Communication: Where Nature Meets Nurture." In *Nonverbal Communication: Where Nature Meets Nurture*, edited by Ullica Segerstrale and Peter Molnar, 1–21. New Jersey: Lawrence Erlbaum, 1997.

Segerstrale, Ullica, and Peter Molnar, eds. *Nonverbal Communication: Where Nature Meets Nurture*. New Jersey: Lawrence Erlbaum, 1997.

Sheets-Johnstone, Maxine. *The Phenomenology of Dance*. Madison: University of Wisconsin Press, 1966.

Shorr, Joseph, Gail Sobel-Whittington, Pennee Robin and Jack Connella, eds. *Imagery: Theoretical and Clinical Applications*. Vol. 3. New York: Plenum, 1983.

Silverman, Hugh J., and James Barry Jr., eds. *Merleau-Ponty: Texts and Dialogues*. Atlantic Highlands, N.J.: Humanities Press, 1992.

Singer, Jerome. *Daydreaming: An Introduction to the Experimental Study of Inner Experience*. New York: Random House, 1966.

———. "Towards the Scientific Study of Imagination." In *Imagery: Theoretical and Clinical Applications*, vol. 3, edited by Joseph Shorr et al., 3–27. New York: Plenum, 1983.

Singer, Linda. "Merleau-Ponty on the Concept of Style." *Man and World* 14 (1981): 153–63.

Smith, Michael B. "Transcendence in Merleau-Ponty." In *Merleau-Ponty, Interiority and Exteriority, Psychic Life and the World*, edited by Dorothea Olkowski and James Morley. Albany: State University of New York Press, 1999.

Stewart, Jon, ed. *The Debate between Sartre and Merleau-Ponty*. Evanston, Ill.: Northwestern University Press, 1998.

Strawson, Peter. *Freedom and Resentment and Other Essays*, 103–16. London: Methuen, 1974.

Tiemersma, Douwe. "'Body-Image' and 'Body-Schema' in the Existential Phenomenology of Merleau-Ponty." *Journal of the British Society for Phenomenology* 13 (1982): 246–55.

Tolstoy, Leo. *What Is Art?* Translated by A. Maude. Oxford: Oxford University Press, 1955.

Van den Berg, J. H. "An Existential Explanation of the Guided Daydream in Psychotherapy." *Review of Existential Psychology and Psychiatry* 2 (1962): 5–35.

Vasari, Giorgio. *The Lives of the Artists*. Translated by George Bull. Harmondsworth: Penguin Books, 1965.

Vlastos, G. "On Heraclitus." *American Journal of Philology* 76 (1955): 337–68.

Walker, Katherine Sorley. *Eyes on Mime*. New York: John Day, 1969.

200 Bibliography

Walton, Kendall. *Mimesis as Make-Believe: On the Foundations of the Representational Arts*. Cambridge, Mass.: Harvard University Press, 1990.

Warnock, Mary. *Imagination*. London: Faber & Faber, 1976.

———. "The Imagination in Sartre." In *Existentialist Ontology and Human Consciousness*, edited byWilliam McBride, 103–16. New York: Garland Press, 1997.

Weiss, Gail. *Body Images: Embodiment as Intercorporeality*. New York: Routledge, 1999.

Welsh, Talia. "The Logic of the Observed: Merleau-Ponty's Conception of Women as Outlined in His 1951–1952 Sorbonne Lecture, 'The Question of Method in Child Psychology.'" *Symposium* 5, no. 1 (2001): 83–94.

Westphal, Merold. "Situation and Suspicion in the Thought of Merleau-Ponty: The Question of Phenomenology and Politics." In *Ontology and Alterity*, edited by Galen Johnson and Michael B. Smith, 158–79. Evanston, Ill.: Northwestern University Press, 1990.

White, Alan. *The Language of Imagination*. Cambridge: Basil Blackwell, 1990.

Wittgenstein, Ludwig. *Philosophical Investigations*. Edited by G. E. M. Anscombe. Oxford: Basil Blackwell, 1958.

Yamagata, Yorihiro. "The Self or the Cogito in Kinaesthesis." In *Self-Awareness, Temporality, and Alterity*, edited by Dan Zahavi, 9–19. Boston: Kluwer Academic Publishers, 1998.

Yeo, Michael T. "Creative Adequation: Merleau-Ponty's Philosophy of Philosophy." Ph.D. diss., McMaster University, 1987.

Young, Iris. "Asymmetrical Reciprocity: On Moral Respect, Wonder, and Enlarged Thought." *Constellations* 3, no. 3 (1996): 340–65.

———. *Throwing Like a Girl and Other Essays in Feminist Philosophy and Social Theory*. Bloomington: Indiana University Press, 1990.

Zaner, Richard. *The Problem of Embodiment*. The Hague: Martinus Nijhoff, 1964.

Index

aboriginal communities and nature, 126
Abram, David, 124, 135, 143
absence: of body, 24–26, 149; in perception, 47
acting, professional, 26
aesthetic experience, 7–8
aesthetics. *See* art
affective relations, 108–9
air, 10, 124–25
ambiguity: in body, 15, 18–19, 139–41, 143; of experience, 93–96; and neurosis, 96; in perception, 34–36, 143–44
amputation, 20–21
Anaximander, 125, 152
anchorage, 15–16
animism, 144
anonymity of individual, 105, 179 n. 4, 179 n. 5
anthropocentrism, 188 n. 42
Antrobus, J. S., 71
apeiron, 125, 152, 153
appearances, 11, 138, 141–42
archetypes, 132–33
art, 6, 7–8, 51–66; Being approached through, 155; body and significance of, 59–66; elemental images and, 130–31; expressive function of, 55–56; Impressionist, 39, 51, 55; meaning of, 56; Merleau-Ponty and, 52; mimetic function of, 52–54; Renaissance, 51; representation/expression dialectic in, 56–59; style in, 62; technical innovations in, 53–54. *See also* dance; film; literature; poetry
athletics, 61

Bach, J. S., 65
Bachelard, Gaston, 123–24, 126, 154, 157, 183 n. 11
Balzac, Honoré de, 52
Barbaras, Renaud, 42, 44–45, 128–29, 131, 133, 153
Barrault, Jean-Louis, xi, 14
Baudrillard, Jean, 4, 130, 133, 134
becoming, ontology of, 134
behaviorism, 16–17
Being, 137–59; appearing of, 11, 138, 141–42; body and, 145, 156; brute, 141–42; chaos theory and, 187 n. 25; color and, 127; difference as constitutive of, 134; elements and, 127–30, 135, 153; fire and, 125; flesh and, 138, 142–43, 149–51; flesh of the world as bridge to, 127; general expression of, 142; imagination and understanding of, 137; imagining body and, 156–58; language and, 158–59; meaning and, 133–34, 133–34, 156; narcissism of, 157; phenomenology of, 138, 141–42; philosophical inquiry into, xi; as possibility, 152–53; question of, 156, 188 n. 42; self-imagining of, 156–57; transcendence and, 147. *See also* ontology
Bellugue, Paul, 14
Benhabib, Seyla, 112–15
Berkeley, George, 139
Block, Ned, 8, 73
body, 13–31; aesthetic value and, 59–66; ambiguous experiences involving, 15, 139–41, 143; asymmetry of nature and, 144–46; Being and, 145, 156; expressive

capacity of, xi–xii, 2–3, 14, 28–30;
language and, 30; as lived, 18; metaphor and embodiment, 166 n. 35;
perceptual world in relation to, 43–50;
phenomenological analysis of, 14–15;
relation to nature of, 135; and self-
reflection, 145; traditional theories of,
16–17; transcendence of, 147–48;
visceral aspect of, 148–49. *See also*
body at this moment; body concept;
body image; body language; body
schema; flesh; imagining body;
virtual body
body at this moment, 19
body concept, 19
body image, 19, 27–28, 165 n. 28
body language, 28–29. *See also* gestures
body schema, 6–7, 18–31, 162 n. 9; ambiguity in concept of, 18–19, 139–41;
body image versus, 165 n. 28; in
daydreams, 86; genesis of, 165 n. 27;
Merleau-Ponty's definition of, 19; new
body habits and, 21–22; phantom limb
phenomenon and, 20–21; role in
perception of, 45–46; spatial orientation
and, 84; specular image and, 27–28;
virtual body as aspect of, 6–7, 22–30.
See also virtual body
bracketing, in phenomenological analysis,
76–77
brain, 20, 25–26
Brandenburg Concertos (Bach), 65
Breuer, Josef, 9
Brown, S. L., 71
Brunelleschi, Filippo, 53
brute Being, 141–42
brute essences, 153–55
Busch, Thomas, 118, 134, 142
Butler, Judith, 114, 117

caress, 106, 109, 111
Casey, Edward, 4, 8; on imagination,
69–70, 74, 79–80, 82, 86–87, 151–52,
177 n. 46; on psychology, 93
Cézanne, Paul, 40, 52, 55, 57, 58–59, 62, 157
chaos and chaos theory, 149–50, 152, 187
n. 25
Chardin, Jean-Baptiste-Siméon, 54, 62
chimpanzees, 23–24
cinema. *See* film
Cleveland, Sidney, 20–21
Cohen, Richard, 162 n. 9
Cole, Jonathan, 165 n. 28
Coleridge, Samuel Taylor, 4
color: effects on body of, 44; elemental
quality of, 126–27; identification of,
37–39; in Impressionist painting, 39,

57–58; particularity of, 129–30; role in
perceptual structure of, 46–48
color areas, 38
consciousness: imagination and, 70, 75–76;
in psychoanalytic theory, 92; role in neurosis of, 93–94; and transcendence, 146
Copeau, Jacques, 13–14
creativity: in art observers, 66; in
perception, 48–49
cultural factors in self development, 115–19
cultural relativism, 129
customary body: as body schema, 19–20;
dialectic with virtual body of, 26–30, 101

dance, 60–62
Dastur, Françoise, 76
daydreams, 6; functions of, 69; guided, 9,
97–98; spatiality of, 85–86; subjective
aspects of, 85–86. *See also* dreams
deconstructionism, xi
Decroux, Etienne, 13–14
Déjeuner sur l'herbe, Le (Manet), 55
Deleuze, Gilles, 162 n. 9
Dennett, Daniel, 73
Denny-Brown, D., 165 n. 28
Derrida, Jacques, xi
Descartes, René, 53, 168 n. 1
Desoille, Robert, 9, 97
difference: Being's self-differentiation,
134; elements and, 128–29; meaning
and, 133–34; nature and, 128–29;
ontological, 141; between self and
Other, 111–12, 114–15; sexuality and,
118; social position and, 116–17. *See
also écart*
Dillon, Martin, 94, 108–9, 112, 144–46, 152
directionality of spatial perception, 82–86
double sensation, 15–16, 105, 138, 139
dreams: relation to reality of, 90–91; spatiality of, 82–83. *See also* daydreams
Dreyfus, Hubert, 22
Duchamp, Marcel, 52
duck-rabbit image, 87–88

earth, 10, 124
Eastern philosophy, 186 n. 20
écart: flesh and, 142, 145; nature and, 128;
self/Other and, 111–12, 114–15; sexuality and, 118; transcendence and,
147–48. *See also* difference
Ecole du Vieux Colombier, 13
Ekman, Paul, 167 n. 38
elemental images, 130–35; colors as,
126–27; hierarchy among, 129–30;
meaning and, 130–35; metaphor and,
131–32; simulacra and, 130–31
elements, environmental, 10, 121–35; as

Index 203

archetypes, 132–33; Being and, 127–30, 135, 153; difference and, 128–29; elemental images, 130–35; individual character of, 123–25; laws of, 126, 128, 132, 183 n. 11; perception and, 124, 126–27; philosophical treatment of, 124–25; qualities as elements, 129. *See also* air; earth; fire; nature; water
empiricism, 139
Enfants du paradis, Les (film), 14
environment, natural, 10
Epsom Derby (Gericault), 63
essences of Being, 153–55
expression: art as, 55–56; body and, xi–xii, 2–3, 14, 28–30; representation/expression dialectic, 56–59; symbolic, and neurosis, 93–94
Eye and Mind, xi, 139–41

family resemblances, 5–6
fancy, 8, 67–88, 177 n. 46. *See also* imagination
Fanon, Frantz, 117
Fast, Julias, 28
feminist philosophy: on gender differences and self development, 115–19; and uniqueness of individuals, 114
film: imagining body and, 64; Merleau-Ponty and, 52; mime influenced by, 14
fire, 10, 125
Fischer, F., 98
Fisher, Seymour, 20–21
flesh, 11; Being and, 138, 142–43, 149–51, 156; chaos theory and, 187 n. 25; dynamic nature of, 149–50; Eastern philosophy and, 186 n. 20; hierarchy in, 150; as medium, 139–40, 142–43, 145–46, 149–50; as possibility, 151–52; sentient and nonsentient, 145–46; separation as characteristic of, 142–43; transcendence of, 147–48. *See also* body
flesh of the world, 127–28, 135
Flynn, Thomas, 81
Fodor, Jerry, 8, 73
foreshadowing, perceptual, 43
for-itself, 146–47
Foucault, Michel, 162 n. 9
Fragonard, Jean-Honoré, 54, 62
freedom: acquisition of habits and, 22; imagination and, 70
French Royal Academy of Painting and Sculpture, 54, 55
Freud, Sigmund, 4, 9; and art, 52, 57; on body, 162 n. 9; psychoanalytic theory of, 91–93

Gallagher, Shaun, 27, 165 n. 27, 165 n. 28
Garelli, Jacques, 42, 149, 154

gender differences and self development, 115–19
George, Stefan, 158
Gericault, Theodore, 63
Gestalt psychology, 7, 19, 34, 43, 169 n. 11
gestures, 29–30, 161 n. 2, 167 n. 38. *See also* body language
Ghiberti, Lorenzo, 53
Gilgen, Albert, 84
Gilligan, Carol, 115–16
Gould, Glenn, 65
gymnastics, 14

habits, 22
hallucinations, 98–100
Hegel, G. W. F., 111, 137
Heidegger, Martin: on Being/appearances relation, 141; on bridge, 121–22; and four elements, 124, 135; on language and Being, 158; on perception of objects in space, 82; on possibility, 150
history, interpretation of, 95
Horenstein, S., 165 n. 28
horizon, perceptual, 94
Humanism and Terror, 95
Hume, David, 4, 7, 68–69, 73
Husserl, Edmund, 3, 4, 7; on body/world relation, 156; and imaginative variation, 154; lifeworld as concept for, 43; and mathematization of nature, 53; and phenomenological analysis, 14, 76–77; on phenomenological and symbolic domains, 141

idealism, 139
illusions, optical, 35, 36, 87–88
imagination: Being approached through, 137, 155; body image and, 27–28; expressive capacity of body and, 28–30; fancy as aspect of, 87, 177 n. 46; flesh as, 151; functions of, 3–5; general theory of, 5–6; as ground of truth and knowledge, xi–xii; historical treatment of, 3–4; and imagining body, 26–30; material, 124; Merleau-Ponty's theory of, 3–4; and neurosis, 96–98; in phenomenological analysis, 76–77; possibility and, 151–52; and psychosis, 98–101; relation to perception of, 67–88; theories of, 68–73; types of, 78; and virtual body, 6–7, 22–26. *See also* fancy; mental imagery
imaginative variation, 76–78, 154
imagining body, 26–30, 46–50, 59–66, 85–86, 156–58
Impressionism, 39, 51, 55
intellectualism, theory of body in, 16–17
interdisciplinarity, xii

204 Index

interpersonal relations, 9–10
intrauterine experience, 107–8, 110, 112
invisibility. *See* visibility and invisibility
Irigaray, Luce, 107–8, 110, 112, 114

Jay, Martin, 108
Johnson, Mark, 166 n. 35

Kant, Immanuel, 4, 7, 68–69, 76–77
Kearney, Richard, 5
Keltner, Dachler, 167 n. 38
kinesics, 28
kinesthesis, 44–45, 60–62
Klee, Paul, 52, 143
Koehler, Wolfgang, 34
Koffka, K., 34
Kohler, W., 23
Kosslyn, Stephen, 8, 72, 82

Lacan, Jacques, 4, 10, 104, 106–7
language: archetypes and, 133; Being and,
    158–59; body and, 30; difference and,
    128; elemental images and, 131; gestures
    and, 29–30, 167 n. 38; intersubjective
    relations through, 110; material embodi-
    ment of, 134; meaning in, 29–30, 167 n. 37
laws: of elements, 126, 128, 132, 183
    n. 11; of perception, 37, 183 n. 11; of
    synesthesis, 37
learning, 23
Lebrun, Jocelyn, 155
Leder, Drew, 148
Lefort, Claude, 147–48
Leibniz, Gottfried Wilhelm, 150
Lever, J., 116
Levin, David Michael, 107, 112
lifeworld, as context for perception, 43–44
literature, 65–66. *See also* poetry
lived body, 18
Loeschke, Maravene Sheppard, 29, 60
love, 106
Love, Nancy, 114, 115

Madison, Gary, 3, 48, 134–35, 156, 169 n. 6
Malevich, Kasimir, 56
Mallin, Sam, 41, 169 n. 7
Malraux, André, 52, 56, 57
Manet, Edouard, 55
Marceau, Marcel, vii, xi, 14, 31
material imagination, 124
material meanings of things, 122–24
Matisse, Henri, 62
Mazis, Glen, 76, 109, 161 n. 4, 187 n. 25
McCleary, Richard, 177 n. 46
meaning, 130–35, 156
Meltzoff, Andrew, 165 n. 27
memory, 21

mental imagery, 8, 67–74 79–88
Merleau-Ponty, Maurice: art in philosophy
    of, 52; body in philosophy of, 2–3;
    early philosophy of, 161 n. 4; on mirror
    stage, 106–7; ontology in philosophy
    of, 137–38; perception in philosophy
    of, 33, 169 n. 6; phenomenology as
    practiced by, 35–36, 154;
    psychoanalysis in philosophy of, 91
Merleau-Ponty, Maurice, works by: *Eye
    and Mind*, xi, 139–41; *Humanism and
    Terror,* 95; "On Sartre's *Imagination*,"
    75; *Phenomenology of Perception*, xii,
    2, 3, 14–22, 25–26, 29–30, 34–40,
    43–49, 58, 75–79, 82–84, 88, 90–91, 94,
    96, 98–101, 105–6, 133, 156, 158, 168
    n. 2, 183 n. 11, 186 n. 20; *The Primacy
    of Perception*, xii, 54, 58, 63, 78, 105–6,
    125, 128, 130–31, 135, 139–41, 143, 151,
    157, 165 n. 27; *Sense and Non-Sense*, 40,
    57, 64, 65, 157; *Signs*, xii, 46, 48, 49,
    53, 54, 56, 58, 62–63, 66, 106, 118, 133,
    153, 156, 186 n. 20, 187 n. 26; *The
    Structure of Behavior*, xii, 2, 16–17, 20,
    23–24, 34–35, 42, 47, 48, 75, 77–78;
    *Themes from the Lectures at the College
    de France 1952–1960*, 63, 64, 93, 124,
    167 n. 38; *The Visible and the Invisible*,
    xi, 40–42, 44, 76, 94, 99, 106, 110, 111,
    125, 126–27, 131–34, 142, 143–54, 157
metaphor, 131–32
Métius, Jacques, 53
Meyer, J. S., 165 n. 28
mime, art of, xi, 1–2, 5–6, 13–14, 29, 31,
    49–50, 59–60, 158–59
mimetic theory of art, 52–54
Minkowski, Eugene, 98
mirror: and alternative points of view, 23;
    as analogy of reflective behavior,
    109–10; gender differences and mirror
    stage, 116; Lacan and mirror stage in
    psychogenesis, 10, 104–5, 106–7; and
    self-Other relationship, 103, 105–6;
    virtuality of image in, 15
Mondrian, Piet, 14
Monet, Claude, 55, 57
Montagne Sainte-Victoire, 55
Moore, M. Keith, 165 n. 27
Morley, James, 9, 85–86, 100
Moscow Trials, 95
motility and perception, 43–44
motion, representation of, 63–64
Mullarkey, John, 162 n. 9
Müller-Lyer optical illusion, 35, 36
multiple-aspect seeing, 87–88
Munchow, Alan, 59

Murray, Edward, 132
music, 64–65

narcissism, 103–4, 157
nature: asymmetry of body and, 144–46;
    Bachelard on, 123–24; elemental
    perception of, 126–27; elements and
    Being, 127–30; embodiment and, 135;
    phenomenology of, 126; psychoanalysis
    of, 122, 126; Sartre on, 122–23. *See
    also* elements, environmental
neurosis, 6, 9; imagination and, 96–98;
    and mirror stage in psychogenesis, 105;
    psychoanalytic explanation of, 92;
    relation of imagination and reality in, 91
Nietzsche, Friedrich, 4
nonverbal communication, 28–29

object: body and subject/object ambiguity,
    139–41; body as, 17–18; virtual body
    and body as, 24–25
ocularcentrism, 108, 110
"On Sartre's *Imagination*," 75
ontology, xi, 11; and anthropocentrism,
    188 n. 42; Merleau-Ponty and, 137–38.
    See also Being
optical illusions, 35, 36
optics, 168 n. 1
Other: denial in mirror stage of, 111;
    relation of self to, 103–6, 110–15
overdetermination, 92–93

painting. *See* art
Panofsky, Erwin, 52
Papousek, Hanus, 167 n. 38
Papousek, Mechthild, 167 n. 38
pathological behavior, 89–102
Peacock, Christopher, 4
perception, 33–50; ambiguity in, 34–36,
    143–44; art and, 51; body role in,
    43–50; creativity in, 48–49; elemental,
    126–27; flesh and, 138, 139; Gestalt
    psychology theory of, 34–35; and
    kinesthesis, 44–45; laws of, 37, 183
    n. 11; Merleau-Ponty and, 33, 169 n. 6;
    phenomenological analysis of, 35–37,
    49; relation to imagination of, 67–88;
    role of imagination in, 7; synesthesis and,
    37–43; traditional theories of, 34, 46; and
    virtual modes of existence, 46–49
perceptual scene, 43, 45–50
Perky, C. W., 73–74, 86
perspective, linear, 53–54
phantom limb phenomenon, 20–21
phenomenology: of Being, 138, 141–42;
    of body, 14–16; Merleau-Ponty's
    version of, 35–36, 154; of nature, 126;

of perception, 35–37, 49; role of
    imagination in, 76–77
Phenomenology of Perception, xii, 2, 3,
    14–22, 25–26, 29–30, 34–40, 43–49,
    58, 75–79, 82–84, 88, 90–91, 94, 96,
    98–101, 105–6, 133, 156, 158, 168 n. 2,
    183 n. 11, 186 n. 20
philosophy: ad hoc approach to, xii;
    postmodern, xi; relation to Being of,
    155; and silence, 158–59
photography, 14
physiological movements and imagination, 71
physiotherapy, body image and, 27
Pissarro, Camille, 55
poetry, 30, 48
Pollock, Jackson, 62
possibility, 150–53
possible worlds, 150, 187 n. 26
postmodern philosophy, xi
presence: in perception, 47; philosophy of,
    xi–xii
pre-Socratic philosophers, 124, 126, 128, 152
pretense, 71–72
Primacy of Perception, The, xii, 54, 58,
    63, 78, 105–6, 125, 128, 130–31, 135,
    139–41, 143, 151, 157, 165 n. 27
Proust, Marcel, 52
psychism, 144
psychoanalysis, 9; Freud and, 91–93;
    Lacan versus Merleau-Ponty over, 107;
    and nature, 122; therapeutic
    applications, 96–98
psychogenesis. *See* self, sense of
psychosis, 6, 9, 98–101
pure description. *See* phenomenology

qualities, perceptual, 7; effects on lived
    experience of, 44; as elements, 129;
    phenomenological analysis of, 40–42;
    in traditional theories of perception, 34;
    as virtual modes of existence, 47–48
question of Being, 156, 188 n. 42

race and self development, 117
reading, body and, 65–66
realism: artistic, 52–55; elemental images
    and, 130–31
reflection. *See* self-reflection
relativism, cultural, 129
representation: elemental images and,
    130–31; expression/representation
    dialectic, 56–59; mimetic function of
    art, 52–54; simulacra and, 130
reversibility: of elements, 128–29; flesh
    and, 138; in experience, 128; self-Other
    relation and, 105–6, 110–15, 179 n. 5

Richir, Marc, 129, 141, 155
Ricoeur, Paul, 131, 135, 154
Rodin, Auguste, 52
Rouen Cathedral, 55
Russon, John, 156
Ryle, Gilbert, 4, 8, 70, 71

Sade, Marquis de, 162 n. 9
Sallis, John, 124, 125, 138, 141–42
Salon des Refusés, 55
Sartre, Jean-Paul, xi, 3, 4, 8; on art, 56; on
    imagination, 68, 70, 72, 74–78, 80–82,
    86–88, 151–52, 177 n. 46; on nature,
    122–23; and phenomenology, 154
Saussure, Ferdinand de, 29, 167 n. 37
Schilder, Paul, 18–19
Schneider (brain injury patient), 25–26
Schröder (psychologist), 98
Schwartz, G. E., 71
science, criticism of, 168 n. 2
self, sense of, 9–10, 103–19; criticism of
    role of vision in development of,
    107–12; gender differences and, 115–19;
    mirror stage in development of, 103–7;
    relation to Other and, 103–6, 110–15
self-reflection, body and, 145
Sense and Non-Sense, 40, 57, 64, 65, 157
sensible world, 36–37, 49, 57–59
Seurat, Georges, 38
sexuality, 118
Sheets-Johnstone, Maxine, 60–61
signifiers, 130
Signs, xii, 46, 48, 49, 53, 54, 56, 58,
    62–63, 66, 106, 118, 133, 153, 156,
    186 n. 20, 187 n. 26
silence, philosophy and, 158–59
simulacra, 130, 133
Singer, Jerome, 8, 9, 67, 69, 71, 84, 97, 102
slime, 123–24
Smith, Colin, 82
Smith, Michael B., 146
space: artistic depiction of, 54; daydreams
    and, 85–86; directionality of perception
    in, 82–86; dreams and, 82–83; human
    significance of, 82; mental imagery and,
    72–73, 79–88
specular image, 27–28
Stalin, Joseph, 95
stereotypes, social, 116–17
Stratton, George Malcolm, 83
Strawson, Peter, 4
Structure of Behavior, The, xii, 2, 16–17,
    20, 23–24, 34–35, 42, 47, 48, 75, 77–78

style, artistic, 62
subject, 17–18, 24–25, 139–41, 147
symbolic expression, 93–94, 167 n. 38
sympathy, 105–6, 179 n. 5
synesthesis: examples of, 37, 39–42, 169
    n. 7

Themes from the Lectures at the College
    de France 1952–1960, 63, 64, 93, 124,
    167 n. 38
therapy, psychological, 96–98
time, in representation of motion, 63–64
Tolstoy, Leo, 55
tools, use of, 23–24
transcendence, 146–48
truth, xii, 134–35

unconscious, Merleau-Ponty on concept
    of, 92–94

van den Berg, J. H., 9, 97
Verry, Pierre, xi
virtual body, 6–7, 22–30; and absence of
    body, 24–26; art understood through,
    63–66; in daydreams, 86; definition of,
    22; dialectic with customary body of,
    26–30, 101; in dreams, 91; generaliza-
    tion of situation and, 23–24; learning
    and, 22–24, 164 n. 21; and pathological
    experience, 89–90, 101; and spatiality
    of mental images, 83–86; virtuality in
    perception and, 48–49
virtuality in perception, 46–49
visceral aspect of body, 148–49
visibility and invisibility, 147–151
Visible and the Invisible, The, xi, 40–42,
    44, 76, 94, 99, 106, 110, 111, 125,
    126–27, 131–34, 142, 143–54, 157
vision, role in psychogenesis of, 107–12

Walker, Katherine Sorley, 31
Walton, Kendall, 8, 71
Warhol, Andy, 51
Warnock, Mary, 4–5, 80, 87, 161 n. 4
water, 10, 125, 128–29
Weiss, Gail, 114, 117
Welsh, Talia, 117
Whistler, James McNeill, 55
White, Alan, 8
Williams, Bernard, 4
Wittgenstein, Ludwig, 5, 87–88

Yeo, Michael, 137
Young, Iris, 112–15, 117